CW00495404

HJT | TRAINING PROFESSIONALS

Mastering the Points Based System

HJT Training is a company limited by guarantee. Registered in England and Wales.
Reg no. 4891943

HJT Training Ltd
107 Fleet Street
London
EC4A 2AB

+44 (0) 20 3766 3860
enquiries@hjt-training.co.uk
www.hjt-training.co.uk

ISBN: 978-1-9164312-1-8

Limited Edition

Introduction to the Points Based System

The Points Based System ("PBS") was first proposed in 2005 and launched in phases between March 2008 and March 2009. It replaced a range of work and study visa categories that had evolved over time on a rather uncoordinated basis, including the Highly Skilled Migrants' Programme, work permit schemes, and quota-based schemes for certain types of low-skilled work. The Highly Skilled Migrants' Programme was an early precursor to the Points Based System and awarded points for qualifications, work experience and past earnings.

As one promoting Minister declared, the hope was to achieve "a firmer, faster and fairer Australian-style points system" with an objective transparent process that was more robust against abuse than its predecessors. The needs of the system have consistently been inspired at least partly by the findings of the Migration Advisory Committee (MAC) which reports regularly on areas of the UK economy suffering from skills shortages and the impact of immigration measures. The MAC has long held that a policy of selective immigration which favours more skilled workers is vital to ensure that the UK continues to be thought of as a good place to do business, invest or study.

As time has passed, more targeted sub-categories have been created, such as the Entrepreneur and Exceptional talent routes within Tier 1. Some options have closed down: for example the Tier 1 (General) and Post Study Work routes, on both accounts due to concerns as to the amount of unskilled work being performed by migrants in the route.

The PBS was conceived as a way of making the application process more certain for all involved. But the flip side was a very significant decrease in the use of discretion. Many migrants have fallen foul of the tough approach taken to the Rules, which are very complex and change frequently; even the blandest of details may have drastic consequences for the individual who falls foul of it. Application forms are very lengthy and there are extremely prescriptive requirements by way of specified evidence, and the remedies when things go wrong are limited. There is no right of appeal and thus there is no access to an independent judge who can look at the merits of cases; a challenge is possible by way of judicial review but that is generally slow, costly, and looks only at the legality of the decision making, not its correctness.

The Brexit process is expected to lead to a to face further overhaul of the PBS. The government plans to maintain a policy by which highly skilled workers seeking to live and work in Britain will be prioritised, whilst low-skilled immigration is curbed. Currently the "restricted" route under Tier 2 permits 20,700 high-skilled workers into the UK each year; the government has indicated that in future it may look at better ways of controlling migration than a restrictive cap.

One objective of the PBS was to improve upon its predecessor which was "complex and difficult to understand". Not everybody would say this objective has been met. One puzzled reader was Lord Justice Jackson in Pokhriyal [2013] EWCA Civ 1568: he opined that the system's "provisions have now achieved a degree of complexity which even the Byzantine Emperors would have envied".

We hope the pages that follow will help legal practitioners to navigate the system's complexities. From late November 2018 the full publication will be available online, updated by reference to changes to the Immigration Rules and to both the Guidance for applicants and for decision makers.

HJT Training has been established for 15 years and over that time we have become the leading immigration training company. We have provided bespoke training packages to Parliamentary staff and the Home Office, and to the judiciary around the world. We are the examining body for the Office for the Immigration Services Commissioner's immigration accreditation scheme and we provide the academic materials for the Law Society's accreditation scheme for publicly funded practitioners.

Chapter 1: General Themes in PBS cases

The Rules and the Guidance

The first thing to say about the Rules is that it is unrealistic to repeat their detail fully in a guide of this nature. Indeed it would be dangerous to do so – they change frequently, and it is their precise wording that matters, not a paraphrase.

Although these guides are reasonably detailed, we do not necessarily repeat everything found within the Rules in this series, although we sometimes get pretty close. We aim to explain the broad concepts of each route and the pitfalls associated with it. We give sufficient detail for the reader to go and read the Rules for themselves, better equipped with the necessary overview before grappling with the precise wording. And we give examples of how to critically interrogate the meaning of the Rules, which often requires sharply focussed reading. When we describe the content of the Rules, which is what we do most of the time, we aim to make their content more intelligible than the original text. This is so you will have the background comprehension to closely study the Rules yourselves in the course of your casework.

As we emphasise throughout our training on the Immigration Rules, it is essential to read the Rules carefully and critically against your client's circumstances.

The Rules provide specific definitions of many of the concepts within them. We can usually find this either within the Rule itself, or in the compendium of definitions in rule 6. When determining the meaning of a Rule, their terms should be construed (see *Mahad* [2009] UKSC16):

> 'sensibly according to the natural and ordinary meaning of the word used, recognising that they are statements of the Secretary of State administrative policy'.

The Guidance

Although the Immigration Rules are very long indeed, they are not the whole story. They are supplemented by Guidance. This material can be very useful: it shows how the Home Office will actually approach a case in practice. There are actually two sets of Guidance available regarding many immigration routes – one is aimed at Home Office staff (i.e. the decision makers) and the other at applicants (so it is intended to accompany the application form). Generally speaking the Home Office's guidance to its own staff is of greater interest to the experience practitioner.

When one reads a particular piece of Guidance, it quickly becomes apparent that the vast majority of it represents a repetition of the Rules: usually literally, occasionally by paraphrase. The sheer bulk of the Guidance becomes rather less intimidating once one appreciates this. Sometimes the paraphrase may be useful because the Rule itself is unclear.

However, there are also extra pieces of information found in Guidance: there may be hints on how the Home Office think about a particular kind of scenario, e.g. by providing practical examples. Or the procedures which will be applied to a particular sponsor may be set out. Or, very importantly, express policy criteria for exercising discretion outside the Rules may be set out: for example, Rule 245AAA, which measures whether a settlement application has continuous lawful residence, provides virtually no discretion *within* the Rule. But the supporting Guidance provides the structure of discretion *outside* it.

The Guidance sometimes sets out additional information as to how a particular requirement is to be satisfied. The landmark Supreme Court judgement in Alvi [2012] UKSC 33, held that all mandatory requirements relevant to a grant of leave, including evidential requirements, must be listed in the Immigration Rules: this decision led to the Home Office putting virtually every requirement that they really cared about into the Rules.

The Home Office cannot operate a policy that is stricter than the Immigration Rules. This is because it is the Rules that have the authority of parliamentary approval, as shown by the Pankina/Alvi litigation. However the Secretary of State may operate policies that cover situations not dealt with under the Rules, and thus may seem more generous than the Rules (so long as they do not directly conflict with them).

And a useful side effect of Pankina [2010] EWCA Civ 719 §28 is that whereas Rules are to be applied strictly, Guidance must be interpreted in a common sense way.

> A policy is precisely not a rule: it is required by law to be applied without rigidity, and to be used and adapted in the interests of fairness and good sense.

These days there is not a great deal of difference between the Rules and the Guidance, and the additions made by the latter to our overall understanding of the Points Based System are rather minimal. For example, the English language sections of some of the published Guidance gives a detailed explanation of the testing procedures that is not found in the Rules themselves. It is now very rare to find a strict requirement to satisfy the core requirements for entry clearance or leave to remain in Guidance that does not derive directly from the Rules.

It can be tempting to use the Guidance as a substitute for the Rules. However, this is bad practice. You should always read both, alert to the fact that the Rules are the bottom line. If there is some lack of clarity, then you can always quote the Guidance at the Home Office if it suits your application: but whilst this may often work (and if it fails *might* lead to a successful if time-consuming legal challenge), the Home Office would usually be entitled to reply "The Rules are the Rules. Our Guidance aims to help. But you should go by the Rules."

As well as the detailed Guidance, there are also brief summaries of each route on the Home Office website, giving a brief overview of the key criteria and means of joining the route: for example this is the one on Graduate Entrepreneurs.

The scheme of the Rules

The Rules follow roughly the same scheme throughout the Points Based System.

- Firstly the Rules in Part 6A set out the key requirements for entry clearance or leave in terms of immigration history, age and so forth: when it comes to the more detailed criteria for the route, they cross reference to Appendices A-C.

- Appendices B-C simply set out the English language and Maintenance requirements. We address those compendiously in our Chapter 1: *General themes in PBS cases.*

- Appendix A firstly addresses the technical requirements, for example the level and form of investment which an Entrepreneur must establish as being available to their business

- Secondly, detailed Tables, of varying complexity and sometimes with the criteria within them divided up into a series of Rows, sets out the principal criteria which must be satisfied

- Thirdly, there are then Notes on the Tables, which explain the criteria within those Tables in more detail

- Fourthly, very detailed provisions outline the specified documents which must be provided before it is accepted that those criteria are met – occasionally specified documents are set out in Part 6A rather than Appendix A, for example the documents regarding pay records for Tier 2 Intra-Company Transfer migrants applying for indefinite leave to remain

In this general overview, we explain some of the recurring themes that are common to some or all of the routes under the PBS, such as the English language and maintenance requirements, leave for dependent partners and children, and then a whole series of concepts that recur throughout the Immigration Rules, ranging from the various limitations on study and switching to the way in which continuous residence is calculated in settlement applications.

You will often find a heading *General guidance for applicants* within the Guidance issued for each route. Although the contents of those sections vary slightly, it gives a general idea of those issues which the Home Office consider are generic in nature. We deal with many of the more important themes below.

Of course, there are many sets of Guidance that touch on generic issues within the system: below we generally refer to the Entrepreneur Guidance to exemplify typical recurring themes, so where we state "para 6" below, we refer to paragraph 6 of that Guidance; "Guidance A11" refers to Annex A of the Guidance.

We reference other sources thus:

- *Immigration Rules via prefix "r" – e.g. r245H refers to Part 6A of the Rules*
- *Appendix A paragraph 84 – A84*
- *Appendix J paragraph 14 – J14*
- *Home Office Tier 2 guidance – Guidance para 23*

Generic concepts within the Rules

Sponsors and Certificates of Sponsorship

The Sponsor is central to the PBS. Some Tier 1 applicants are free from the requirement of Sponsorship (though even then the Tier 1 Exceptional Talent route has a Sponsor component). A licensed Sponsor must satisfy onerous requirements as to their system of reporting and record keeping regarding the migrants for whom they are responsible. For example Tier 2 and 5 Sponsors must report a person who does not turn for the first day of work, if they are absent for more than 10 working days without reasonably granted permission, if the period of engagement ends including resignation or dismissal, if information as to the migrant breaching the conditions of leave comes to light or if there is reason to believe they are engaged in terrorism or other criminal activity; and must also record any significant changes of circumstances such as a job change or salary change, though not a change of job title or an annual pay rise.

The Certificate of Sponsorship, be it a Certificate of Acceptance for Studies (CAS) for Tier 4 students or a Certificate of Sponsorship (CoS) for the Tier 2 and Tier 5 worker routes, is a virtual document like a file on a database. Each has a unique reference number and contains information about the role for which it is issued.

Only one CoS can be issued for a period of leave and once this is done no other Sponsor may issue the same CoS reference number. It may well be advisable to give personal details such as passport number to a prospective Sponsor for whom the migrant will definitely be working. If a migrant does not want to take up the job for which a CoS has been issued, they should notify the Sponsor and request its withdrawal, giving them five days to action the request before sending a reminder. If it is not cancelled, they should contact the Sponsor Licensing Unit at sponsorlicensing@homeoffice.gsi.gov.uk providing relevant details: the Sponsor they no longer want, their own full name and nationality, the CoS to be cancelled and the reason, and the dates of contacting and chasing the Sponsor.

A CoS will expire three months after it is assigned if it is not activated by a person coming to the UK. A CoS may be withdrawn or cancelled at any time by the Home Office or Sponsor and then becomes invalid.

The CAS is equally central to the Tier 4 student route. It is valid to support an application for six months once issued and applications must not be made more than three months before the course's start date. A CAS is valid only for so long as the sponsoring educational establishment retains its licence, and it has to provide specified information regarding the course of studies.

Loss of a Sponsor's licence
A Sponsor may have their licence suspended or revoked for failing to meet the record keeping and reporting conditions. For their sponsored migrants, this means

- If the licence is suspended, the Sponsor may no longer issue new CoSs or CASs, but this does not immediately impact on the migrants working or studying there

- Individuals may apply for further leave during a period of suspension – however the application will be held pending the suspension being (hopefully) lifted

- If the Sponsor's licence is revoked, then presuming the migrant is not suspected of complicity in the issues leading to revocation, their leave should be curtailed to 60 days from notification of curtailment (or they will be allowed to retain their existing leave if they have less than 60 days outstanding); they may seek to find a new Sponsor over this grace period. Any CoS or CAS issued becomes invalid upon revocation of the licence.

- Those who have travelled to the UK will be allowed to enter the UK and start their work notwithstanding suspension of a licence; however the recommendation in the Guidance is nevertheless not to travel once the applicant becomes aware of their Sponsor's difficulties. If possible the Home Office will contact such applicants before they travel to advise them of the situation

If a Tier 2 or Tier 5 Sponsor is taken over by another organisation then the new employer must apply to become a licensed Sponsor within 28 days of the takeover. Otherwise leave will be curtailed in line with the regime above. CoSs will become invalid if no Sponsor application is made. If such a Sponsor does not renew their licence, leave will similarly be curtailed, and CoSs will become invalid.

Premature termination of employment will have similar consequences as to the treatment of outstanding leave.

Specified documents
Throughout the Points Based System, there is a requirement for specified documents to be provided. As Rule 39B sets out, these are mandatory: an equivalent document or an explanation as to the possible availability of such documents in a covering letter will not do. There is no provision to correct defects in an application apart from the provisions of Rule 245AA.

Translations must be provided if the original is not in English or Welsh, with confirmation of accuracy, date, the full name and original signature of the translator or the translation company's contact details (see for example PBS Dependent Guidance para 13).

Correcting applications
There are limited remedies available under the Points Based System when things go wrong. The most important one is the discretion for a decision maker to request further documents under Rule 245AA, which addresses "Missing documents" (it is commonly called the "evidential flexibility" Rule). If the decision maker has failed to consider whether such a request was appropriate, then it is possible to argue that the decision is flawed.

Biometric residence permits (BRPs)
From 18 March 2015, those applying for entry clearance to come to the UK for more than six months are treated as also applying for a BRP. Accordingly they must provide fingerprints and a facial image alongside their application by having their fingerprints and photograph taken at a visa application centre. They can collect the BRP from their nominated post office if their application succeeds, which must be collected within 10 days of arrival; in the meantime a vignette is added to their passport giving 30 days of entry clearance.

Passports
Clearly holding a passport is a central part of an immigration application. Under the PBS, a passport is also the key to gaining points for English language speaking where one's nationality might bring some benefit, such as a presumption of language competence under Appendix B (on the basis that courses within certain countries can be presumed to have been taught in English).

Switching into a route
As always in the Immigration Rules, the provisions which control the ability to change immigration route are found in the destination Rule rather than in the category being exited. So one would not find the routes that a Tier 4 student could switch into within Tier 4: one would have to look at the "leave to remain" provisions of every route within the PBS, and find whether or not they include Tier 4 students as a potential entry point. The Ctrl-F search function found in most web browsers will come in very useful here.

Example

John is the partner of Betty. She is a Tier 2 worker. He is present as her PBS dependent. He wishes to join the Tier 2 route himself without leaving the UK and wants to know if this is possible.

We need to look at the switching controls in Tier 2. The phrase used in the Rules to describe PBS dependents is by reference to their relationship to a "Relevant Points Based System Migrant". We do find partners of RPBSMs in Tier 2, but only with respect to their ability to switch into the route from Tier 4 (r245HD(b)(i)(5)). So this proposal is a non-starter. However he could always return abroad and apply for entry clearance.

Student switchers and suitable Sponsors
There is a general restriction on the circumstances in which students can switch into other PBS categories. Thus students present under Tier 4 General may only extend their leave under Tier 4, and may only switch into the Investor or Entrepreneur routes on having a suitable Sponsor. This requires that they are (or were last) sponsored by a UK recognised body, one in receipt of public funding as a higher education institution, an overseas higher education institution to undertake short-term UK study, an Embedded College offering Pathway Courses, or an independent school (you can see the restrictions in rules r245ZX(b), 245ED(c)(xvi), 245DD(e)(xxi) respectively).

Part 6A of the Rules cross references to Rule 245A, which is the general provision in Rules addressing this issue. It requires

- Unconditional written consent

- In the form of a letter on official headed notepaper bearing the official stamp of the organisation and issued by an authorised official

- Confirming that the organisation gives its unconditional consent to the applicant remaining in the UK for an unlimited time

Limitations on study – ATAS clearance certificates
Particular routes often permit migrants within them to study. However, there are limitations on the kinds of study that can be conducted, particularly because of the international effort to control studies in postgraduate qualifications in certain sensitive subjects, knowledge of which could be used in programmes to develop weapons of mass destruction. This is addressed via cross references to Part 15 of the Rules.

Part 15 just includes one long Rule, r417, which sets out that

- If a person is studying one of the courses listed in para 1 of Appendix 6 of the Rules (for example Biology), then

- They may not do so via

  - undergraduate or postgraduate research leading to a Doctorate/Masters, or

  - a Taught Masters in certain other subjects (listed in para 2 of Appendix 6, for example Physics), or

  - a period of study or research exceeding six months at a higher education institute as part of an overseas postgraduate qualification

- Unless they have obtained a valid Academic Technology Approval Scheme clearance Certificate from the Counter-Proliferation Department of the Foreign and Commonwealth Office issued before their studies began

Care arrangements for child applicants
Some of the routes allow for the possibility of applicants under the age of 18 – for example a precocious young businessperson may apply to be a Tier 1 Entrepreneur. Where the route permits child applicants, they must be at least 16 years old. There are then a number of requirements as to their care where they are under 18:

- The parents, or parent with sole legal responsibility, or legal guardian, must support the application

- Confirm that they consent to the proposed care arrangements for the child during their time in the UK (245DB(o)-(q)/245DD(q)-(s)) (the full details for such a letter appear in the PBS Dependents Guidance para 63ff)

- As the Guidance explains, if the child is to live with someone who is not their parent or a close relative as defined in the Guidance, the accommodation will count as a private fostering arrangement such that the local authority must be notified and must give their approval to the care being adequate (e.g. see the Entrepreneur Guidance for applicants page 48)

Appendix H Countries
Appendix H lists a number of countries whose nationals benefit from a dispensation on the extent of supporting evidence that they have to provide, so long as they are applying from the relevant country or applying for further leave in the UK.

The countries are Argentina, Australia, Barbados, Botswana, Brunei, Canada, Chile, Japan, Malaysia, New Zealand, Oman, Qatar, Singapore, South Korea, Trinidad and Tobago, United Arab Emirates and United States of America.

Dual nationals who hold one of these country's nationalities also benefit, so long as they are applying from the relevant country or for further leave in the UK.

Residence in Jersey, Guernsey and the Isle of Man
Residence in these islands can count towards an entitlement to settle in the UK under some PBS routes, where the residence was in an equivalent route to the route on which the indefinite leave to remain application is grounded, and so long as there were no excess absences outside the UK or those islands inconsistent with Rule 245AAA – this dispensation is found in r245AAA(e).

Overstayers
The general scheme of the Rules is that "where paragraph 39E of these Rules applies, any current period of overstaying will be disregarded".

Rule 39E provides that

- Where an application is made following the refusal of another application (made in time, or within 14 days of leave expiring) and any subsequent section 3C leave, administrative review or appeal procedures have expiring, the relevant period is within 14 days of leave expiring – i.e. where the second application is a rectification effort following straight on from a refusal, one is permitted 14 days overstaying as of right

- Where an application is made in other circumstances, the period is within 14 days of leave expiring but *only where the Secretary of State is satisfied* that there was a good reason beyond the applicant's control (or their representative's): such reason must be supplied with the application

Example

Barney is present as a Tier 1 Entrepreneur and applied for an extension of leave recently. His application has just been refused because he failed to provide the appropriate evidence to prove that he had invested the necessary funds into the business. He in fact possesses that evidence, so wants to make a further application. As this appears to be a recent refusal, hopefully Barney is within the 14 day period where overstaying is automatically condoned where the new application is made directly following an application's refusal. Accordingly he does not need to seek the exercise of discretion in his favour: overstaying of up to 14 days will not be held against him.

If, alternatively, Barney had made a perfect application but one day after his leave had expired, the representations supporting his application would need to provide a good reason beyond his control justifying the lateness.

Criminal record certificate (CRC) – Entry clearance routes only
The CRC is only required for entry clearance routes. Relevant features are:

- A CRC must be obtained from the relevant authority in any country in which they have been resident for 12 months or more, whether continuously or in total, in the last decade, whilst aged 18 plus (you can see an example at r245DB(r))

- A person who cannot provide a CRC may seek exemption from the requirement which the Home Office may grant *if it is not reasonably practicable* to obtain one (245DB(r))

- If no CRC is provided, then the decision maker may contact the applicant or their representative in writing, seeking a CRC, or explanation of one's absence (245DB(s)). The response must be received within 28 calendar days

- The PBS Dependents Guidance (para 15ff) explains the required information that must be provided in a translation of any such document, which will be necessary when the original is not in English. CRCs are only valid if dated within six months of the Entrepreneur application date (para 22). Failure to provide a valid CRC without good reason may lead to refusal on the general public policy grounds.

Regulated financial institutions
A regulated financial institution is one which is regulated by the appropriate regulatory body for the country in which the financial institution operates (A43) (often known as the home regulator: see Entrepreneur Guidance for applicants A16).

Appendix P to the Rules lists financial institutions which the Home Office will not accept as a suitable fund-holder, because they are unable to make satisfactory verification checks there.

A person subject to any applicable financial sanctions regime must provide confirmation from HM Treasury that the funds are transferable and disposable in the UK (Guidance page 51).

Calculating conversion rates
Many rules require the holding of a certain level of funds. Sometimes funds held abroad qualify. Funds in a foreign currency will be converted to pounds sterling (£) using the spot exchange rate which appeared on www.oanda.com on the date on which the application was made (A119).

Date of application
The Immigration Rules make provision for calculating the precise date of an immigration application or its variation (r34G). This depends on how the application is sent:

- Royal Mail post – posting date as shown by the tracking information provided by Royal Mail or, if not tracked, by the postmark date on the envelope

- Made in person via a paper form – the date on which it is received at a Home Office premium service centre

- Paper application form sent by courier or other postal services provider – the date of delivery to the Home Office; or

- Via the online application process – the date on which the online application is submitted whether or not a subsequent appointment is made at a Home Office premium service centre

Refusal for missing documents
Rule 245AA is very important, because it so often represents the only avenue under which a PBS applicant may effectively challenge a refusal. It is sometimes referred to as the "evidential flexibility" Rule, though this term can be confusing – at times the Home Office have had a policy (which they titled "evidential flexibility")

that is different and more generous than the “missing document” Rule. It seems that the policy and the Rule have been identical since at least 1 October 2013.

Rule 245AA provides that further information may be sought from the applicant in certain circumstances: essentially where they have indeed submitted the *specified documents* but where:

- specified evidence is missing from the documents; or
- a document is in the wrong format (for example, if a letter is not on letterhead paper as specified); or
- a document does not contain all of the specified information.

Until 5 November 2018, Rule 245AA also permitted a request to be made to a missing document within a series: for example where one of a series of bank statements was omitted. Another dispensation that has been consigned to history was the possibility that an original document might to be sought where only a copy had been supplied. However from that same date Rule 39B permits copy documents rather than originals to be supplied as part of the Home Office’s new application process (procedures will be introduced to allow originals to be scanned): accordingly the need for that discretion is presumably reduced. Notable features of Rule 245AA are that

- The discretion only arises where there is some imperfection in the specified documents supplied: not where a specified document is missing altogether
- The discretion may be exercised essentially where a document is in ***the wrong format*** eg not on letterhead paper, or ***does not contain all of the relevant information***
- There is a fast turnaround for the information to be provided (7 working days)
- The discretion need not be exercised where it is anticipated that the failing within the original application is not material because it will be refused for another reason – whether the SSHD will routinely refuse to use the discretion where there are *two* flaws, each of which would be individually potentially rectifiable were it the *only* difficulty, remains to be seen
- There is also a second discretion within Rule 245AA: this allows the application to be granted where the missing information can be found “elsewhere” (presumably within other documents with the application, or perhaps online from reliable sources)

Example

John’s Tier 4 student extension application is refused because the second page of a four-page series of bank statements is missing. Khurshad is refused because the last page of a four-page series of bank statements is missing.

Before 5 November 2018, John should have been given a chance to provide the missing document, as a page was missing which was part of a series; however in Khurshad’s case, the end of the sequence was missing and thus discretion would not have been exercised. From 6 November 2018, they are both losers, as the “missing-document-in-a-series” discretion has been abolished.

Jahan's entrepreneur application is refused because the independent lawyer's letter confirming the availability of third party support omits the name of the legal representative who wrote it. This is a case where document has been provided but not all of the specified information has been provided therein: accordingly discretion can be exercised under Rule 245AA(b)(iv)

Johnson's entrepreneur application is refused because a letter from his bank does not show that it is regulated by the Financial Conduct Authority and the Prudential Regulation Authority. Discretion can be exercised here, without even seeking further information from Johnson, if the website of the bank contains the relevant information: Rule 245AA(d).

Expedited applications
There are procedures by which applications may be expedited. It is important to be confident that the application is a straightforward one, however: any complications may lead to the decision maker being unable to complete consideration on the day, which may waste the premium fee.

Entry clearance applications may be expedited via the Priority Service or Super Priority Service (the latter aims to make decisions within 24 hours of receiving the papers). In-country applications may be made via the Premium or Super Premium Service. The former involves a fee, £590 at the time of writing. The latter gold star service (£10,500 plus an extra component depending on the precise application) involves a courier collecting the applicant's application forms and documents; premium service staff will visit the applicant to obtain their biometric information (fingerprints and photo) and their signature.

The general refusal reasons
Even though a person may satisfy the requirements of points accumulation via the Appendices, and have survived the "genuineness" tests, they may still be refused under the general refusal provisions found in Part 9 of the Rules. These cover all kinds of possibilities, but generally focus on honesty within the present and past applications, immigration history, good character, criminal history, and ability to provide adequate evidence of identity and ability to depart the UK at the end of their leave.

The general refusal reasons specify that an applicant *can*, or sometimes *must*, be refused leave if one of the general grounds for refusal applies. This is notwithstanding the fact that they have already satisfied the core criteria of the route under which they are applying.

An application may meet all the category specific requirements of the rules, but still fall to be refused under the General Grounds. This is a very technical area, and the HJT ebook on the *General Grounds for Refusal* addresses this in depth.

Common problems arising in this area include:

- Clients may have been refused settlement due to inconsistencies between the income claimed on their HMRC tax returns and in their immigration extension applications

- English language test results may have been cancelled because a provider (usually ETS) has declared the results invalid

- Omissions in application forms may lead to the decision maker to consider that there has been a material failure to disclose something relevant: for example, a failure to mention convictions, past refusals of a visa, or the possession of earlier travel documents (which may be taken to imply that such travel documents may have contained inconvenient information)

A lengthy ban may follow a decision based on grounds of dishonesty. Our very detailed guide to *The General Refusal Reasons* addresses all these issues.

Verification of documents

Documents supplied in support of the application will not necessarily be taken at face value, and are subject to verification. The Guidance explains the process (e.g. the PBS Dependent Guidance at 27 onwards; for Tier 4 General applicants the information appears in Annex 2 to the Guidance). Essentially

- Verification checks will be made where there are *reasonable doubts* backed by *clear reasons* about the document being genuine – "*based on the facts we have*"
- They will be made with employers, an embassy or high commission, government departments in the UK or abroad, banks, universities or professional bodies
- There is a rather obscure further process known as "other checks" where less cogent suspicions appear to justify checks being made
- Verification checks may inevitably delay the progress of the application
- Passports will always be verified. Sometimes verification checks will be omitted notwithstanding concerns about a document because there are other reasons for refusal
- There are three possible outcomes
    - **The document is confirmed as genuine** – in which case the application will be considered as normal
    - **The document is confirmed as false** – in which case the application will be refused under the general refusal reasons, though it will probably also be refused because no points can be awarded regarding the criteria which that document was aiming to support
    - **Verification check inconclusive** – if checks do not confirm or undermine a document's genuineness, then the application will proceed to decision. The suspect document will not be awarded points, but if other non-suspect documents were put forward then the application may still succeed
- Results of verifications of falseness will be reported via a standard Document Verification Report form

Extension and indefinite leave to remain requirements

Whatever stage an applicant is at, it always pays to look ahead. There are particular requirements for maintaining job creation and investments within the Entrepreneur and Investor routes, for example, and a client should be advised as to how to ensure they give themselves the best shot at being able to extend their stay or settle in the UK. Though they should also be warned that the Rules can always change, and the case law says that that a disadvantaged migrant has no complaint here in most cases.

Appendix B: English language requirements

The English language requirements are dotted around the various provisions within the PBS.

- Tier 1 and Tier 2 applicants under the Points Based System cross reference to Appendix B in order to define the relevant English language requirements.
- Tier 4 applicants

- Must be able to demonstrate, without an interpreter, such proficiency in the English language as the studies identified in their CAS indicate should be expected, via examination or interview (however the Rule states they will not be subjected to a test at that level) (r245ZV(ca), r245ZX(da))

- For their CAS to be valid, it must contain details of how their Sponsor assessed their English language proficiency including test scores for reading, writing, speaking and listening where appropriate (A116(vi))

- Beyond this, we deal with the English language proficiency of students in Chapter 6: Tier 4 Students

➢ Settlement applicants must meet the criteria for Knowledge of Life and Language in the UK: Appendix KoLL

How the scheme of Appendix B works
As always, each Appendix provides core criteria that have to be satisfied, which are set out in Tables. Those Tables are then glossed by Notes.

Tier 1 and Tier 2 migrants may satisfy the requirements by any one of five routes:

➢ Being a national of a listed majority English speaking country

➢ Having obtained an academic qualification

➢ Having passed an English language test

➢ Meeting the requirement in a prior successful application

➢ Transitional arrangements

Each of these routes to showing English language proficiency is likely to have a substantive requirement as to what precisely must be shown but also evidential requirements, which give painstaking detail of the form and content of the evidence that will satisfy the test. Sometimes a full understanding of the requirements can be gained only via reference to other sources beyond Appendix B, for example the list of approved English language test providers in Appendix O. As ever, there is also Guidance: we have taken the Entrepreneur Guidance as the reference point for general points regarding language skill as its contents are similar to that for other the Tier 1 and 2 routes.

Once we reach Appendix B, we find two tables. Table 1 addresses the level of English language proficiency required by Tier and sub-category, specifying whether the requirements adhere to entry clearance and/or leave to remain. In general the requirements are the same for both stages of the application process; however Tier 2 General cases are glossed by a requirement found in paragraph B5.

For example, a Tier 1 Entrepreneur needs to show level B1 proficiency of the Council of Europe's Common European Framework for Language Learning (see Row B). Whereas a Tier 2 Minister of Religion has to demonstrate prowess at level B2 (see Row E).

Paragraph B5 explains that a Tier 2 (General) migrant must display level A1 proficiency if they entered that route by certain paths: from Tier 2 (General) under the pre-6 April 2011 Rules, or as a qualifying work permit holder, representative of a news agency, airline operational ground staff or Jewish Agency employee, who has not since been granted entry clearance/leave in another route.

Example

Jane applies for leave to remain as Tier 1 Entrepreneur. She is aware that she has to show aptitude at Level B1 of the common European framework. She relies on a certificate from the Learning Resource Network (LRN) that she passed a few months ago for non-immigration purposes. It shows she has Level B1 language proficiency.

Jane's application will probably be refused: LRN are not listed as a qualified provider under Appendix O.

Acquiring points under Appendix B

Points may be acquired via a series of five alternative means, set out in Table 2, which is in turn glossed by various further requirements as to how each of the means in question is to be evidenced. The requirements (see for example this explanation from IELTS) will either be at A1 (basic level), B1 or B2 (respectively lower and higher proficiency for speakers whose expertise is sufficient for them to be thought able to get by independently in the language):

- **Being a national of a listed majority English speaking country** if the applicant has B1 level competence and provides their passport/identity document or letter from an authority in their country of origin if neither is available (B6) – the Guidance explains that applications can succeed absent a passport only if it has been lost, stolen, expired and returned to the relevant authorities or been sent to another part of the Home Office (English language Guidance – Tiers 1 and 2 (Version 13.0), page 9)

  The countries (listed at B6(i)) are: Antigua and Barbuda, Australia, The Bahamas, Barbados, Belize, Canada, Dominica, Grenada, Guyana, Jamaica, New Zealand, St Kitts and Nevis, St Lucia, St Vincent and the Grenadines, Trinidad and Tobago and USA

Example

Daniel is a citizen of Antigua. His application for entry clearance has been refused because he did not provide NARIC evidence that his Masters degree was taught in English.

The refusal is unlawful. Antigua is listed in B6(i) as one of the English speaking countries. So long as Daniel provided his passport on the application (or, exceptionally, an explanation for not having done so), he should have been awarded points for language.

- Having obtained an academic qualification (not a professional or vocational qualification) which is proved via

  - Firstly evidence as to the qualification level (B7(i)), Either:

    - A UK Bachelor's degree, Master's degree or PhD, or

    - Its foreign equivalent as certified by UK NARIC both as to level and language of teaching, or

    - Where the applicant is a national of one of the listed majority English speaking countries (not including Canada, as some degrees there are not taught in English) and UK NARIC has deemed that the qualification to be the equivalent

- Secondly, evidence as to the holding of the qualification (B7(ii)-(iii)):

    - The certificate, or an academic transcript (or letter for PhD studies) giving the applicant's and institution's name, award title and confirmation that it has been or will be awarded, and the date the certificate will be issued (or confirmation that the original cannot be reissued) (the Guidance usually states that the letter must bear the institution's stamp, be on headed paper, and issued by an authorised official)

    - The information from UK NARIC confirming certification or deeming of equivalence

- Where the requirement is for level A1 proficiency, firstly evidence as to the qualification level (B8(i)):

    - Either a UK Bachelor's degree, Master's degree or PhD, or

    - Where UK NARIC has deemed the qualification to be the equivalent for qualifications taught outside the UK

- And secondly, evidence as to the holding of the qualification (B8(ii)-(iv)):

    - The same specified documents itemised above as to certificate/transcript and

    - A letter from the awarding institution giving the same details as those documents and confirmation the subject was taught in English

    - Information from UK NARIC confirming deeming of equivalence of the foreign qualification with UK standards

- Graduate Entrepreneurs benefit from a dispensation (B9) that there is no need to provide such evidence of a qualification taught in English if their UK higher education institute provides the specified details of the qualification

Example

Edward is a citizen of Ghana wishing to seek entry clearance to the UK. He has a Masters degree from Accra University.

Ghana is not one of the listed English speaking countries. As the course was taken at an educational establishment outside the UK, Edward needs to obtain UK NARIC confirmation (via a letter from them) that the degree was taught or researched in English to the appropriate level of the Council of Europe's CEFL.

Ranjiv is an Indian citizen who is applying under the Graduate Entrepreneur route; his sponsoring UK higher education institute where he previously studied qualifies as a Sponsor that can identify and nurture business talent.

He does not need to provide evidence of English language proficiency so long as his Sponsor's sponsorship letter clearly shows the details of the relevant qualification that he has obtained with them.

- **Having passed an English language test** and providing the specified documents to show this

    - The test must have been provided by a specified English language test provider approved by the Secretary of State, these being listed in Appendix O, which contains a single table naming the acceptable tests separated into two classes, those taken in the UK and those taken abroad, and then identifying the accepted tests by title, organisations providing the test (IELTS SELT Consortium and Trinity College London) and actually making the awards (Cambridge English Language Assessments and Trinity College London), the levels such tests cover, their period of validity, and the documents to be provided for verification of test success (since 6 April 2015, all tests are verified via a unique reference number via the IELTS SELT Consortium online system rather than via paper copies)

    - From 6 April 2015 there was significant reform of the English language testing system, and from that date only certain tests are accepted as reliable, which means that some individuals will have to retake tests (English language Guidance pages 16-19)

    - The Guidance sets out the general process for taking tests

        - They are booked online

        - They may be sat only with acceptable evidence of identity ie valid passport, EU identity card, and a Biometric Residence Permit. Some individuals cannot access the testing process because they lack a relevant identity document, as where the Home Office has kept their passport

        - The Home Office Guidance on Retention of Valuable Documents explains that s17 of the Asylum and Immigration (Treatment of Claimants, etc.) Act 2004 gives a power to retain passports which is exercised where a migrant is suspected to be liable to removal and retaining the passport may facilitate removal, for example where they are an overstayer, illegal entrant, have been refused leave to remain (whether or not they have a right of appeal), a removal decision has been made, or their leave has been curtailed to 60 days (e.g. because their Sponsor has lost their licence).

        - In Freedom of Information Reference 40803 the Home Office sets out that they would return the identity document to allow a person to sit a test where they have extant leave, including s3C leave, or EEA free movement rights, but that documents will not be returned where they are an overstayer or an application has been refused; where an appeal is pending then normally the passport will be returned

- Results are given via a Secure English Language Test unique reference number (Guidance pages 18)

- Those applying under transitional arrangements may provide paper documents providing the test result details, though must nevertheless be confident that the test provider's online verification system will confirm the result to the Home Office

- The test result must identify the applicant, qualification and its date, the test centre and the test result's period of validity (B10)

- The qualification must establish the required proficiency from Table 1 in speaking and listening if the target is A1, or for all speaking, listening, reading and writing for levels other than A1, unless the applicant is exempted from sitting one component due to disability (B10A)

Example

Han is a citizen of China applying for the Tier 2 General route. He has taken an English language test which he wants to rely on to support his application. He took the test with Integrated Skills in English awarded by Trinity College London 18 months ago, achieving B1 proficiency.

His provider is eligible (Appendix O); his marks are sufficient (Appendix B Table 1) and that same Table also shows that his test remains valid for another few months. One would need to check his results carefully ensuring that results are shown for all four components (reading, writing, speaking and listening – only where the proficiency target is A1 would speaking and listening suffice).

Remember that it is the electronic record to be accessed by the decision maker rather than the paper qualification which really matters.

- Those **meeting the requirement in a prior successful application** can acquire the relevant points in various ways (though not if any false representations were made in the course of that application (B15))

  - For all applicants, as an Entrepreneur or Business person, or as a Post-Study Worker or HSMP participant (B11)

  - For all applicants (B12),

    - As a Minister of Religion under the Rules in place from 19 April 2007,

    - As a Tier 2 Minister of Religion who was granted leave having shown English language proficiency for being a national of a majority English speaking country, a degree taught in English, or passing an English language test, or

    - As a Tier 4 (General) student whose CAS was assigned from 21 April 2011 for a course of at least degree level study

- For all applicants except Tier 2 Minister of Religion, having shown level B1 proficiency in the course of being granted leave (B13) as a

    - Tier 1 Graduate Entrepreneur or

    - Tier 2 (General) migrant under the Rules from 6 April 2011, or

    - Tier 4 (General) student whose CAS was assigned from 21 April 2011

- For a person now applying under Tier 2 (General) or as a Tier 2 Sportsperson, having been granted leave (B14) as a

    - Minister of Religion (but not as a Tier 2 Minister of Religion) under the Rules in place from 23 August 2004, or

    - Tier 2 (General) migrant having shown English language proficiency for being a national of a majority English speaking country, a degree taught in English, or passing an English language test

There are additionally some transitional arrangements by which points will be awarded (without any reference to A1 or B1 proficiency levels) to individuals who have been present in the UK for a long term time, for:

- ➢ Those now applying as Tier 2 (General) migrants who last held leave as a qualifying work permit holder, representative of a news agency, airline operational ground staff or Jewish Agency employee, who has not since been granted entry clearance/leave in those same routes nor as Tier 2 ICTs or under Tier 2 (General) (B16)

- ➢ Those now applying as Tier 2 Ministers of Religion who have previously been granted leave as Ministers of Religion, Missionaries or members of religious orders, and have not since been granted leave as such under the Rules from 28 November 2008, or as Tier 2 Ministers of Religion (B17)

- ➢ Those now applying as Tier 2 Sportspersons who have previously been granted entry clearance/leave as qualifying work permit holders and have not since been granted leave other than as such, or as Tier 2 sportspersons, under the Rules from 28 November 2008

Appendix C: Financial maintenance requirements

Applicants under the Points Based System have to demonstrate that they possess various sums of money in order to show they can maintain and accommodate themselves. The Guidance emphasises that this is to ensure that there is no burden on public funds during their time in the UK.

Appendix C has a series of Tables which set out the levels of money that must be held. There are general provisions at 1A regarding where funds must be held, and the content of bank or building society statements or passbooks and the period over which they must be produced, and the evidence required to show that funds are under their own control. There are in addition some specific requirements for each of the Points Based System routes, which are much more extensive for Tier 4 students (whose precise source of funding must be evidenced) and Tier 4 child students (the requirements for whose care arrangements, as well as maintenance requirements, are detailed in Appendix C).

We have produced our own tables to simplify things showing the general position, though our subsequent text shows how Appendix C then glosses those core requirements.

Meeting the financial requirements: non-student routes

Class of Points Based System Migrant	Entry clearance requirements	Leave to remain requirements	Period over which funds must be held
Tier 1 Investor	No requirement	No requirement	N/A
Tier 1 Entrepreneur (the funds must be additional to the investment funds for Appendix A: C3)	£3,310	£945	90 days
Tier 1 Graduate Entrepreneur	£1,890		90 days
Tier 2 all categories	£945	£945	90 days
Tier 5 Temporary Worker	£945	£945	90 days
Tier 5 Youth Mobility	£1,890	Check this	Within 31 days of the application date

Meeting the financial requirements: Student routes

Class of Points Based System Migrant	Entry clearance requirements	Leave to remain requirements	Period over which funds must be held
Tier 4 Child	Sufficient funds to pay boarding fees including lodging for an academic year If studying at a non-residential independent school and is in a private foster care arrangement (see notes below) or staying with and cared for by a close relative,	The same as the entry clearance route The same as the entry clearance route	28 days

	sufficient funds for fees for an academic year, a maintenance and accommodation undertaking from the caregiver, and funds of £570 a month up to nine months If studying at a non-residential independent school and staying with an accompanying parent, sufficient funds for fees for an academic year, and funds of £1,560 a month if there are no other children, £625 monthly per additional child otherwise, up to nine months As Tier 4 General if aged 16/17 and living independently and studying at a non-residential independent school (months are rounded up for course length: C20)	The same as the entry clearance route The same as the entry clearance route	
Tier 4 General	Full course fees if less than a year in duration otherwise fees for the first year; up to nine months of maintenance of £1,265 monthly for Inner London, £1,015 otherwise (months are rounded up for course length: C12A)	Full course fees if less than a year in duration otherwise fees for the first year; up to nine months of maintenance of £1,265 monthly for Inner London, £1,015 otherwise If applying for leave to remain on the Doctorate Extension Scheme, £2,530 for at least two months, for Inner London, £2,030 otherwise If applying for leave to remain as a postgraduate doctor or dentist on a recognised Foundation Programme or as a Student Union Sabbatical Officer, £1,265 for each remaining month up to two months for Inner London, £1,015 otherwise	28 days

For example, a Tier 1 Entrepreneur must show possession of funds of £3,310 (entry clearance) or £945 (leave to remain) for their maintenance (Appendix C), to qualify for the necessary 10 points. This is additional to the sums shown for available funding for their business (C3). The sum must be shown for the principal applicant and each dependent (C/1A(g)).

Example

Harbinder, a single man, applies for entry clearance as a Tier 1 Entrepreneur having put together an immaculate application with respect to the Appendix A requirements, attesting to £203,000 of funds being available to him.

He writes in his covering letter that he relies on the same bank statements to show his ability to maintain himself as to show the availability of investment funds for the business.

His application will be refused. He cannot rely on the same funds for investment and maintenance, leaving him a few pounds short of the requirements for the latter, given the target is £3,310.

The requirements for the funds are that:

- They are held as cash funds (under the applicant's control) for the relevant period leading up to and including the application date (C/1A), the balance being calculated if in a foreign currency using the spot exchange rate for the application date as shown by www.oanda.com (C/1A(e))

- The same level of funds must be available for each applicant where dependent partners and children are making applications at the same time (C/1A(g))

- They are evidenced by consecutive (i.e. no gaps: (C/1B(a)(i)(1), (C/1B(a)(iii)(7)) bank/building society (excluding overdraft facilities: (C/1A(l))) with an end date taken to be the closing balance on the most recent statement, not earlier than 31 days before the application date (C/1A(h)); if in a joint account, then the applicant must be named as an account holder (C/1A(k))

- In the event that multiple bank statements are produced from different accounts, then in the past the Guidance has indicated that these will be aggregated and the date of the closing balance most favourable to the applicant will be taken

- Funds held in a financial institution that is not trusted by the Home Office will not count: these are listed in Appendix P

- If funds relied on were obtained whilst the applicant was in the UK, this must have been during a valid period of leave without any breach of conditions (C/1A(d))

- Save for Tier 4 migrants, the funds must be under the applicant's own control (C/1A(f))

The fund-holding must be evidenced by consecutive bank/building society statements, or a building society pass book giving similar information, for the relevant period:

- The bank etc. statements covering the relevant period of time (which must not be ATM mini-statements (C/1B(a)(v))) must show the account number, their date, the name and logo of the institution, any transactions over the period in question (C/1B(a)(iii)); they must be on the institution's letterhead or, if they are electronic statements, they should be supplied alongside a headed covering letter from the institution or its official stamp

- If provided for dependents, they must show their name and if a child dependent they must show the name of the UK-resident parent (C/1B(iii)1))

- Alternatively a letter from the institution may provide all of these details, including, for foreign accounts, one from the home regulator from the country in question (C/1B(c))

Example

Billy, a single man, applies for leave to remain as a Tier 1 Entrepreneur. He satisfies the Appendix A requirements without question. He provides bank statements for six months leading up to the application, without any missing documents, ending a month and a half before the application is posted.

Billy's application is defective: whilst he has provided 90 days worth of bank statements, the end point is too early: it is around 45 days before the application date when it should not be more than 31 days earlier.

Graduate Entrepreneurs:

- May score points for funds provided for Appendix A purposes where the sum in question is confirmed by the Department for International Trade as having been awarded in their endorsement letter (C2(c))

A Tier 4 migrant

- Must additionally confirm that the funds are available for their use studying and living in the UK, and that the funds will remain available to them (save for their inevitable use to meet course fees and living costs (C1A(ca))) – funds will be treated as available to them only when the documents confirm that they are (C13) (depending on the source being their own funds, their parents, or an official sponsor):

  - Held by them in a sole/joint bank account

  - Held by their parents/legal guardians (in which case proof of the link between applicant and source of funds must be provided via birth/adoption certificates or court order, plus a letter from the responsible adult confirming the relationship and their consent to this use of funds (C13B))

- Have been, or will be made available by an official financial sponsor such as HM Government, the home government, the British Council, any international organisation, international company, University or Independent School (in which case the Certificate of Acceptance Checking Service entry must confirm details of this official Sponsor, or a signed, dated, headed letter must be provided from the sponsor giving their name and contact details and confirmation of the sponsorship and its duration (C13D))

➢ May rely on funds via a student loan, in which case they may provide proof of funds via a loan letter from a FCA/PRA regulated financial institution in the URK or for overseas accounts from the official regulatory body of the place where the funds are held, dated within six months of the application and showing

- Its date, the applicant's name, name and logo of the institution, the money available

- That it is unconditional on any requirement save for obtaining Tier 4 leave,

- That it is provided by the national or state government or regional or government-sponsored loan company or is part of an academic or educational loan scheme

- For funds backing entry clearance applications, that they are or will be available and will be paid to the applicant or sponsor before travelling and that the living costs component will be available to them on arrival, or if the loan is from a national government, that it will be available to them on arrival in the UK

➢ Must provide the specified documents by way of bank statements, etc., but where they have a Tier 4 Sponsor and hold a passport from an Appendix H country (and if applying for entry clearance are doing so from that country), they may simply confirm the funds are available: the Home Office then reserves the right to request the documents (these are known as the *differentiation arrangements* in the PBS Dependent Guidance 25ff)

➢ Must show higher sums for maintenance if studying in Inner London: at the University of London, or within the City of London or former Metropolitan Police District, which receives a lengthy definition at C12AA (remarkably there was a different definition of Inner London for applications made before 12 November 2015: the Guidance to Home Office staff states that "You can check if the educational establishment is in inner London by entering the postcode into the 'About my vote' website")

➢ A deposit paid on account for accommodation costs may count towards the required maintenance figures up to £1,265 (C13A)

➢ Where fees have been wholly or partly paid, the CAS must confirm this or a paper receipt from the Tier 4 Sponsor must be provided (C13C)

Example

Aloysius applies for entry clearance as a Tier 4 student. He has provided confirmation that he has paid the fees for his 12-month course and additionally has provided evidence of his sponsoring father's bank balance of £12,000 for the calendar month preceding his application, via two bank statements from the same account. You need to check whether this is sufficient evidence of maintenance, by reference to the Table for Tier 4 students in Appendix C.

It would be important to determine where he is studying: if within (the complex definition of) Inner London including its metropolitan area, he needs to show maintenance of £1,265 a month for up to 9 months, if studying elsewhere, only £1,015 a month up to 9 months. He has enough funds for study outside inner London, as the target to hit would be £9,135, but not enough for Inner London study, being £11,385.

And check those bank statements to ensure they cover every day of the 28-day period: whenever more than one statement is provided, there is always the chance of the odd day going astray (C1A(c)). As the statements cover the calendar month preceding application, the most recent presumably is dated within 31 days of the application date and is therefore satisfactory (C1A(h)).

As this is a case of third party support, there must be written consent provided from the parent for the use of funds for study purposes: C1A(ca) read with C13(ii).

Tier 4 child migrants

These applicants

- Enjoy the usual dispensation if from an Appendix H country regarding proof of holding maintenance funds – i.e. they must be provided on request but need not be put forward automatically (C16B)

- Count as privately fostered if cared for full-time by persons other than their parents/close relatives for more than 28 days (C17) – close relative is a grandparent, brother, sister, step-parent, uncle (brother or half-brother of the child's parent) or aunt (sister or half-sister of the child's parent) who is aged 18 or over (C18)

- If so fostered, the care arrangements must be evidenced by a letter from, and confirming the relationship between, all responsible parents/legal guardians and applicant, the basis of the former's legal responsibility, their consent to the Tier 4 application and the living arrangements, and to their travel to the UK for entry clearance applications (C19(a)) – and there must be agreement from the local authority and a copy of the exchange of correspondence between parents/legal guardians and local authority (C19(d))

- If the child is not living independently and is aged under 16 they must provide a signed written letter from their intended carer (accompanied by their passport, proof they are settled in the UK via current passport/travel document, certificate of naturalisation)

- confirming the care arrangements

- giving the carer's contact details, address where they will be living, confirmation that this is a private address and not a commercial enterprise

- explaining the relationship between parent/guardian and carer, the former's agreement to the care arrangements including the address where the child will live

- confirming that £570 is available monthly for up to 9 months

- listing any other people to whom the carer has offered support (C19(b))

➢ Face the same provisions for maintenance (with an elevated threshold for those studying in Inner London) as Tier 4 migrants where studying independently aged 16 or 17 (C19A)

➢ Face the same restrictions as Tier 4 migrants as to availability of funds held by them, their parents/guardians or from an official financial sponsor (C21, C21C), and are similarly able to offset an appropriately evidenced accommodation deposit against the maintenance requirement (C21A-C21B)

Tier 2 applicants may score points for funds, alternatively to meeting the maintenance requirement above (C5(b)-(c)), if

➢ They have entry clearance or leave as a Tier 2 Migrant, or as a work permit holder, representative of a news agency/broadcaster/newspaper, overseas-owned airline operational ground staff or Jewish Agency employee

➢ Their Sponsor is A-rated and has certified on the CoS that should it become necessary they will maintain and accommodate them for the first period of employment, to the tune of at least £945

Tier 5 (Temporary Workers) migrants may also benefit from the latter dispensation if their Sponsor so certifies (C9).

Dependents of Points Based System Migrants

There are particular rules covering the means by which dependent spouses and children of PBS migrants obtain leave themselves. These are found in Part 8 of the Rules (i.e. the part addressing family members generally) rather than within Part 6A dealing with the PBS. Certain rules reflecting general immigration policy are cross-referenced into play, with a view to preventing partners entering the route if aged under 18 (r277) and ensuring that neither partners nor children enter in circumstances that involve the endorsement of entry based on polygamous relationships where there remains another person alive who has migrated to the UK as the spouse of the sponsor (r278, r296).

The Rules are supported by Guidance for Home Office decision makers Family members of PBS Migrants and for applicants (Dependent Policy Guidance).

Only partners and children are eligible: as the Guidance explains, other relatives do not qualify under the Rules. There is supposedly some guidance to be found at the link *Applications submitted on a PBS (Dependant) form for relatives who are neither the partner nor the child of the main applicant*, though at the time of writing there appears to be no such link.

The Rules define a number of characters:

Relevant Points Based System Migrant (RPBSM) – i.e. the principal, who has been granted leave under the PBS routes

Partner of a Relevant Points Based System Migrant – their partner

Child of a Relevant Points Based System Migrant – the latter's child

How the partner route works
This is an entry clearance only route (r319B(a)), except for those who satisfy these three requirements:

- Are not visa nationals (r319B(b)(i))
- Are the partners of RPBSMs entering as Tier 5 Temporary Workers in the creative/sporting sub-category for engagements of less than three months (r319B(b)(ii))
- Can show that they meet the requirements of the route notwithstanding the absence of a visa (r319B(b)(iii))

The requirements for partners (spouse, or civil, unmarried or same-sex partner: we just state "partner" for convenience below) are found in a single rule (r319C), without the usual split between the requirements for entry clearance and leave to remain. An applicant must show that

- They do not fall foul of the general refusal reasons (r319C(a))
- They are the partner of a **RPBSM who is already present with leave or is accompanying them** with entry clearance (r319C(b)(i)-(ii)), or
  - **Settled or settling British citizen PPBSM** – where the RPBSM has indefinite leave to remain or is in the process of being granted it, where the applicant is simply applying for further leave to remain including circumstances where they are being refused settlement for failing the UK life and language requirements (r319C(b)(iii)) and was last granted leave as a dependent of a RPBSM or as a partner of that person in some other immigration route before they entered the PBS (r319C(b)(iii)(1)-(2)), or
  - **British citizen PPBSM** – where the RPBSM previously held indefinite leave to remain as a RPBSM and is now a British citizen where, as in the last scenario, the applicant is making an extension application including where they are compelled to do so because of a UK life and language mishap (r319C(b)(iv))
  - Where the applicant is the unmarried or same-sex partner, they must also show that any previous relationship/marriage has permanently broken down, that they are not so closely related as to bar marriage, and they have been living together in a relationship akin to marriage/civil partnership for at least 2 years (r319C(c))
- The relationship must be genuine and subsisting (r319C(d)) and they must intend to live together permanently throughout their stay in the UK (r319C(e))
- The applicant must not intend to remain in the UK for longer than the RPBSM (r319C(f))
- They must meet the relevant maintenance requirements unless the RPBSM is in the Tier 1 investor or exceptional talent route (r319C(g)): these are found in Appendix E

- Where applying for further leave, they must not be on temporary admission/release or on the immigration bail which replaces temporary admission (r319C(h)(ii-iii)), and must not have last have had entry clearance/leave as a visitor (including coming via Ireland as a visitor), as a short-term student, parent of a Tier 4 (child) student, unless the RPBSM is in, or is joining, the creative/sporting sub-category of Tier 5 (Temporary Worker) (r319C(h)(i))

- They must not be an overstayer other than provided for by Rule 39E (r319C(j))

- Where aged over 18 and applying for entry clearance, they must provide a criminal record certificate for countries in which they have been present for 12 months in total in the last decade (r319C(k)) where the RPBSM is a Tier 1 Entrepreneur/Investor, or is present as a Tier 2 (General) Migrant in the list of health professionals in r319C(k)(1)(c)

- A RPBSM who is a Tier 4 General student must be of a certain calibre within that route (r319C(i)); i.e. a full-time:

  - Government-sponsored student for a course exceeding six months in length (r319C(i)(i)) or on the doctorate extension route (r319C(i)(iii))

  - Post-graduate student for a course of 9 months or longer, sponsored by a UK recognised body or in receipt of funding as a higher education institution from England's Higher Education Funding Council or an equivalent in Wales, Northern Ireland or Scotland (r319C(i)(ii))

Additionally, where the RPBSM is a Tier 4 General student, who is applying for entry clearance or leave for a course of six months or more (r319C(i)(iv)), then the RPBSM and their partner must be applying together for further leave (r319C(i)(iv)(3)) and

  - The RPBSM must hold entry clearance/leave of six months or longer or last held such entry clearance/leave within the three months before this application (r319C(i)(iv)(1)) and

  - The applicant partner must hold entry clearance as the partner of a RPBSM for a course of six months or longer, or have last had such leave within the three months before this application (r319C(i)(iv)(2))

Examples

Anila is the wife of Sarabjit. He is coming to the UK as a Tier 2 (General) migrant. They want Anila to travel and live with him in the UK.

Anila is the spouse of a RPBSM (all PBS migrants qualify subject to the restrictions for Tier 4), and Sarabjit would be "at the same time, being granted entry clearance" as her (r319C(b)(ii)). She must intend to remain in the UK for no longer than him, and the funds in Appendix E must be available.

Imagine that Anila had not previously joined Sarabjit, and he has now become a British citizen, a year after obtaining ILR in the UK.

Anila could not join him under the PBS partner rules: although she would be the spouse of a person who previously held leave as a RPBSM before becoming a British citizen (r319C(b)(iv)), she herself has not previously held leave as his partner, either whilst he was a RPBSM or otherwise (r319C(b)(iv)(1) or (2)). She would have to apply under the Appendix FM route to join a settled person in the UK.

Anooshka is the wife of Imran, who is already present in the UK as a Tier 2 (General) migrant. She has come to the UK as a visitor and wants to know if she can switch into leave as the partner of a RPBSM.

She cannot do so: a visitor cannot switch (r319C(h)(i)).

Davinder is in a long-term relationship with Marilyn who has leave to remain as a Tier 4 Migrant pursuing a Masters level degree course lasting two years, and wants to join her in the UK. She is government sponsored.

In order to be a qualifying Sponsor, Marilyn must satisfy the r319C(i) requirements: this is easy enough in her case, as her government sponsorship means she qualifies (under one of the most confusingly numbered of all Rules, r319C(i)(i)).

He will need to join her via the unmarried partner sub-category: this will require that he provides evidence of any previous relationship having broken down, that any blood relationship is not too close, and that they have previously cohabited for two years: r319C(c).

Now imagine that the facts above are the same, except that Marilyn is only studying at bachelor's degree level without government sponsorship of any kind, and is halfway through her three year course with leave granted for the length of the course. Davinder would only qualify if they met the requirements of r319C(i)(iv), the sweeping-up provision for students. However that sub-route requires the partner to already be present in the UK with leave as the partner of a Tier 4 migrant: r319C(i)(iv)(2). So he would not qualify.

So let's imagine Davinder had indeed been present with Marilyn throughout her bachelor's degree studies, and that they have come to an end. She wants to apply to do a further degree which she considers appropriate to expand her CV, although not at Masters level.

The application looks hopeful: although the only sub-route is the rather forbidding text of r319C(i)(iv), Marilyn would indeed be applying to study for longer than six months, and would have previously held leave within the three months before the application for study purposes exceeding six months (r319C(i)(iv)(1)) and Davinder would have had held leave of similar quality alongside her r319C(i)(iv)(2). They would have to be applying together (r319C(i)(iv)(3)), which on these facts would not be a problem.

Length and conditions of leave for a partner of a RPBSM

Entry clearance/leave will be granted

- In line with the RPBSM or for three years if the RPBSM has, or is being granted, indefinite leave to remain or has become a British citizen (r319D(a))

- Subject to conditions:

  - No recourse to public funds, and police registration if required under r326 (r319D(b)(i)-(ii))

  - No employment as a doctor/dentist in training, unless they hold a primary degree in medicine/dentistry from a UK recognised or listed UK institution (or one which holds a Tier 4 Sponsor licence), or have previously been granted entry clearance/leave to so work and have a letter from the Postgraduate Deanery or NHS Trust that they have been working on a training programme/post approved by the GMC or the Joint Committee for Post Graduate Training in Dentistry (r319D(b)(iii))

  - No employment whatsoever if they are granted leave under the last of the student sub-categories of applicant partner identified above, i.e. where they made a joint application to extend leave with the RPBSM to pursue a course exceeding six months in length where they both had been granted leave in the previous three months for such purposes (r319D(b)(iv)) – however the partner may work where the RPBSM is applying for, or has leave, to continue studying the same course for which they had previously been granted more than 12 months leave

  - No employment as a professional sportsperson/coach (r319D(b)(v))

  - No study other than as permitted in Part 15 of the Rules (r319D(b)(vi))

Indefinite leave to remain as the partner of a RPBSM
The requirements are:

- Not falling for refusal under the general refusal reasons or being an illegal entrant (r319D(a))

- Being the partner (all references here being to the broad definition given above comprising all four kinds of partner) of a RPBSM who has, or is being granted, indefinite leave to remain or has become a British citizen having previously held indefinite leave to remain as a RPBSM (r319D(b)) (the Guidance emphasises that ILR must have been obtained via the PBS route not via long residence: page 34 of 83)

- Having last been granted leave as the partner of such a RPBSM (r319D(c))

- Have been living together as partners (including whilst living lawfully in Jersey, Guernsey or the Isle of Man) for

  - Two years if the applicant previously had leave under the Rules in place before 9 July 2012 as the RPBSM's partner whilst the principal was a RPBSM, or as their partner whilst the RPBSM had another form of leave under the Rules, and has had continuous leave as a RPBSM partner since then (r319D(d)(i))

  - Five years during which time they have been in a relationship for the entire period, and most recently had leave as a RPBSM partner, consistently satisfying certain requirements of the route: genuine and subsisting relationship with an intention to live together permanently whilst residing in the UK in circumstances where any previous relationship has broken down and without a general refusal reason arising and whilst the RPBSM has been within a PBS route (r319D(d)(ii))

- For leave granted from 11 January 2018, they must not have been absent from the UK for more than 180 days during any 12 month period in the relevant continuous period, save for evidence-backed periods abroad assisting with a national or international humanitarian or environmental crisis overseas (r319D(d)(ii)(d))

➢ They must remain in a genuine and subsisting relationship with an intention to live together permanently whilst residing in the UK (r319D(e-(f))

➢ The knowledge of UK life/language requirements in Appendix KOLL must be met (r319D(g))

➢ They must not be an overstayer other than provided for by Rule 39E (r319D(i))

How the child route works
This is an entry clearance only route (r319G(a)), except for those who satisfy the same three requirements identified above for partners (i.e. essentially where they are non-visa nationals entering as Tier 5 sporting/creatives for short engagements and can show they satisfy the route's requirements (r319G(b)). Once again the requirements are found in a single rule (r319H), without the usual split between the requirements for evidence and leave to remain. They must show that

➢ They do not fall foul of the general refusal reasons (r319H(a))

➢ They are the child of a RPBSM or the RPBSM's partner who is already present with limited or indefinite leave (or holds British citizenship having previously had ILR) or is accompanying them with entry clearance (r319H(b)(i)-(ii))

➢ They are aged under 18 at the application date or if over 18 and applying for leave to remain, have previously been granted leave as the child of a RPBSM or their partner, or the child of a person who subsequently became a RPBSM (r319H(c))

➢ They must not be married, in a civil partnership, have formed an independent family unit, or be living independently and if aged over 16, must provide documents to such effect (r319H(d)) - those documents are

- Two forms of proof of residential address from a list in the Rules dated within a calendar month of the application date, details of rent/board payments, and if living away from the family home, an explanation of the reasons for this backed by an authorised letter from the place of study and matching bank statements from child and parent confirming the parental support and origin of funds for three months (r319H-SD(a))

- The Guidance gives examples of living independently: living away from the family other than due to study, being in full time employment, or ostensible financial independency (e.g. where income exceeds expenditure) (page 56 of 83)

➢ They must not intend to remain in the UK for longer than the RPBSM (r319H(e))

➢ Both their parents must be lawfully present in the UK (and not as visitors) or be making applications at the same time (r319H(f)) unless

- The RPBSM is the sole surviving parent or

- The RPBSM has and has had sole responsibility for the child's upbringing

- There are serious and compelling reasons making it undesirable to refuse the application and suitable arrangements have been made for the child's care

➢ They must meet the relevant maintenance requirements unless the RPBSM is in the Tier 1 Investor or Exceptional Talent route (r319H(g)); these are found in Appendix E

➢ Where applying to extend their leave, they must not be on temporary admission/release or be on immigration bail (r319G(h)(ii-iv)), and must not have last have had entry clearance/leave as a visitor (including coming via Ireland as such), as a short-term student, unless the RPBSM is in, or is joining, the creative/sporting sub-category of Tier 5 (Temporary Worker) (r319G(h)(i))

➢ They must not be an overstayer inconsistently with Rule 39E (r319H(m))

➢ If the RPBSM is a Tier 4 General student, then they must be of a certain calibre within that route (r319H(i)), studying full-time and being a:

- Government-sponsored student for a course exceeding six months in length (r319H(i)(i)) or on the doctorate extension route (r319H(i)(iii))

- Post-graduate student for a course of twelve months or longer, sponsored by a UK recognised body or in receipt of funding as a higher education institution from England's Higher Education Funding Council or an equivalent in Wales, Northern Ireland or Scotland (r319H(i)(ii))

- RPBSM who is applying for entry clearance or leave for a course of six months plus (r319H(i)(iv)), where the PBSM and their partner are applying together for further leave (r319H(i)(iv)(3)) and

    - The RPBSM holds entry clearance/leave of six months or longer or last held such entry clearance/leave within the three months before this application (r319H(i)(iv)(1)) and

    - The applicant child holds entry clearance as the child of a RPBSM for a course of six months or longer, or last had such leave within the three months before this application (r319H(i)(iv)(2))

➢ If born in the UK to a RPBSM and their partner, they must provide a UK birth certificate showing the names of both parents (r319H(k))

➢ All arrangements for their care and accommodation in the UK must comply with relevant UK legislation and regulations (r319H(l))

➢ If the child falls foul of the bar on being a visitor or a short-term student, then their application may still succeed if they are applying for entry clearance (r319H(j)) and

- They were born during the RPBSM's last entry clearance/leave (if the RPBSM is a student, such leave must exceed six months in length)

- They were born during leave granted to the RPBSM for resitting examinations or repeating a course module or during the leave given for the purpose of the original studies

- They were born within three months of the expiry of the most recent leave

Example

Janice is the 14 year old daughter of Marilyn. Marilyn plans to come to the UK as a Tier 2 (General) worker, and has the necessary sponsorship lined up. Marilyn is separated from her husband John, who remains in the country of origin.

Rule 319H normally contemplates child applications only where both applicants are in the UK lawfully. As only one parent is in the UK, the only route is 319H(f), which requires, beyond the establishment of the child/parent link, that Marilyn has sole responsibility for Janice or that there are otherwise serious reasons making it undesirable to refuse her entry.

Pablo is the son of Juanita and Marty, respectively a Tier 1 Entrepreneur and her husband who is a PBS dependent; Pablo entered the UK with them two years ago when they were granted entry clearance in the Entrepreneur route over three years ago. They are now planning to extend their leave. Pablo is now aged 18 years and six months.

Pablo is entitled to apply as a child dependent, notwithstanding he is now an adult, because he is "over 18 and applying for leave to remain" and has leave as the child of a RPBSM: r319H(c).

Hubert is the 12 year son of Jacinta. Jacinta is present in the UK as a Tier 1 Exceptional Talent migrant. Given the nature of his RPBSM, Hubert does not have to pass the Appendix E financial requirements: r319H(j).

Rudy is the child of Eleanor and Henry, citizens of the USA who are coming to the UK as a Tier 5 Temporary Worker and their dependent partner. Eleanor and Rudy do not require entry clearance, so long as they meet the requirements of the route generally, as they are not visa nationals and the RPBSM is entering under r245ZN(b): r319B(b), 319G(b).

The maintenance requirements for Points Based System dependent partners and children

The maintenance requirements are found in Appendix E.

- This incorporates the requirements for timing and content of bank statements and other evidence required to establish the reality of the maintenance relied upon in Appendix C (E(aa)), including the calculation for the end date of supporting bank statements (E(m))
- The funds must be demonstrated as available to the RPBSM or applicant (E(c))
- The funds are additional to those relied upon by the RPBSM if they are applying at the same time (E(e))
- Funds obtained during UK residence count only where such residence was lawful without breaching any conditions of leave (E(h))

- Financial institutions listed in Appendix P are deemed unacceptable (E(ia))

- In general applicants must provide the specified documents by way of bank statements, etc., but where they are applying alongside their Tier 4 RPBSM and hold a passport from an Appendix H country (and if applying for entry clearance are doing so from that country), they may simply confirm the funds are available: the Home Office then reserves the right to request the documents (E(j))

- Available funds will be calculated via a conversion using www.oanda.com (E(k))

- Where there are multiple applications being made, by the RPBSM and one of more dependents or simply by multiple dependents, then all dependents will be refused if any one of the group fails to show sufficient funds for maintenance (E(l))

- Overdraft facilities do not count (E(q))

There are some route specific criteria:

- Just as applies for principal applicants, Entrepreneurs may not rely on their business's investment funds to meet the maintenance requirements for dependents (E(ab))

- Tier 4 dependents

    - Must confirm the funds are, and will remain, available to them or their RPBSM for living expenses (E(ba)(i)(3)) – for children, the funds must be shown as available to them, the RPBSM or the other parent living lawfully in the UK

    - Where funds are coming from an official financial sponsor who is also covering the maintenance costs of dependents (such as HM Government, the home government, the British Council, any international organisation, international company, university or independent school), that sponsor must confirm this by letter (E(n))

    - If their applications were made before 12 November 2015, the figures are £615/£450 for inner London and other study (Guidance page 44 of 83)

- For Tier 2 (General) and Tier 5 (Temporary Worker), funds will be treated as available where the Sponsor is A-rated and certifies they will maintain and accommodate if required (for at least £630) up to the end of the first month of leave, either by endorsing the CoS or by letter confirming the applicant's name, Sponsor's name and logo, and any limitation on their undertaking (E(i)): if applying at the same time as the RPBSM, the latter must provide a valid CoS reference

- The dependents of a Tier 2 RPBSM may score points for funds (or to put it more clearly, are exempt from evidencing maintenance funds), alternatively to meeting the maintenance requirement, where the RPBSM is applying alongside them simply because they are switching employer, or as a work permit holder, representative of a news agency/broadcaster/newspaper, overseas-owned airline operational ground staff or Jewish Agency employee (E(o)) – the same proviso applies where they are not applying at the same time, but in the last application leading to a grant of leave the RPBSM was exempted for the same reasons (E(p))

➢ Graduate Entrepreneur dependants may score points for funds provided for Appendix A purposes where the maintenance for dependents is confirmed by the Department for International Trade as having been awarded in their endorsement letter (E(ib))

Category of RPBSM	**Funds required**	**Length of time funds must be held**
Tier 1 Investor/Exceptional talent migrant	None (E(ab))	Not applicable
Tier 1 Graduate Entrepreneur	£1,260 (E(a)(i))	90 days (E(g)(ii))
Other Tier 1	£1,890 (E(a)(ii))	90 days (E(g)(ii))
Other PBS categories	£630 (E(b)(ii))	90 days (E(g)(ii))
Tier 4 (General)	£845 for each month of stay which would be granted where the RPBSM is studying in Inner London for up to 9 months (E(ba)(i)) £680 for each month of stay which would be granted for up to 9 months (E(ba)(ii))	28 days (E(g)(ii))

Examples

James is the spouse of Jemimah, who is present as a Tier 1 Entrepreneur. He wishes to join her in the UK as his present job in the USA has finished; he enjoys life in the UK where he previously stayed for a couple of years.

He will need to demonstrate funds of £1,890 (E(a)(ii)). The funds must be established as available to him James or Jemimah (E(c)). He must show they are available for 90 days (E(g)(i)), demonstrated via a complete set of bank statements ending no more than 31 days before the application (E(m)). It is important to check that he is not relying on funds gathered from a period when he was present in the UK unlawfully or in breach of conditions (E(h)).

Cedric is the partner of Edith; she is present in the UK in the Tier 4 (General) category as a government-sponsored student. They are both Australian nationals.

As Australia is an Appendix H country, Cedric need not provide the specified documents (by way of bank statements as required by Appendix C at para 1B (E(j))) along with his application; however the Home Office may still request those documents should they wish to do so.

Length and conditions of leave for a child of a RPBSM
Entry clearance/leave will be granted

- In line with the parent (RPBSM or their partner) whose leave expires first, or for three years if both parents have, or are being granted, indefinite leave to remain or have become British citizens (r319I(a)(i)-(ii))

- Subject to conditions:

  - No recourse to public funds, and police registration if required under r326 (r319I(b)(i)-(ii))

  - Where the RPBSM is a Tier 4 general migrant applying for leave of less than 12 months or is pursuing studies below degree level, no employment whatsoever (r319I(b)(iii))

    - if the applicant is granted leave under the last of the sub-categories of a Tier 4 student's child, i.e. where they made a joint application to extend leave with the RPBSM to pursue a course exceeding six months in length where they both had been granted leave in the previous three months for such purposes (though they may work where the RPBSM was, or is being, granted further leave to continue a course for which they had previously been granted more than 12 months' leave) or

    - if the applicant was granted leave under the provisos for children who fell foul of the restriction on being present as visitors

  - No employment as a professional sportsperson/coach r319I(b)(iv))

Indefinite leave to remain as the child of a RPBSM
The requirements are:

- Not falling for refusal under the general refusal reasons or being an illegal entrant (r319J(a))

- Being the child of a RPBSM or their partner who has, or is being granted, indefinite leave to remain (r319J(b))

- Having last been granted leave as the child of a RPBSM or their partner, or having been born here as the child of such (r319J(c))

- They must not be married, in a civil partnership, have formed an independent family unit, or be living independently and if aged over 16, must provide documents to such effect (r319J(d)) – those documents are identified above

- Both parents must be lawfully settled in the UK or being granted indefinite leave to remain unless (r319J(e)):

  - The RPBSM is the sole surviving parent, or

- The RPBSM has and has had sole responsibility for the child's upbringing, or

- There are serious and compelling reasons making it undesirable to refuse the application and suitable arrangements have been made for the child's care, or

- One parent is being granted ILR at the same time as a RPBSM, the other is lawfully present in the UK or being granted leave alongside the applicant, where the applicant was granted leave as child under the Rules in place before 9 July 2012

➢ The knowledge of UK life/language requirements in Appendix KOLL must be met (r319J(f))

➢ If born in the UK to a RPBSM and their partner, they must provide a UK birth certificate showing the names of both parents (r319J(g))

➢ All arrangements for their care and accommodation in the UK must comply with relevant UK legislation and regulations (r319J(h))

➢ They must not be an overstayer inconsistently with Rule 39E (r319J(i))

Applying for indefinite leave to remain

Many of the routes within the PBS provide for a migrant to apply for settlement. It is easy to tell whether the route in question does or not: there will be a distinct section addressing ILR applications. Thus we can see that in most Tier 1 routes, there will be access to ILR. So when one reads through Part 6A of the Rules, it quickly becomes apparent that there are some routes that do not offer access to settlement: Tier 4 students, for example, and most migrants under Tier 2, except for Intra-Company Transfers who have been here under the Rules before April 2010. Until April 2018, there is even a route that only exists for settlement purposes: Tier 1 General, which accordingly contains no provision for initial grants or extensions of leave.

The Rules explain precisely what period of prior leave needs to be clocked up before an application is made. That criteria is sometimes found in Appendix A (for Investors and Entrepreneurs, see Tables 6, 9A and 9B) and sometimes within Part 6A of the main Rules. There is sometimes scope for accelerated settlement, as in the Entrepreneur route where a significant number of jobs have been created (see Appendix A, Row 4 of Table 6) or in the Investor route where investment has been on a particularly large scale (see Table 9A at row 3).

The most distinctive feature of ILR applications for PBS migrants is the continuous residence requirement found in Part 6A of the Rules, at r245AAA.

Continuous residence requirement: only 180 days of absence allowed

Part 6A of the Rules sets out some general requirements regarding the meaning of *continuous residence* for Points Based System applicants seeking settlement. The key passages of the Rule are as follows:

> **245AAA.General requirements for indefinite leave to remain**
> For the purposes of references in this Part to requirements for indefinite leave to remain ...:
> (a) "continuous period of 5 years lawfully in the UK" means ... residence in the United Kingdom for an unbroken period with valid leave, and for these purposes a period shall not considered to be unbroken where:
> (i) the applicant has not been absent from the UK for more than 180 days during any 12 month period in the continuous period ...

Features of this Rule are:

- The regime is reasonably generous as to how much residence abroad it permits, in that one can be out of the country for almost half of any particular year;

- Otherwise the Rule is strict, in that the application will be refused for any greater absences

- There may be a single break due to a national or international environmental or humanitarian crisis overseas, such as the Ebola crisis (before January 2018, only Ebola-related breaks were condoned by the Rule) – and the Sponsor must have consented to the absence (r245AAA(a)(i))

- The Applicant must have leave on their departure and return (r245AAA(a)(ii)), however breaks in leave will be disregarded in these scenarios: where

    - Leave expired no more than 28 days before a successful further entry clearance application was made before 24 November 2016: in this scenario, the break will be disregarded, both the period of up to 28 days pre-application, and the period whilst the application was considered and granted, pending re-entry

    - For applications made on or after 24 November 2016 by applicants who make a successful entry clearance application whilst they have continuing limited leave granted, the period spent abroad with continuing leave and period pending return shall be disregarded

    - For applications made on or after 24 November 2016, a further application was made within 14 days of leave expiring and a good explanation within the ILR application for the delay

    - Leave had expired, a further application for entry clearance was made and refused, but a further application made within 14 days of the refusal or within the permitted administrative review period succeeded

- Short periods of overstaying are disregarded where protected by Rule 39E, i.e. because up to 14 days of overstaying were condoned, either automatically or by the exercise of Home Office discretion (r245AAA(a)(iii))

- Other short periods of overstaying are disregarded for applications made before 24 November 2016 and within 28 days of the expiry of leave (r245AAA(a)(iv))

- Save for migrants in the Investor, Entrepreneur, Exceptional or Highly Skilled Migrant routes, absences must be for a purpose that is consistent with the applicant's basis of stay here, including paid annual leave, or for serious or compelling reasons (r245AAA(c)) (the Guidance points out that those benefitting from the "serious or compelling proviso" would be other modern PBS routes, plus work permit holders, overseas business representatives, overseas government employees, airport-based operational staff of overseas-owned airlines or domestic workers in private households)

- The continuous period is treated as ending on the date which is most beneficial to the applicant out of the following: application date, decision date, or any date up to 28 days after the application date (r245AAA(d))

- Residence may have been in Jersey, Guernsey or the Isle of Man, where the residence was pursuant to leave for an equivalent purpose, and provided the last period of leave before the settlement application was spent in the UK with leave under the relevant category (r245AAA(e))

- Although not dealt with in this Rule, PBS dependents granted leave from 11 January 2018 will be under a similar "180 days" residence requirement: we addressed this when dealing with PBS dependents, above

The Rule changed *for applications made from 11 January 2018*, with an implication for the calculation of continuous residence that is of uncertain effect. Previously the Rule stated:

> the applicant has been absent from the UK for a period of 180 days or less in any of the five consecutive 12 month periods preceding the date of the application for leave to remain,

Whereas, as we just saw, it now says

> the applicant has not been absent from the UK for more than 180 days during any 12 month period in the continuous period

The practice under the previous version of the Rule has been to calculate the periods of absence during each of the calendar years running up to the application date. This provided the useful possibility of timing the application so as to exclude periods of excess absence, or at least to share them between particular years, with a view to demonstrating that there was no excess absence in any of the five annual periods running up to the application date. However, one reading of the more recent wording is that applicants would have to calculate their absence during *every single possible* 12-month period over the last half decade.

Indeed, the Guidance recognises this possibility, stating:

> you must consider absences from the UK on a rolling basis, rather than in separate consecutive 12-month periods

A version of the Guidance addressing this change stated this (though it was not retained in the Version 17.0 Guidance effective from July 2018):

> You may also consider granting outside the rules if an applicant provides a letter setting out reasons why they believe changes to how the 180 days are counted will cause them exceptionally harsh consequences.

The Guidance - calculating continuous leave explains how discretion may be exercised outside of the Rule:

- Absences (beyond those referenced in the Rule) due to serious and compelling reasons can be condoned where down to circumstances beyond the applicant's control (backed by written evidence of the relevant crisis and ensuing travel disruption), e.g.

  - serious illness of the applicant or a close relative
  - a conflict
  - a natural disaster, for example, volcanic eruption or tsunami

  Absence for employment or economic activity reasons is expressly *not* considered exceptional

The Guidance also makes other points:

- Applicants may rely on the time from when entry clearance was originally granted until they arrived in the UK as part of their continuous residence period: they will be treated as absent during that period, but providing it does not carry them over the 180-day limit, this avenue may bring forward the date at which settlement is obtained

- Only whole days of absence count: so days which include periods of travel to and from the UK are, usefully, excluded from the calculation

- Any time spent working offshore on the UK continental shelf, beyond the 12 mile zone defined as UK territorial waters, does not count toward the continuous qualifying period, for example on ships or oil rigs, so it is treated as a period of absence from the UK

- Absence must be established to be for purposes consistent with the leave granted: holidays within relevant contractual limits and other short trips abroad are not required to meet this requirement, though employers should nevertheless confirm the periods of annual leave and any additional periods of permitted absence (Tier 2 migrants are allowed to have a further holiday period in between jobs where an application to change Sponsor succeeded). Absences of up to 30 days may be condoned even without an employer's letter depending on all the circumstances

- Absences for the purpose of employment outside the UK "which demonstrates that the UK employment is secondary" are not permitted and will break continuous residence

- If continuous residence is broken, then it will be necessary to rebuild it from scratch, making further extension applications

The Guidance states that possible reasons for condoning late applications would be

- Serious illness causing a delay in making an extension application, established by medical evidence

- Travel or postal delays

- Inability to provide a document for reasons outside their control: e.g. because the Home Office held documents and failed to return them on time, or because replacement documents required because of theft, fire or flood did not materialise in time due to postal delays

Until 13 December 2012, Chapter 6A of the Immigration Directorate Instructions as it was from November 2011 contained an "Annex B - Calculation of the qualifying period of continuous leave for settlement" which did permit excess absence "for reasons related to the applicant's employment or business in the United Kingdom". It might be thought that somebody who incurred excess absence for that reason, relying on the Guidance, would have a good case. However the Upper Tribunal disagreed in RN [2017] UKUT 76 (IAC).

Examples

Janet is present as a Tier 1 Entrepreneur. She wishes to apply for settlement having clocked up five years of leave under this route. She has another three months of leave presently. She has travelled a lot. When you calculate her periods of absence from the UK, it is clear that in the first year of leave, she was absent for slightly more than 180 days, for reasons related to her business; this included being absent for the first two months of her leave.

Janet will almost certainly, if she makes a settlement application now, be refused for excess absence under r245AAA.

However, she can wait two months for the excess absence to drop out of the five year period of continuous residence before the application date on which she relies. Then she can apply for indefinite leave to remain before her present leave expires.

James is present under Tier 2 General, having had leave in that route for the last five years. He wants to apply for indefinite leave to remain. In the second of his five years of residence, he was abroad for 190 days.

You need to determine the reason for his absence beyond 180 days. If it was due to his employment, it will not qualify. However, if his return was delayed on one occasion (accounting for the excess absence) due to a natural disaster, he may be granted leave outside the Rules (if he puts forward a cogent evidence-backed explanation), under the policy statement in the Guidance.

Knowledge of life in the UK and the English language

These requirements are laid out in Appendix KoLL to the Immigration Rules. Individual rules generally refer to this Appendix thus: "The applicant must have sufficient knowledge of the English language and sufficient knowledge about life in the United Kingdom, in accordance with Appendix KoLL" (for example, take a look at the provisions at the start of Part 6A, for Tier 1 (Exceptional Talent) Migrants: you can see the relevant provision at r245BF(e)).

Under Appendix KoLL, applicants must pass the Life in the UK test, and separately evidence that they can speak and understand the English language at minimum B1 level of the Common European Framework of Reference for Languages (CEFR) (equivalent to an ESOL qualification at entry level 3).

The Life in the UK Test requirement is met by sitting and passing an examination with multiple choice questions based on the book *Life in the United Kingdom: A Guide for New Residents.* The ESOL route (i.e. passing an ESOL qualification taught with citizenship materials) is no longer available.

The official website for those booking and preparing to take the test is https://www.gov.uk/life-in-the-uk-testc

The language requirement can be met in several different ways:

By being a national of a country listed in paragraph 2.2(a)(i) of Appendix KOLL (essentially the USA, and then Commonwealth countries in the Caribbean and Australia, New Zealand and Canada)

- By passing a secure English language test in speaking and listening at the minimum level with a provider approved by the HO (as specified in Appendix O – which lists providers and the levels at which their various examinations must be passed, and the duration for which test results stay valid). A full list of tests and test centres is on the GOV.UK website.

- Having an academic qualification at Bachelor's degree or higher level (excluding professional and vocational qualifications) from the UK (backed up by the appropriate academic certificate, reference or transcript showing the award's details) or from a college in a country listed in paragraph 2.2(a)(iii) of Appendix KoLL

- Having an academic qualification at Bachelor's degree or higher level (excluding professional and vocational qualifications) taught in English

- Having already met the B1 requirement in a previous grant of leave, and having had unbroken leave since that grant

Part 3 of Appendix KoLL lays out the exemptions:

- for those aged under 18 or over 65 at the date of their applications, and

- where the UKVI considers that, because of the applicant's mental or physical condition, it would be unreasonable to expect them to fulfil that requirement (a GP or GMC registered consultant must provide the supporting medical evidence).

Some of those who are unable to pass either or both KoLL tests, despite their best efforts, may be able to rely on a reduced requirement after having spent 15 continuous years in the UK (as specified in paragraph 3.2 of Appendix KoLL). They will then need to pass an English language qualification at Level A2 of the CEFR. Nationals of the countries listed at paragraph 3.2(d) must take and pass the Life in the UK test, however long that takes. The specified documents that must be submitted with the ILR application are in Part 4 of Appendix KoLL.

Guidance on the KOLL requirements is at: https://www.gov.uk/government/publications/knowledge-of-life-and-language-in-the-uk

Rule 39C allows the UKVI to interview applicants for settlement to satisfy the Secretary of State that the KoLL requirements are met. If the decision-maker has reasonable cause to doubt (on examination or interview or on any other basis) that any document submitted, by an applicant for the purposes of satisfying the requirements of Appendix KoLL, was genuinely obtained, that document may be discounted for the purposes of the application.

Chapter 2: Tier 1 Representing Entrepreneurs

In this chapter we provide:

- A practical explanation of the way the Entrepreneur and Graduate Entrepreneur Rules operate, explaining the major concepts underpinning the route before presenting the detailed requirements in a user-friendly format

- Highlights of the most useful parts of the Home Office Guidance about Entrepreneurs

- Practical examples and casework tips showing the common pitfalls of the route

- Strategies for avoiding genuineness refusals in advance; and for managing, and challenging, such refusals when they arise

Introduction

For a person with sufficient means and the right frame of mind, the Entrepreneur route represents one of the more accessible ways of entering the UK for business immigration purposes. However, the route is fraught with challenges, ranging from the genuineness test (by which Home Office decision makers assess not only the *credibility* of the application but also its *feasibility* as a business venture), to the fabulously detailed supporting document requirements which are likely to frustrate any but the most devoted reader of small print, to the difficulties in meeting the consistent employment requirements for an extension of leave.

A person may apply in their own right or as a member of a two-person entrepreneurial team. The investment funds may come from the applicant, or from a third party, such as a family member, or from one of the external sources identified by the Rules which independently vet the quality of the business proposal, such as seed funding competitions and UK government departments. Where funds come from a third party, there are numerous details that have to be provided in the supporting documents, including some that are known to unhorse some applicants, such as the need for the bank to confirm that the funds promised to the applicant on this application have not also been affirmed as available to someone else.

The route aims to provide an opportunity for individuals (including two people forming an entrepreneurial team) wishing to invest in a UK business to do so. Unsurprisingly, certain activities are ruled out, particularly property development and management, and also activities that amount to disguised employment such as simply working for another business. The investment may be made into the business via cash funds, a director's loan or shareholding. Those who have already made all or part of the investment before they apply may do so only via investing in a way that shows up in the company accounts. They must provide proof of so doing, bringing into play a broader variety of specified evidence. Investment funds must remain available to the applicant until spent for business purposes.

The general requirement is to hold funds of £200,000. However this is modified in some circumstances, for example where the applicant has sourced funds from certain trusted sources which have independently verified the business, such as winners of seed funding competitions or those backed by UK government departments, and for Graduate Entrepreneurs. The investment funds must go towards the expansion and establishment of the business: thus any element of money that is then paid back to the applicant by way of remuneration does not count. So it pays to scrutinise the proposed investment in the context of the business model.

Although the investment funds may come from a third party, the reliability of such funds has to be affirmed by the bank holding them, confirming that they have not been promised to another enterprise, and by a letter from an independent legal adviser from the country where the money or the third party is located confirming the identity of the person offering funds.

A business plan must be provided in order for the decision maker to understand and assess the application. The business idea can be tested by the Home Office for genuineness: this is as much about assessing the viability of the business as it is about its credibility. If there are concerns about the application, the applicant is likely to be called for interview for their plans to be probed. Thus the applicant must be intimately familiar with the key elements of their business plan, and be able to speak consistently and articulately about their marketing strategy, and to cogently explain how their enterprise will compete with existing businesses. It is the genuineness testing stage which is the main contributor to the high refusal rate in this category: at least half of all applications are refused.

Applicants may apply to join the Entrepreneur route via entry clearance or from within the UK. They may switch into the route from other parts of Tier 1, Tier 2, and sometimes Tier 4, where previously sponsored by educational establishments which particularly impress the Home Office, such as a UK-recognised one or one in receipt of public funding. However, these students may only try and enter the route where their business has been actively backed by such an establishment formally endorsing their enterprise, under the Graduate Entrepreneur route.

There are fewer routes than once were: for example, it used to be the case that Tier 1 General migrants could apply to be an Entrepreneur, but that route closed on 6 April 2015; similarly Post-Study Workers could apply, until their own cut-off of 11 July 2014. Only businesses established before those dates qualify, and so applicants via those routes face additional evidential requirements to satisfy a decision maker that their business was trading and they were making a contribution to the economy at a particular skill level, measured by the National Audit Office's Standard Occupation Codes, before the route closed.

Extensions of leave can be granted within the route, but only for those who can prove they have established two new full-time jobs (either additional to previous staffing levels where a business was taken over, or two such jobs within a new business) for UK-settled workers that have lasted for at least 12 months, within the last grant of leave to remain. Additionally it must be proved that the promised business funds were invested in the previous 12 months leading up to the extension application, and that the business was appropriately registered with companies house or HMRC within six months of joining the route.

The route gives access to settlement, more quickly for those who have created significant numbers of jobs or income (10 or more new jobs, or £5 million more income). Once the Entrepreneur has been in the route for five years (three years under the accelerated proviso), they may apply for indefinite leave to remain.

There is a separate route for Graduate Entrepreneurs, who may apply if they have been endorsed by a UK higher education institution and the department of international trade. They can exit their sub-category into the general Tier 1 Entrepreneur route, and only require £50,000 of investment funds when so doing.

The prudent applicant will ensure that they explain their business in a covering letter, which will also give them the opportunity to address any issues that might be thought to arise from their business plan. The Guidance states this is appropriate for "unusual or particularly complex" cases where the case for scoring points may not otherwise be clear or where an extension application needs to clarify the establishment or joining of a business and the subsequent jobs creation. It then goes on to emphasise that the provision of a letter is no substitute for the provision of the necessary evidence and information within the application itself.

The covering letter may well provide the best opportunity to plug any gaps left by the business plan having regard to the matters listed below that might be taken into account when assessing the credibility of the application: a judge on a judicial review application would certainly expect it to be taken into account by a decision maker.

How do the Entrepreneur Rules work?

The Rules are structured in a distinct way throughout the Points Based System. The Entrepreneur route is set out in Part 6A of the Rules. However, the detailed provisions by which it is satisfied are laid out in Appendices A-C. Appendices B-C simply set out the English language and Maintenance requirements. We address those compendiously in Chapter 1: *General Themes in PBS Cases.*

The real detail of the route lies within Appendix A. Like some other aspects of the Points Based System, the reality is that either one satisfies a particular requirement, or one does not. If one satisfies it, then one gets full points for that aspect of the Rules. And if one satisfies each of the requirements of the Table under which one is applying, then one gets the necessary 75 points to qualify for the targeted form of entry clearance or leave to remain. Applicants must obtain 75 points for whichever stage of the process they are applying under: entry clearance, an extension of leave to remain, or indefinite leave to remain (Tables 4, 5 and 6 respectively).

Note that we identify the provisions of an Appendix A via its letter prefix plus the paragraph number: thus A43 is Appendix A para 43.

The criteria for the route under Appendix A were extensively reworded in January 2018: however, the Home Office position at the time was that this was simply for ease of understanding, and did not imply any change of position.

There are two sets of Guidance:

- Tier 1 (Entrepreneur) Version 21.0 (published for Home Office staff on 5 November 2018) (which we reference as Guidance para ...)

- The Guidance that helps applicants complete the application form (Version 11/2018; to be used for applications made on or after 5 November 2018) (which we refer to as *Guidance to applicants*)

Generally speaking we refer to the former, being that used by the Home Office's own staff (i.e. the Version 20.0 Guidance), which is significantly more extensive.

Entrepreneur route: Key features

Joining a business

This route (245D(a)) is for migrants wishing to

- Establish, or

- Join, or

- Take over

one or more UK businesses.

Although the route allows a person to be involved in more than one business, we will use the singular throughout this chapter for simplicity.

In order to show that they are in a position to set up or expand a business, they need to show that they have money available to them when entering the route. The money must be available as cash rather than assets, where the money has not yet been spent (A40(a)). As r245(c)(i) explains, there are three ways in which it can be established that money is truly available, because it is:

- In the applicant's own possession

- Already invested in the business, and shows up in its accounts
- Available from some third party source who backs up their promise with cogent evidence

They may do so via the main ways in which a business may be established in the UK (245D(b)): as

- A sole trader
- A partnership
- A company

The Tables in Appendix A
Table A includes a series of Tables, numbered 4-6, which set out the key criteria for accessing the route. In general they are set out thus:

- Entering the route, either via entry clearance or switching in-country: Table 4
- Extending one's leave: Table 5
- Applying for indefinite leave to remain: Table 6

Qualifying investments
Not every kind of investment will qualify. Business income must be generated from the supply of goods and services, and not derived from the increased property value or rent:

- **Property development** (i.e. developing property with a view to earning a return through rent or sale) and **property management** (i.e. renting or selling property for profit) are **excluded** ((A39(a)(v))
- The investment may be made in any of three ways (usefully summarised in the *Guidance to applicants* at Annex A, para A26):
    - **Direct cash investment**: which must appear in the business's accounts, not simply as cash in the bank; this form of investment may only take place where it is a company of which the applicant is a director, or a partnership of which they are a member) (A40(d)
    - **Director's loan**: only if it is unsecured and subordinated in favour of the business (A39(a)(iv))
    - **Shareholding**: with a company whose structure permits it to issue shares. The shareholders must be identified – either via the company accounts, or via a copy of the register of members from Companies House
- The business must be a **UK business**: i.e. with a registered office in the UK (unless the applicant is self-employed and there is no business office; multinationals count so long as they have a registered or head office here), trading within the UK economy, with a UK bank account and subject to UK taxation (A39(b)-(c))
- Some kinds of investment are expressly excluded (r245D(c)(ii)):
    - Anything that contributes to the Entrepreneur's **own remuneration**
    - **Buying a business** from a previous owner **where the payment goes to the previous owner**, directly or indirectly, rather than into the business
    - Investing in **businesses other than the one being operated** on a self-employed basis or as a director

- Anything that is **not directly for the purpose of establishing or running** the applicant's own business

In Anjum [2017] UKUT 406 (IAC) an Entrepreneur's application was refused because of the entry clearance officer's view that he was effectively paying the previous owner for their business. However, the UT noted that he was not proposing to engage in the prohibited activity of purchasing "the" business from someone else – rather, he was proposing to acquire another online retail entity which would be added to and amalgamated with his existing online business. This would entail investment in and expansion of his extant business, which was a legitimate form of investment under the Rules. As the President put it:

> This provision of the Rules prohibits the purchase of the business concerned from a previous owner where the applicant intends to draw the purchase monies from the minimum fund of £200,000. The rule states clearly that the expenditure of any part of the funds for this purpose is prohibited.

Example

Arslan wants to obtain entry clearance under the Entrepreneur route. His business plan is to buy property in derelict sites and improve the quality of the accommodation before selling the property onwards. He is confident his plan has mileage and will create jobs in the UK in the building industry.

Arslan has a problem. His proposal will involve property development as defined by the Home Office. He will have to think again.

Criteria for the Entrepreneur route under the Rules

There are broadly similar requirements for entry clearance and leave to remain. You can find them in 245DB for entry clearance applicants; 245DD for those seeking leave to remain. These are

- **Acquiring the relevant points** under the Appendices A-C (the precise paragraphs addressing entrepreneurs are given in the Rules: 35-53 of A, 1-15 of B, 1-2 of C) (245DB(b)-(d)/245DD(b)-(d))

- The **unconditional written consent** of the Government or Agency that previously sponsored them if they were have Tier 4 leave, or were last granted leave under Tier 4 – i.e. as a student – and sponsored by a government or international scholarship agency (245DB(e)/245DD(f))

- A **genuineness test**, applicable both to business establishment activities and to the source of investment funds, to determine the viability and veracity of the business proposal, including whether or not the activities amount to disguised employment rather than entrepreneurial activity. It applies both to new businesses and to extension applications (245DB(f), (h)/245DD(h), (j))

- A **business plan** is required (partly to help the decision maker understand the nature of the business; but also to test the genuineness of the application) (245DB(g)/245DD(i))

- There is **the possibility of an interview** to further investigate the case: and refusal may follow if a request to attend is not taken up, unless a reasonable explanation is provided for failing to do so (245DB(n)/245DD(p))

- The applicant must be **at least 16 years old**: there are specific provisions addressing this in Chapter 1: *General Themes in PBS Cases*

- Providing a **criminal record certificate** (245DB(r)): an entry clearance only requirement

- The person must not fall foul of **the general grounds for refusal**(245DB(a)/245DD(a)): whilst there are some additional grounds applicable to the Points Based System routes, these do not bite on Entrepreneurs aside from those in the Graduate Entrepreneur route

Example

Jimmy is a computing genius aged 16 and 2 months. With the support of his parents, who live in Silicon Valley whilst he is privately educated in the UK, he wants to set up a software development company aimed at producing mobile phone apps for young people. His parents will often visit him in the UK, but he will stay with his father's best friend from university in London.
Jimmy's care arrangements amount to private fostering so require local authority approval, of which the Home Office should be notified.

Recurring themes

Switching for in-country applicants
There are limitations expressed in the usual way as to who can switch into this route (245DD(e)). One may do so from

- Other parts of Tier 1, including the Post Study Work route, albeit that that closed to new entrants on 11 July 2014

- Those who previously held leave on the HSM programme (it expired long ago, but there are still some individuals with HSM leave, usually as a result of its legacy of special arrangements put in place following legal challenges)

- Tier 2

- Tier 4 (Child) students; Tier 4 (General) students who are or were last sponsored by a UK recognised body, one in receipt of public funding as a higher education institution, an overseas higher education institution to undertake short-term UK study, an Embedded College offering Pathway Courses, or an independent school (this is very restricted, however, as they can only rely on funds from seed funding competitions or from a UK government or devolved government department: Table 4 at 1(b)(ii)-(Iii) read with A36(b));

- Visitors undertaking permitted activities as a prospective entrepreneur

Overstaying

We address Rule 39E and the provisions for overstayers in our Chapter 1: *General Themes in PBS Cases.* The basic idea is that 14 days of overstaying are automatically tolerated where a person has just been refused their last application; where an application is made in other circumstances by an overstayer, they will have to justify the delay this to the Home Office who will have to positively exercise discretion in their favour if the application is to get off the starting blocks.

Criminal record certificate (CRC)

The CRC is only required for the entry clearance route. We deal with it generally in Chapter 1: *General Themes in PBS Cases.* Essentially it must be obtained from any country where the applicant has previously been resident for a year more in the last decade; they may seek exemption from the requirement if there is some reasonable justification for this.

Example

Claudia has applied to be a Tier 1 Entrepreneur via the entry clearance route. She forgot to provide a criminal record certificate with her application. The Home Office did not write to ask her for one, but simply refused her application instead for failure to provide a mandatory document.

You could apply for administrative review on the grounds that the Home Office should have provided an opportunity for her to provide a CRC, as per the Rules.

Consent of the Government or Agency that previously sponsored an applicant

Students who are, or were, sponsored by a government or international scholarship agency, must obtain that body's consent to an immigration route that implies long term stay in the UK such as the Entrepreneur route. Part 6A of the Rules cross references to Rule 245A, which is the general provision in Rules addressing this issue.

Rule 245A requires

- Unconditional written consent
- In the form of a letter on official headed notepaper bearing the official stamp of the organisation and issued by an authorised official
- Confirming that the organisation gives its unconditional consent to the applicant remaining in the UK for an unlimited time

Regulated financial institution

A regulated financial institution is one which is regulated by the appropriate regulatory body for the country in which the financial institution operates (often known as the "home regulator": *Guidance to applicants* A16).

Appendix P to the Rules lists financial institutions which the Home Office will not accept as a suitable fund holder, because they are unable to make satisfactory verification checks there: obviously funds held in such entities would not be awarded points (*Guidance to applicants* para 10).

A person subject to any applicable financial sanctions regime must provide confirmation from HM Treasury that the funds are transferable and disposable in the UK (Guidance page 51).

Calculating conversion rates
Funds in a foreign currency will be converted to pounds sterling (£) using the spot exchange rate which appeared on http://www.oanda.com on the date on which the application was made (A44).

Example

Jipal wishes to apply for entry clearance as an Entrepreneur relying on £200,000 of funds held in Indian Rupees in a bank in his country of origin. He has calculated that he has sufficient funds, though it is a close thing.

Make sure that the calculation used the daily rate for the date of application as shown by www.oanda.com and not via any other online currency converter.

Entrepreneurial Teams
Two (but no more than two) applicants may make a joint application as an ET. They must still evidence the requirements set out in the Tables and the specified supporting documents. Specific criteria are then that (A52):

- They have equal control over the funds and business

- They are both named in each other's application and in the specified evidence (including their Points Based System reference numbers) (the Guidance recommends that each application includes a full copy of the other team member's application)

- Neither has previously been granted leave as an Entrepreneur on the basis of investment or business activity linked with any applicant, other than each other, if the same funds are being relied on as in a previous application

- No funds can be relied on save those that satisfy the requirements just mentioned, *unless* they come from joint account with one applicant's spouse/civil partner/partner of two years' cohabitation, so long as the relevant partner is not *themselves* applying under the Entrepreneur category (A53). The object of this Rule is to prevent the same funds from underlying multiple applications from different people

- Where the applicant is not the sole member or director in their business, they should confirm the names of the other directors/members, and whether they are Tier 1 Entrepreneurs (and if so, the dates they took up their role, whether they are applying under the Team provisions themselves, and if they are relying on points for job creation, if so, identifying the jobholders in question) (A53)

Although there is no requirement for both team members to apply at the same time, simultaneous applications are a good idea, because of the requirement for supporting evidence to be relatively recent in date in order to count as a valid specified document, and given the frequency with which the Rules may change.

Given that selection of a team partner is one aspect of the proposed business, it is presumably a matter that can be questioned under the genuineness provisions as much as any other aspect of the Entrepreneurial proposal. So it would be a good idea to think about how the composition of the team looks to a decision maker, bearing in mind:

- The track record in education and business of each prospective team member: ("what does person B add to the skill set of person A"?)
- How long they have known one another, and how they met: there is nothing inherently lacking in credibility by the fact that they meet via a business matching service, but this should nevertheless be explained
- Whether other putative team members were identified and found wanting by each applicant

When Team members come to apply for an extension of leave, they may both rely on the same evidence of job creation.

Example

Amrit and Avtar wish to apply as Team Members under the entry clearance route relying on £200,000 of funds with a view to setting up a business importing fine art tapestries. Amrit has £100,000 of funds in his personal account in India. Avtar has £50,000 in his own personal account and £50,000 in a joint account with his wife Rupi. Rupi has plans to make her own Entrepreneur application to pursue her ambitions in the fashion business.

As Team Members can rely on the same funds to score points, the volume of funds is acceptable, so long as both applicants have access to them. However, although Avtar is entitled to rely on funds in a joint account with his spouse, he may not do so if she makes an Entrepreneur application in her own right.

Tier 1 Entrepreneurs in businesses with other Tier 1 Entrepreneurs

An applicant who is not the sole partner/director in the business must state the names of the other partners/directors, identifying whether they are also Tier 1 Entrepreneur migrants, and if they are, then further information must be given: the date they entered the route, whether they are making a Team application, and if they have made (or will be making) an application claiming points for job creation, in which case they must name the jobs created.

Whereas Team Members can each rely on the same job creation (i.e. two full-time jobs lasting at least 12 months between them), multiple Tier 1 Entrepreneurs who have invested in the same business, outside of a Team application, must each provide evidence of additional job creation (A53).

Example

Hank applied for entry clearance as an Entrepreneur. He relied on funds from a third party, his uncle Madison. His application is refused solely because the letter from Madison's bank did not confirm that the institution was not aware of the funds being promised to another person.

Rule 245AA permits the decision maker to request further information where a specified document is provided, but does not contain all relevant information. An administrative review application should flag up the issues, inviting the decision maker to request the further information if a perfected bank letter is not available at the time the review application is made.

Genuineness testing

Introduction to genuineness

Although when the routes were first addressed, the Points Based System Rules aimed to simply award points on an objective basis, over time a series of credibility and viability tests have been inserted into them.

Genuineness is considered at the final stage of the process. The Rules make it clear that the Home Office reserves the right throughout the PBS to test an application for genuineness on a reconsideration even though the original refusal did not raise the issue: no doubt because it saves resources to refuse applications on simple "knock-out" grounds like missing documents without entering into this more complicated enquiry (245DB(m), 245DD(o)).

Refusals on these grounds will be based on the evidence that was before the decision maker. If the decision maker considers they require any information beyond that supplied with the original application, then they have options:

- They may request further documents, which must be supplied within 28 days of the request's date (245DB(k), 245DD(m)) or

- Invite the applicant to interview (245DB(n), 245DD(p))

The Guidance contains extensive provisions about the procedure where the decision maker has "*doubts over the credibility of an application*" in an Entrepreneur case under the heading *Genuine Entrepreneur Test*. This explains that

- Genuineness tests can be considered simply on the material provided on the application, though a decision maker contemplating this way forwards "must consult a manager to make sure that the proposed course of action is fair and proportionate"

- Where further information is sought, a request should be made giving the applicant 28 calendar days from that date to submit the evidence sought

- An interview will be appropriate if a paper consideration is considered inadequate

- A standard test form must be completed considering the pros and cons of the application

- Types of evidence that might be evaluated in assessing genuineness are

- a curriculum vitae (CV) to assess the applicant's previous experience in the field and in business
- a business plan and any market research to assess how much consideration the applicant has put into starting their business – this information can be purchased as a package, so plans that appear general may provide an indication of how genuine the applicant is
- evidence of appropriate accreditation, registration or insurance for the relevant business section (if the business is established)
- financial information overseen by a bank, for example a small business loan
- hierarchy charts of larger businesses
- evidence of advertising
- contracts showing trading, if the business is established
- tax documentation (for example, returns or evidence of registration with HMRC) but only if the business is actually trading – non-trading businesses may still be registered (but you must note that applicants switching from Tier 1 (Post-study work) will not score points for working in a skilled occupation if their business is not trading)
- affidavit from any mentors – for example if the applicant is being mentored by member of the British Business Angels Association
- evidence of previous businesses owned by the applicant
- details of trading premises, and permissions if the business is trading in the applicant's home
- evidence of investment
- evidence of job creation

In Anjum [2017] UKUT 406 (IAC) the UT criticised an Entrepreneur interview for failing to carry out the essential probing and follow-up questions that were essential to a fair interview. In particular, the interview record showed that there had been confusion between the applicant's existing business's turnover before and after he had acquired a new business to add to it. Furthermore the questions had not taken account of the basis on which the firm's financial planning would proceed, which had been set out in the business plan.

Example

Herbert has applied for an Entrepreneur visa and has been interviewed. He was asked a series of questions about his business plan. He has now been refused because he lacked knowledge of the financial and employment projections in his business plan, and because the plan did not identify the competitors that the entry clearance officer's googling suggested would face the business.

If Herbert attended the interview without a good understanding of his own business plan, then this is an unsurprising refusal. So long as the questions were fair (e.g. they did not expect an unreasonable degree of recall of figures), it is hard to criticise a decision of this nature. Applicants often succumb to the temptation to adopt template business plans: however, if they do so, it is important that they make additions and variations to such plans to reflect the realities of their own business.

However, if the googling exercise took place after the interview and its results were not put to Herbert for comment, then the process would be unfair. Experience indicates that it is this kind of argument which is more likely to succeed on judicial than administrative review.

Strategies to address a genuineness refusal
Genuineness refusals often come as a surprise to the applicant. Only once the difficulty is identified will they appreciate the desirability of putting forward more evidence in order to identify the concern subsequently raised by a decision maker. As there are no longer appeals against PBS refusals, the only remedies are administrative review and judicial review.

- Administrative review only permits the provision of fresh evidence in relation to allegations of dishonesty made with reference to the dishonesty aspects of the general refusal reasons (i.e. Part 9 of the Rules) and does not permit further evidence to be advanced when it is the substantive criteria of the PBS Rules themselves (i.e. Part 6A of the Rules) – such as the genuineness tests — upon which the refusal is based

- Judicial review is normally restricted to the evidence that was before the original decision maker

- So neither remedy readily gives an opportunity to provide further information than the documents and representations that accompanied the application, plus further information that was given following a request for more documents/information and/or an interview

- Accordingly the best option may be to make a further application within the condoned 14 days of overstaying, providing further information – this is especially worthwhile when there is some hope of changing the decision maker's mind next time round, for example where a business plan has been criticised for lack of detail and can be improved in order to answer the criticisms made this time

- Of course, there are some Entrepreneurs with appeals against refusal emanating from the era before March 2015 when there remained a right of appeal

    - Those appeals were limited, by s85A of NIAA 2002, to the evidence that accompanied the application

    - Accordingly, when appeals are heard, there should be no post-application evidence: no new documents, no witness statement for the appeal, and no oral evidence. Credibility is to be assessed via examination of the interview record. See generally Ahmed [2014] UKUT 365 (IAC) and Olatunde [2015] EWCA Civ 670

    - Indeed one might wonder quite how it is that the Home Office interview record is admissible as it is a post-application document – presumably the thinking is that the application, whilst usually frozen at the date it is made, is held open in those cases where further investigation is necessary

    - Post-application evidence is admissible, however, if it is relevant to the fairness of the decision making process; for example if the Appellant's argument is that there was something unfair about the process

Lines of argument in genuineness cases

If an administrative review has been made and failed, and you consider that the only option is to make a legal challenge to the decision making process via judicial review, then the best lines of attack will usually be to

- Concentrate on the *fairness* of the process rather than providing answers after the event ("the decision maker should have raised this at interview" rather than "the reasoning of the decision maker is irrational because they looked at things the wrong way round"). The latter kind of argument very seldom works in a judicial review application. This is because on judicial review, unless relevant evidence has been overlooked or the process has been unfair, it is necessary to show that the decision is irrational. Decisions such as Mushtaq IJR [2015] UKUT 224 (IAC) show that

    - The UT expects immigration interviews need to be fair

    - Interviews serve two purposes, enabling applications to be probed and investigated and giving the applicant a fair opportunity to respond to potentially adverse matters. Sometimes the Home Office's own guidance sets out the relevant procedures that should be followed

- Criticise the decision maker's failure to use the tools given them in the Rules by which further information might be received: this may involve

    - Attacking the failure to interview or invite further information/documents

    - Where there was an interview, or further information was sought, carefully checking whether the issues that ultimately motivated the refusal were properly raised such that the applicant had a reasonable opportunity to answer the concerns

- If the refusal letter alleges dishonesty in the application (rather than, for example, a simply stating that the business plan is too vague to be credible), then the burden of proof is on the decision maker to show dishonest intent. In so doing, the relevant question is whether sufficiently cogent evidence was before the decision maker, bearing in mind the requirement that evidence of "sufficient strength and quality" and having appropriate regard to "inherent probabilities": see generally Giri [2015] EWCA Civ 784 at [36]-[38]

Where the decision maker relies on the contents of interview records to show that an applicant is vague or that their application is otherwise lacking in plausibility, it will be essential to obtain a copy of the record in order to assess the allegations for yourself. The Home Office will usually provide a copy, though sometimes judicial review proceedings need to be at least threatened in order to prompt them.

Some refusals criticise the progress made in establishing a business. However, when the Rules identify the purpose of the Entrepreneur route, Rule 245D(a) states

> This route is for migrants who wish to establish, join or take over one or more businesses in the UK.

So the business activities are essentially prospective in nature – they may well crystallise only after the application is made (and, indeed, after it is granted, given the obvious difficulties people may face in presenting a credible face to potential clients and colleagues absent a visa). Strictly speaking, it is not appropriate to criticise a person's plans for lack of advancement when the Rule does not require the business be under way at the time of the application. Nevertheless a failure to move the business forwards is likely to be viewed critically.

Example

Mr Chan applies for entry clearance as a Tier 1 Entrepreneur with a view to running an online fashion business making the most of cheap design costs in his home country, China, which could be sold to fashion businesses in the UK. His application is refused because it is not considered that his business is viable: he lacks experience of online fashion and he did not appear to have made contact with potential customers in the UK. He has been advised he has a right to seek administrative review of the decision.

When advising Mr Chan as to his options, it is necessary to consider the quality of evidence provided on the original application carefully. If he provided evidence showing that he had experience of the same or an analogous business, and of having established contact with possible buyers, which the decision maker overlooked, that would be a strong ground for administrative review. If he did not do so, then a fresh application would seem much more promising.

Protecting an application against refusal on genuineness grounds
The best way of dealing with these provisions is to anticipate them in the original application, and if an applicant is called in for interview, to anticipate common lines of enquiry. The Rules and guidance provide inspiration on this.

The scope for refusal is significant, focusing not just on the business enterprise itself, but on the funding behind it. Additionally, it is clear that the assessment is not simply based on honesty (i.e. "we do not believe you are really going to put this proposal into practice") but on viability (i.e. "we have read your plans, we think they are unrealistic bearing in mind the competition and/or your lack of experience").

The Rules hold out the possibility of refusal on the grounds that any of these aspects of the application lack genuineness:

- Intention to establish/take over a business (245DB(h)(i), 245DD(h)(i))
- Intention to invest the money in the business in question (245DB(h)(ii), 245DD(h)(ii))
- The claimed investment money being truly available to the business (245DB(h)(iii), 245DD(h)(iii))
- The reality of the investment (245DB(h)(iv), 245DD(h)(iv))
- Intention to set up a business as opposed to work in the UK (245DB(h)(v), 245DD(h)(v))

Home Office thinking on the availability of the funds is illuminated by this extract from the Guidance:

> It may also be appropriate to test if the funds remain available to the applicant at other stages, for example where the Immigration Tribunal has sent a case back to the Home Office for reconsideration and the evidence of funds originally provided by the applicant is significantly out of date.

The Rules now make the provision of a business plan compulsory (245DB(i), 245DD(i)): so one can expect that to be at the centre of the decision making on genuineness, particularly with regard to the detail of the planned enterprise and the market research undertaken. Other factors will be the source of the investment funds, previous educational and business experience, immigration history and previous activity in the UK, meeting relevant accreditation/registration/insurance requirements (indeed the Guidance expressly refers to *compliance with the requirements for the chosen business sector*), and anything else the decision maker considers relevant (245DB(j), 245DD(j)).

Casework Tip

Entrepreneur refusal reasons based on credibility and viability are known to raise issues such as the following. So make sure your client has thought about these issues as part of the preparation of their application and before any interview.

(a) A lack of recollection shown at interview of websites visited as part of their market research, an inability to recall the name of financial advisors, giving figures for earnings for the applicant and any intended staff that are inconsistent with the figures given in business plans, generally any inconsistency between representations or interview and business plans; inability to name regulators;

(b) A failure to negotiate prices and establish relationships with suppliers and end clients or to identify the person who would design and maintain their business's website;

(c) A lack of arrangements for storage of stock;

(d) Speculative predictions of business activities, both as to processes and sales/turnover/profit;

(e) A lack of capacity during periods when the proposed entrepreneur is not available to the business;

(f) A lack of experience of the relevant industry;

(g) A lack of experience of managing one's own business;

(h) A failure to adequately assess the competition;

(i) A failure to develop the business as indicated by the business plan;

(j) A failure to provide a detailed explanation of the business's activities (particularly when relying on what may be a partially generic business plan which does not really fit with the contracts provided as proof of business activities);

(k) Spending significant time working in employed roles rather than in the business (implying that too little time is spent on the business for it to be a viable one);

(l) Working only for one client firm (suggesting that in reality this is a case of disguised employment rather than true entrepreneurship): the Guidance to applicants at A41 is based on the government's Employment Status guidance, and sets out the relevant considerations in determining whether activities claimed to be self-employment are actually employment by another name: relevant factors will be control over one's working tasks and hours, whether running costs are paid by the contractor, and their degree of independence generally;

(m) Minimal activity in the business (this and some other concerns may be explained by the fact that the business is effectively on hold pending the result of the application/appeal process)

To those examples, which tend to focus on the business itself, we can add those related to the investment funds:

(n) An unexplained failure to transfer any of the money held by way of investment to the business;

(o) An investment by a third party which is not commensurate with their means and/or with the business's apparent potential

The general grounds of refusal

Any of the general grounds for refusal are in theory available in an Entrepreneur case. There are also a few Points Based System-specific refusal grounds, though these have limited applicability to this route as they focus on the kind of mishap that tends to undo sponsored migrants. HJT has an ebook addressing this subject in detail, *The General Refusal Reasons,* so for now we just make a few general points.

Possible general refusal mishaps that may befall Entrepreneur applicants are:

- An allegation that false documents have been provided, e.g. an enquiry is made regarding a supporting bank letter as to the availability of funds abroad and a Document Verification Report indicates that there is no account matching that stated in the letter – when the Home Office allege dishonesty, the burden of proof is on them, as set out above where we mention the authority of Giri (Rule 320(7A))

- An entry clearance application might be refused because of past immigration misdemeanours during a previous sojourn in the UK – these include the mandatory bans under Rule 320(7A) and the provisions for previously contriving in a significant way to frustrate the purposes of the Rules (320(11)) (so if the client has previously been present in the UK and are now seeking a visa from abroad, make sure you check whether they overstayed and the circumstances of their departure, given that varying forms of exit attract subsequent bans on return of differing lengths)

Initial applications to join the route – Table 4

Appendix A comprises a series of Tables which set out the general requirements of the route, and then itemises, in brain-numbing detail, the precise requirements, including the ***specified*** evidence. The points required for initial applications are found in Table 4 (A36). Those for extension applications are found in Table 5 (A37) and for indefinite leave to remain applications in Table 6 (A38).

Table 4 sets out requirements in a series of rows:

- **Available funds (Row 1)**: A series of levels of available funds, and constraints on their source, depending on who is backing the business and the immigration status of the applicant

- **Regulated financial institutions (Row 2)**: Table A also requires that funds are held in regulated financial institutions

- **Money disposable/held in the UK (Row 3)**: The money must be disposable in the UK; and on an application for leave to remain, the money must be held in the UK

Availability of funds

The general requirement for funds available is access to a sum not less than £200,000 (Table 4(a)).

However, there are then a series of exceptions (funds cannot be mixed from different sources: A40(f)):

- Where the funds emanate from impressive sources (essentially ones which show that an objective and independent expert body is backing the business), there is a reduced sum: only £50,000 where funding comes from FCA-regulated venture capital firms (VCFs), or from Entrepreneurial seed funding competitions (ESFCs) or UK Government Departments (UKGDs) (Table 4(b))

- Having just described these funding sources as prima facie impressive, it must be recognised that closer analysis shows a lack of due diligence: for example Arshad [2016] UKUT 334 (IAC) where one particular VCF had, at the very least, wholly overcommitted itself as to the ventures that it sought to support – indeed there are some tantalisingly redacted passages in the Guidance about VCFs

- There are specific controls on **various classes of student**, including Tier 4 (A36(b)): they may enter the route with only £50,000, but will only be awarded points under certain parts of Table 4. This limits the sources of funds upon which they can rely: not their own or third party funds, but only funds from ESFCs or UKGDs (Table 4(b)(ii) and iii))

- **Graduate entrepreneurs** may apply with a fund of only £50,000 (Table 4(c))

- **Tier 1 General migrants may apply**, relying on either £200,000 (or £50,000 from the credible backers just mentioned), but only where their business was established as of 6 April 2015 (A36(c))

- There is a similar control for former **Tier 1 post study workers** (this can be seen in older versions of the Rules at A36B, the route having closed it no longer appears in Appendix A): they face the same restriction on funding sources as for students, but additionally, they may rely on their own funds, and not the usual £200k but only £50,000: however, this route closed, such that it was available only to businesses established as at 11 July 2014 (see the older Table 4, (b)(ii) and (iii), and (d))

- Where individuals are relying on funds from **ESFCs, UKGDs or VCFs**,

    - An applicant may be able to rely on a mixture of eligible funds, e.g. partly from an ESFC and partly from a UKGD (Guidance under heading "£50,000 funding", which goes on to make the point that those wishing to mix personal funding with funds from these special classes of investor would have to use the £200,000 route under Table 4)

    - Both team members applying as part of an Entrepreneurial Team must qualify for the funding in question: e.g. if one team member is switching from post study worker and one from Tier 2, relying on £200,000 of their own funds, but they cannot show business activity before the route closed to PSWs, then only the application of the Tier 2 migrant can be granted

The reality of business activities prior to the cut-off dates for post study workers and Tier 1 general migrants is measured by the requirement to show that they were "continuously engaged in business activity" other than simply working for another business under a contract of service, which is shown by

- Registration with HMRC as self-employed, or with Companies House as a director or partner in an existing limited liability partnership (LLP) (a disqualified director will be barred, A39(d)) and

- Working in a core business whose activities are at RQF occupation level 4 or above (these are listed in Appendix J): the activities in question exclude administration, marketing or website functions for the business itself.

Example

The Guidance gives this example: a software sales business might qualify if the applicant mainly carries out software development, whereas a taxi business managed by the applicant would not qualify simply because the applicant manages their own business, because their main activity is providing a taxi service, which would represent activity at a lower skill level when measured via a SOC code than the PBS accommodates (page 59)

There are further restrictions on the funds available for investment:

- They must be available *in addition* to the funds required for maintenance, found in Appendix C for principal applicants and Appendix R for their dependents (A39(a)(i))

- Whilst they may come from a third party, any such third party must not be another Tier 1 Entrepreneur migrant, nor the applicant's own business, nor a close family member of another Tier 1 Entrepreneur applicant (A39(a)(ii)): this latter restriction, introduced in January 2018, may be important because many applicants under this route have traditionally relied on funds supplied by immediate relatives – however, the bar operates only in relation to family members of another applicant, not to the applicant's own family. Disconcertingly, there is no definition of "close family members" apparent in the Rules as they stand, nor in the Guidance.

Much more detailed provisions then explain precisely what specified evidence is required in each case (A41).

Money must be disposable in the UK
Money is disposable in the UK if

- All of the money is held in a UK based financial institution or

- If the money is freely transferable to the UK and convertible to sterling (A40(g))

Access to funds
The possession of accessible funds must be established in a very particular way. For those applicants who hold funds for the purpose of the business which have not been invested in the business yet:

- The funds must be held as cash (A41(a)(i))

- The money must have been held for 90 consecutive days ending no earlier than 31 days before the date of application, unless the funds are coming from a third party or UKSFC or UKGD, in which case they must have the funding available to them at the date of the application and all the specified documents for those forms of fund must be provided (A41(a)(ii))

- The money must be either held in a UK regulated financial institution or be transferable to the UK (A41(a)(iii))

- The money must remain available to the applicant until spent for business purposes – the Home Office reserve the right to request further evidence to confirm this availability (A40(e))

- "Available" means in the applicant's own possession, in the financial accounts of their business, or available from the third party (r245D(c))

Prior investment of the funds
For those who have invested funds in the business, then in so far as they have done so, they need to evidence this via the very specific acceptable documents for evidencing investment rather than those attesting to the bare availability of funds. The documents aim to demonstrate both the sum invested and that the investment is in the context of establishing a new business or taking over an existing one. These documents are listed after Table 5, i.e. in a different location in Appendix A.

Those who have part-invested the funds must evidence the non-invested funds via the "*Available money*" provisions (A41); and the invested funds via the "*Investment of funds*" provisions (A45).

The manner in which the investment must be proved represents a very significant restriction on the *form of investment*. This is because the specified evidence requirements only permit it to be evidenced via the company accounts. The Guidance stresses this: any money spent for business purposes must be shown in the accounts (page 69).

So, for example, simply putting funds in the company bank account would not suffice as an eligible investment.

Any such investment must have been made in the 12 months before the application date (or 24 months if hitherto a graduate entrepreneur) (A39(a)(iii)). So if funds were invested longer ago than that, they are no longer eligible to support an Entrepreneur application: a fresh investment must now be made in the year running up to the application (e.g. *Guidance to applicants,* Annex A at A19).

Example

Emily has put forward bank statements showing the funds available to support an Entrepreneur application of £210,000, which is being made on the basis of her consultancy work for her firm, Emily Enterprises. She provides bank statements showing the investment.

Her solicitor, who is on the ball, notices that the bank statements are in the name of Emily Enterprises. Accordingly they are the wrong sort of evidence. Whilst personal bank statements would be fine as the money does not have to have been invested into the company *yet*, if the money *has been invested*, then it is the specified evidence for having already made an investment which must be supplied.

The specified documents showing access to funds
Now Appendix A becomes very pernickety in its requirements. There are a series of requirements, set out as a series of sub-sections. They were re-ordered, though apparently not altered, in the January 2018 changes to the layout of Appendix A.

They are usefully headlined in Table 4A, which cross-references to the requirements for each species of money: seed-funding (Row 1), Venture Capital Firms (Row 2), Third party funds (Row 3), and the applicant's own money (if held for at least 90 days, Row 5; if held for up to less than 90 days, which excludes funds from Venture Capital Firms, Row 4). Here are the documents for the five categories:

- For **money held for less than 90 days before the application date (ending no more than 31 days before the application date)** other than SFC funds or UKGDs (i.e. where the investment funds are held in the applicant's own bank account but where they have arrived so recently from a third party that both the third party and the applicant have to evidence their source) (Table 4A Row 4, and 41(a)(vi-vii), and (ix) or (x) as applicable depending on whether the funds are held abroad or in the UK):

    - The same documents set out for third party support, as below

    - For money held outside the UK, a letter from each financial institution where funds are held, issued by an authorised official, confirming the amount of money being made available, and that the institution is not aware of the said sum being promised to any other person: obtaining such a statement has been said by many applicants to be impossible, but the Tribunal upheld it as a lawful requirement in Durrani [2014] UKUT 295 (IAC) as did the Court of Appeal in Iqbal [2015] EWCA Civ 169: the information now required from a bank may be easier to obtain because the Rule specifies the requirement much more precisely than it did in the version challenged in those decisions. There is a specimen template at Annex D of the *Guidance to applicants*, Document 1.

    - For money held within the UK, recent personal bank/building society statements:

        - Covering the required consecutive days ending no more than 31 days before the application date

        - Statements must be dated, from a FCA/PRA regulated institution, showing cash funds, in the applicant's own name, issued by an authorised official on the institution's official stationery showing its name and logo, the applicant's name and account number

    - Electronic statements must be accompanied by a supporting headed bank letter that is stamped or confirms their authenticity

- For **money held for 90 days before the application date (ending no more than 31 days before the application date)** other than SFC funds or UKGDs (i.e. where the investment funds are held in the applicant's own bank account for the whole 90-day period, and have not arrived more recently from a third party) (Table 4A Row 5, and 41(a)(ix) or (x) as applicable depending on whether the funds are held abroad or in the UK):

    - For money held outside the UK, a letter from a financial institution giving the same details as in the last set of bullet points

    - For money held within the UK, the same bank statements requirements as in the last set of bullet points

- For **funds from UKSFCs/UKGDs** - Table 4A Row 3, A41(i)

    - For UKGDs, a letter from an authorised official or intermediary public body if a UKGD has devolved such powers to it

    - For UKSFCs, a letter from an authorised official

- Such letters must confirm the money available and the identity of its source (UKGD/UKSFC, etc.)

> For **funds from VCFs** (Table 4A Row 2, A41(a)(ii)-(v), (vii))

- Confirmation of the amount of money

- Confirmation the VCF is FCA regulated and its register entry permits it to arrange, deal in or manage investments or alternative investment funds

- A letter from a director, partner or fund manager confirming the strategy, structure and financial exposure of the fund, the rationale for the investment being a genuine and credible proposition, detailing the due diligence conducted in relation to the investment, a copy of the completed term sheet – the Guidance (page 89) gives significantly more detail on this

- A letter from a UK-qualified accountant (other than the applicant, should the applicant happen to be one) validating the financial condition of the fund

- A dated letter from a legal advisor (who is not the source of third party support) confirming that they are authorised to practice in the country where the third party or the money is located, confirming the signature is of the person stated for each third-party declaration and that it has been signed and is valid

> For **third party support where the third party still holds the funds** – Table 4A Row 3, A41(vi)-(viii) (there is a specimen template at Annex E of the *Guidance for applicants*, Document 2)

- Dated written declaration that the amount of money in sterling that has been available for UK business investment, naming the parties, signed by donor and applicant, stating their relationship, and that the money will remain available pending its transfer

- If the third party is another business in which the applicant is a director or self-employed, evidence of the applicant's status in that business and that they are its finances' sole controller, and if they are not, another authorised official of the business must sign too

- A dated letter from a legal advisor (who is not the source of third party support) confirming that they are authorised to practice in the country where the third party or the money is located, confirming the signature is of the person stated for each third-party declaration and that it has been signed and is valid

> There are then some generic requirements as to the content of documents (A41(b)):

- Any letter must be on official headed paper

- Be dated no earlier than three months before the application date (save for the bank letters and bank statements, which must be no earlier than 31 days before the application date)

- Stating the applicant's name, and team partner's name, where relevant, or the name of the applicant's business

- Giving relevant contact details of the author (address, postal code, telephone and email) – and, for a third party, their identity document number, place of issue, and date of issue and expiry, or that of their authorised representative

- Bank statements must show the account number

➢ Finally there are some specific requirements depending on the form of investment:

- Where all or part of the money is being made available to the business rather than to the applicant personally, a Companies House document showing the business's registered or head office, and that the applicant is a director, or, if the business is a partnership, that they are a member (A42)

- Where the investment has already been made, in all or part, then the documents attesting to investment and to establishment/joining of a new or existing basis rather than bare availability of funds must be provided (A43)

Example

Jemima wants to apply for leave to remain under the entry clearance route. She has lined up funds of £200,000 to support her application, which has been supplied to her by her parents two months ago. She wants to make her application immediately if possible and wants to know if there are any obstacles to doing so.

The application is possible. However the timing and source of the funds needs consideration. If the application is made now, given the funds have been transferred to Jemima within 90 days of said application being made, she would have to satisfy the requirements for documents proving the availability of third party support as well as the documents attesting to having the funds in her possession.

This may or may not prove a problem: for example some banks may fuss about making the necessary statement confirming their understanding that the funds in question have not been promised to another person. So if she waits another 30 days, the requirements for supporting documents would lighten somewhat. Of course, her application can still be refused under the *genuineness* provisions if the decision maker is concerned as to where the money came from – so it would be a good idea to provide evidence of the source albeit that it would not have to satisfy every aspect of the specified documents for third party support.

Casework Tip

Always think carefully about the source of the funds. At one time it was thought that the closer the relative, the more credible the gift: funds from parents were very understandable; and some cultures readily encourage gifts from other relatives. However, the prohibition on funds from close family members introduced from January 2018, will require such thinking to be revisited.

Whatever the source of funds, it must always be remembered that the provision of funds is not an "investment" in the usual sense – ownership and control of the funds is being wholly given up, without any corresponding receipt of shares or other interest in the business. So it is always advisable to obtain evidence of the motive of the individual. Under the Rules, genuineness testing extends to the source of funds.

Specific evidence of business activity prior to the Entrepreneur route closing for Tier 1 General applicants

- For an applicant last granted leave under Tier 1 General, detailed evidence of the required timing and level of business activity (i.e. relating to the core requirements identified at A36(c)) (A44):

    - Job Title and SOC Code under Appendix J (the applicant must assign a SOC Code themselves, using the Office for National Statistics system: sometimes it may be a challenge to find the right SOC Code, and the Ctrl-F function in one's web browser may well come in useful to search for particular functions; we provide further information on SOC Codes in Chapter 5: Tier 2 Sponsored Workers).

    - Proof of activities before the route closed: via one of these:

        - dated advertising or marketing material (if online then other than on the business's own website)
        - dated printouts from the business' website showing the service/product provided (though this is only acceptable where the applicant owns the domain name)
        - dated articles from newspaper or other publications showing the business's activity
        - proof of appearance for marketing purposes at a trade fair, or
        - personal registration with a UK trade body linked to the relevant occupation

    - Proof of trading before the route closed:

        - One or more contracts showing trading from before the date that the route closed until the application date, naming the business and its service, the parties and their full contact details, and its duration or (for a rolling contract) confirmation from the customer or their representative that it had not been terminated as at three months before the application date – in Shebl [2014] UKUT 00216 (IAC) at [5] the UT held that a contract

might include multiple documents, extending beyond the document containing the principal terms and into supplementary letters and related materials
  - Letter(s) from UK financial institutions where a business bank account was held confirming trading dates

- Applicants must show that they registered their business thus and that they maintained their registration from 6 April 2015 until a date no earlier than three months before their application:

  - HMRC registration for the self-employed
  - For directors, confirmation from Companies House of the company's filing history page and a Current Appointment Report listing the applicant as a director or partnership member of an actively trading business, and their date of appointment; or for past directorships relied on to show the overall chain of activity, similar information showing continuous office-holding for the relevant period, including the report-filing history

- Applicants must also demonstrate that the business held a UK bank account(s) of which they were a signatory from 6 April 2015 until a date no earlier than three months before their application, via bank statements or letters, generally satisfying the requirements for such documents identified above

- And that the business has been subject to UK taxation and has continuously been actively trading, via evidence of making tax returns to HMRC, via self-assessment or corporation tax, according to whether they are self-employed or a partner, or a company director

Example

Ellery applied to switch into the Entrepreneur route from Post Study Worker. His application was made on the basis that his business was established in June 2014; he provided various pieces of evidence to establish this, including a record of holding a stall at a trade fair in late June 2014 and a contract with a supporting letter saying that the services therein were ongoing. The application fell down the back of a filing cabinet at the Home Office for some time, but has now come to light, and been refused. The decision maker does not accept that the evidence Ellery supplied sufficed to establish business activity prior to July 2014, because:

(a) Printouts from his firm's website are rejected as he did not own the domain name;
(b) The contracts for service did not specify the date over which it ran;
(c) A newspaper article mentioning the firm is undated.

You need to carefully review the evidence provided: there are several routes by which Ellery might have provided satisfactory evidence, and there may be evidence that satisfies the requirements that has been overlooked by the decision maker. The refusal letter raises two issues: business activity and trading. Nevertheless, on what we have been told so far, the refusal appears unfounded:

(a) Ellery only needed to provide one of the five acceptable forms of evidence, so the fact the website evidence is ruled out does not prevent other evidence sufficing: the trade fair evidence was sufficient to show business activity as it is one of the five permitted means of so doing.

(b) The contract (one of the two forms of evidence admissible to establish trading) is in fact acceptable given that a supporting letter confirmed the services therein were still being provided

(c) The deficiency as to the lack of date on the newspaper article might be fatal where that was the only piece of evidence which could satisfy the requirements – but in this case it is not determinative given the trade fair evidence has already satisfied the relevant criteria

Table 5 and Extension Applications

Table 5 sets out the criteria for extending leave for those who have leave in the Entrepreneur route, or who have held such leave in the last 12 months.

It is set out similarly to Table 4. There are four rows within Table 5:

- **Investment of funds due (Row 1)**: To have invested the funds (£50k or £200k) on the basis of which the original application was granted

- **Timely registration of business post-arrival (Row 2)**: Registered with HMRC as self-employed, or with Companies House as a (non-disqualified) director, or member of an existing partnership, within six months of entry if granted entry clearance in the category if the date of entry is ascertainable or otherwise within six months of the date of grant of leave to remain

- **Current registration of business (Row 3)**: Registered with HMRC as self-employed, or with Companies House as director, or member of an existing partnership, within three months of the application

- **Job creation (Row 4)**: the applicant must have either

  - Established a **new** business(es) that has created at least two full time jobs for persons settled in the UK

  - Taken over an existing business(es) resulting in a net increase in employment for persons settled in the UK by creating the equivalent of at least two new full time jobs

  - The jobs must have existed for at least the last 12 months

  - Where the last grant of leave was as an Entrepreneur, the jobs must have existed for at least 12 months during the most recent period of leave (this Table 5 requirement can sink unwitting applicants who thought they had safely "banked" historic employment from a prior period of leave)

  - The jobs must be full-time and involving at least 30 hours weekly (A49(a))

  - Two or more clearly identified part-time jobs may be aggregated to count as a single full-time job, but a job that exceeds 30 hours weekly may not be counted towards another job (A49(b)) – however any combination of jobs must be clearly identified in the application (A49(f))

  - Jobs that have not existed for 12 months cannot be combined to make up a 12-month period (A49(e)) – there is a transitional arrangement for those who entered the Entrepreneur route before 6 April 2014, whereby they may benefit from a slightly more generous appraisal of job creation: then Table 5 stated "the jobs must have existed for at least 12 months of the period for which the previous leave was granted"

- A single job need not consist of 12 consecutive months: it may include six months in one year, and six months in the next, so long as it is the same job (A49(c))

- Jobs need not to have existed at the date of application provided they existed for at least 12 months of the last grant of leave (A49(d))

- The jobs must comply with all relevant UK legislation including the national Minimum Wage and the Working Time Directive (A49(g))

To qualify as a "new business", the enterprise must have been established no earlier than 12 months before the start of a period during which the applicant held continuous leave as an Entrepreneur including the last grant of leave (A46). For a person entering the route as a Graduate Entrepreneur, the period is 24 months.

Those provisions are then extensively glossed by the following paragraphs.

Investment of funds under Table 5
The investment must have been made no more than 12 months before the present application (A39(c)).

Then the specified documents to back up these requirements are set out (A45):

➢ A registered company required to produce audited accounts must produce those accounts (A45(a)) (there is information on the GOV.UK website under *Life of a company* that explains the requirements for producing audited accounts)

➢ A business that is not required to produce audited accounts must provide (A45(b))

- Unaudited accounts

- An accounts compilation report from an accountant who is a member of the UK Recognised Supervisory Body (these documents are designed to inform the decision of Directors to sign the finalised accounts)

➢ The accounts must show the investment being made (A45(c)):

- in the applicant's own name, or

- where the funds came from seed funding competitions or UK or Devolved Government Departments, a letter accompanying the accounts must confirm the investment was made on the applicant's behalf

- where the funds came from a third party beyond those just mentioned, the accounts must confirm the investment was made on account of the applicant's activity

➢ An applicant who has funded the investment via a director's loan must produce (A45(d)):

- Matching entries for the loan in the company accounts and the applicant's bank statements (where the loan was made after 19 November 2015) – the Guidance for decision makers now states that this must be clear via "readily identifiable transactions" in the applicant's bank statements

- A legal agreement between the applicant and the company showing the loan terms including interest rate and period, confirming that the loan is unsecured and subordinated to other creditors

➢ If the investment was funded via funds from ESFCs, UKGDs or VCFs, then a letter satisfying the criteria that are set out for original applications must be produced, showing that the investment was duly made (except it need not be dated within three months prior to the application) (A45(c)) – and the investment must show up in the company accounts. A VCF must confirm that the date of transfer and that it remained registered with the FCA at the relevant time (A45(g))

➢ The accounts provided must be dated and show the size of the investment from the applicant (and their name must appear in the accounts); they must be dated and signed off by an accountant in line with statutory requirements (A45(f))

➢ A share capital investment must be shown via the shareholder's names, the amount and value of the shares (on the purchase date) in the applicant's name as it appears on the application – if the name does not appear in the accounts then a printout of the Company's register of members must be produced from Companies House (A45(e))

➢ If the business investment includes an element of residential property, then the applicant must provide an estimate of the value of the living accommodation from a surveyor who is a member of the RICS, produced in the three months running up to the application (A45(i))

The Guidance has in the past recognised that a true Entrepreneur may have moved onto another business and no longer be part of the one upon which their application was originally based – however the fact that the original investment was made must still be evidenced.

If points have previously been awarded for having made the investment under the Entrepreneur route, then the evidence need not be provided again (Table 5).

Examples

Daniel has invested his £200,000 of funds in the business he has established before making his Entrepreneur application. He provides various documents to establish this. However, the business's annual accounts do not show his name as an investor.

Accounts do not necessarily give this information when produced in standard format. However, there is no reason why the accountants cannot be requested to provide this information: this is an example of the need to take timely advice and plan ahead. Where accounts have been provided without this requirement, then if an application was refused on this basis, one might expect a decision maker to have requested further documents under Rule 245AA, given that specified documents have been supplied albeit that they are missing required information

Establishment of a UK business
There are then a set of requirements to confirm establishment of a UK business (A47-A48) for

- Business premises in the UK
- Being signatory to the business's bank account
- Proof of being subject to UK taxation

These requirements replicate those set out above under the initial application provisions.

Timely registration of business post-arrival
The applicant must provide (A47):

- Evidence of registration with HMRC if self-employed;
- Evidence of registration with Companies House if a Director or partnership member, via the company's filing history and his personal appointments history, no more than six months after the specified date (i.e. six months from proven entry if granted entry clearance in this route, or from the date leave to remain was granted: see Table 5)

Current registration of the business
The applicant must show (A48), that he was registered as self-employed, or a Director or partnership member, no more than three months ***before*** the application date, via a Current Appointment report showing his date of appointment.

Job creation
The required evidence is set out at A50. To fully appreciate its meaning, one needs to understand how it is that employers report tax to HMRC. They have to make Full Payment Submissions to HMRC each time they pay their employees. This is an electronic return which contains details of all payments made to employees (and their name, NI number and tax code) in the pay run, employee income tax and national insurance contributions, details of any starters or leavers during the period of the pay run. HMRC tracks this information throughout the tax year to confirm that each employee's PAYE and NIC liabilities are being deducted correctly. They must provide:

- Proof of PAYE income tax reporting across the full period of employment for which points are claimed, and showing total payments to settled workers as well as the tax deducted and date that work started. From 6 October 2013 all businesses were required to report Real Time-Full Payment Submissions which confirm the report of PAYE to HMRC, via
  - Printouts of Employee Payment Records (for periods up to 5 October 2013), HMRC P45/P46 forms showing start date (unless the EPRs show this),
  - Printouts of Real Time-Full Payment Submissions confirming PAYE income tax being reported (for periods before 6 October 2013)
  - For periods from 6 October 2013, Printouts of Real Time-Full Payment Submissions as above

  It is probably best to err on the side of caution, and provide the full coding that underlies the software's reporting, even though it is somewhat meaningless to the untrained eye.

- Duplicate payslips or wage slips for each settled worker for the full employment period for whom points are being claimed, confirming the hourly pay rate and any changes therein

- Proof of settled status:

  - British passport showing biometric data,

  - A birth certificate showing born in the UK or Colonies before 1 January 1983

  - For those born in the UK from 1 January 1983, a birth certificate showing this plus documentation proving a parent had settled status and including a marriage certificate if the parent is the father, showing marriage to the mother

  - For employees who are EEA nationals and their spouses, biometric pages of passports or EEA residence documents including marriage certificate proving the relationship

  - For overseas nationals with settled status, biometric passport pages plus stamp showing grant of leave or BRP or other official Home Office documentation confirming status

- For Directors, Company House filing history and their personal appointments history showing they were a Director at the time the relevant employees were employed

- For the self-employed, the same documents as they require to establish business activity set out above: i.e. HMRC registration, evidence in relation to being signatory to a UK bank account, and self-assessment tax returns, showing the dates that the applicant became self-employed, the names on the Employee Payment Record or Real Time Full Payment Submission, the names on the bank account, and the address of the business

- For a person taking over or joining a business that employed workers before they joined, evidence proving the net employment increase via employment records for the year before they joined and the year of job creation:

  - Duplicate HMRC Full Payment Submission sent under Real Time

  - P35s for any period before Real Time reporting began

- Before the January 2018 recasting of the route, this was also required: a dated letter from a validly licensed accountant who is a member of one of the listed professional bodies confirming job creation, the name and contact details of the business, the applicant's status in it, the number and date of posts created and the hours worked, confirmation of whether workers were employed before the applicant joined, and confirmation that they will verify the information provided to the Home Office on request

Some further points arise from the Guidance:

- Self-employed Entrepreneurs must directly employ the new workers as employees; whereas companies must show two new posts have been created (Guidance page 103)

- Self-employed contractors do not qualify – they must be PAYE contributors (Guidance page 103)

- Although workers may be replaced when they leave without the post being disqualified for points, if there is a gap in employment between a worker leaving and being replaced, then that period will not count towards the 12 months of employment required: only periods when the worker is in the post count (Guidance page 104)

- Where a further period of leave is sought after an initial extension, it is not necessary to have established a further two jobs beyond those initially created – so long as the two jobs each amount to 12 months of full time employment within the last period of leave (Guidance page 104)

- For those under the pre-6 April 2014 transitional arrangement with its slightly more generous appraisal of job creation: this example is provided (Guidance page 105):

    - One worker for 24 months
    - One worker for 18 months and one for six months
    - Four workers for six months each

- Helpfully there is a specimen template *Job Creation Table* at Annex E of the *Guidance to applicants* showing the best way of presenting the information

Casework Tip

Always make sure that you present the evidence of job creation in a coherent way. The Annex F table certainly takes you some of the way there. But the really well-prepared applicant might well want to go further, and actually produce a reconciliation table that adds up the hours worked for each eligible worker, and shows that hours in excess of the 130 hours permitted each month can be discounted without threatening their ability to meet the target. Not only does that make things easy for the decision maker to understand, it also means that the person submitting the application is completely confident that they have provided the right evidence.

Mechanics of entry and leave granted

This is an entry clearance only route, so the entry clearance must be obtained before travelling (245DA). As seen above, applications may be made by in-country switching from another route, or from abroad, via entry clearance. The application is made online: the *Guidance to applicants* gives a link – see *General information on making an application*).

Initial applicants will be granted leave for 3 years and 4 months (or three years if already in the UK), with a prohibition on recourse to public funds, a requirement to register with the police (where required by Rule 326 – essentially where a person is a national of one of the countries listed in Appendix 2 of the Rules and is given leave for more than six months), and no employment other than working for the business(es) the applicant has established, joined or taken over (245DC).

Extensions of leave will carry the same conditions as just identified and be granted (245DE):

- for two years to those previously granted leave as an Entrepreneur
- for three years for those switching from another route

As far as employment is concerned, rule 245DC (and its equivalent for leave to remain applications) states

> no employment other than working for the business(es) the applicant has established, joined or taken over, but working for such business(es) does not include anything undertaken by the applicant pursuant to a contract of service or apprenticeship, whether express or implied and whether oral or written, with another business

This provisions aims to prevent entrepreneurs working in a de facto employment relationship with another employer whilst claiming to be self-employed: the objective of the Rules is to prevent disguised employment (i.e. to avoid this route being used to dodge the need for a sponsored worker under Tier 2), where effectively the "entrepreneur" is being hired by another business to perform labour for them, or fill a vacancy.

Leave can be curtailed, in addition to the reasons under paragraph 323, if the migrant has not registered themselves as self-employed, or their new business, or as a director of an existing business within six months of being entry clearance, entering the UK or being granted leave to remain.

Indefinite leave to remain applications: Table 6

The Rules for settlement under the Entrepreneur route follow the same scheme as that with which we are now familiar.

- Firstly the Rules in Part 6A set out the key requirements for indefinite leave to remain
- Secondly, a detailed Table, this time Table 6 with four Rows, sets out the principal criteria which must be satisfied as to business activity and job creation
- Thirdly, very detailed provisions outline the specified documents which must be provided before it is accepted that those criteria are met

The basic idea is that settlement may be obtained after five years spent within the Entrepreneur category, during which time the core requirements of investment, registration and business activity have been met.

That period is relaxed to three years where

- 10 or more new jobs have been created or
- Additional income of £5 million plus (over the last period of leave, so it may be spread over more than one year) has been generated in a new business, or via an increase in an existing business's profits

An application may be made up to 28 days before the qualified period is attained; an earlier application may be refused (see generally *Guidance to applicants*). If leave runs for more than five years before the settlement application, then the decision maker will focus on the most recent five year period (*Guidance to applicants* page 32).

Settlement: The core Rules

Under Part 6A, the applicant

- Must not fall foul of the general refusal reasons, and must not be an illegal entrant (245DF(b))

- Must obtain 75 points under Appendix A – there is no requirement under Appendices B or C to meet (245DF(c))

- However that does not mean there is no English language requirement: instead, the requirements of Appendix KoLL must be met (245DF(d))

- Must not be in breach of immigration laws save for the usual proviso that overstaying within the ambit of Rule 39E will be disregarded (245DF(e))

- Once again there is a genuineness test (245DF(f)-(j)), featuring an across-the-board assessment of every aspect of the applicant's past and present situation, including

    - Sources of money, financial accounts, business activity
    - Job creation
    - That the applicant "genuinely intends to continue operating one or more businesses in the UK"

- An interview may be required, and a request to attend for one must be complied with, subject to providing a reasonable explanation (245DF(k))

The Table 6 requirements
The Table 6 rows address:

- Investment (Row 1): the sum for which points were awarded in the last grant of leave must have been demonstrably invested – if points were previously awarded for actual investment, then this need not be evidenced again

- Current business registration (Row 2)

    - Evidence of registration with Companies House if a Director or partnership member, or with HMRC if self-employed, *within three months* of the present application

    - That same evidence must show that the requirement was met within a set period: *either* within six months of entry if the applicant was granted entry clearance in the Entrepreneur category (if the date of entry is ascertainable) *or* within six months of the date of grant of leave to remain: however this evidence need not be provided if points were awarded for registration under Table 5 in the previous application

- **Job creation**: a certain number of jobs must have been created

    - At least two full time jobs for settled persons, which have lasted for at least 12 months during the most recent grant of leave if said leave was as an Entrepreneur

    - A variable number of jobs, specified as "X", but linked to the volume of job creation or business income below

- **Continuous period of leave**:

    - As an Entrepreneur,

        - For three years if at least 10 new full time jobs have been created

- For three years if *a new UK business* has been established with income from *business activity of at least £5 million* during a three-year period during which the applicant has leave as an Entrepreneur; or *an existing UK business* was taken over and a *net increase of at least £5 million business activity* income is shown, during a three-year period during which the applicant has leave as an Entrepreneur, compared with the previous three years

- Otherwise for 5 years

- During which period there has been continuous residence in the UK with absences no greater than 180 days in any period of 12 calendar months

- Time spent in an equivalent business immigration category in Jersey or Guernsey can count, so long as the last grant of leave was as a Tier 1 Entrepreneur in the UK and so long as there are no excess absences as just defined

- Some people are refused indefinite leave to remain because they have been abroad for more than 180 days in one of the last five years, so breaching the residence requirements of the Points Based System route.

The specified evidence to satisfy Table 6
As usual, there are specified documents for evidencing the settlement requirements. The relevant section is headed "Settlement on the basis of £5 million business activity" (A51):

- The £5 million income increase *in a new business* must be shown, in relation to the three-year period claimed, by audited or unaudited accounts showing the value of business activity

- The £5 million income increase *in an existing business* must be shown by

  - Dated audited or unaudited accounts showing the accountant's name and signed off in line with statutory requirements *and*

  - An accountant's letter from a validly licensed accountant who is a member of one of the listed professional bodies (A39(e)) containing business name and contact details, an explanation of the applicant's status in the business, confirmation of the gross net business activity and the net increase, and that the accountant is licensed to practice in the UK and will confirm the letter's content to the Home Office on request

- The same requirements for registration with HMRC if self-employed or as a director/ partnership member as set out for the extension route

- The same requirements for job creation as set out for the extension route

Example

Emmanuel is present as a Tier 1 Entrepreneur having previously been granted an extension of leave in this route. He has been present in the UK for six years under the Entrepreneur route, having missed out on the opportunity to apply for settlement sooner because of a break in his continuous residence early on during his first period of leave in this route. He comes to see you with a view to making a settlement application now: he was last given an extension of leave 10 months ago, running until 14 months from now. He has now achieved five years on the trot without breaking his continuous residence.

Emmanuel still faces a problem with a settlement application. He has to show that he created or maintained two jobs in the last extension of leave that lasted for 12 months. However, given that his present grant of leave has not yet endured for 12 months, he does not satisfy the requirement that "the jobs must have existed for at least 12 months during the most recent grant of leave." Luckily for him, so long as he keeps those employees working for him, he has plenty of leave to remain within which to make good the missing two months.

The continuous residence requirement is dealt with in detail in Chapter 1: *General Themes in PBS Cases.*

Applications outside the Rules

So far we have addressed applications made wholly under the Rules. However, the Home Office always has a discretion to depart from the Rules. It seems fair to say that this is rarely exercised. Nevertheless, it is always open to an applicant to request that discretion be exercised. The Home Office is under a public law duty to consider such requests. The administrative review process expressly excludes arguments outside the Rules and guidance. However, a refusal to exercise discretion may, in relatively extreme circumstances, be found unreasonable by a judge on judicial review.

One difficulty with applications that go off track can sometimes be that arguments become more sophisticated at every stage of the process. In so doing, they become increasingly divorced from the original basis of the application. Sometimes lawyers wish to argue that the Home Office should have considered whether a particular provision of the Rules should have been waived given the circumstances of an individual case. However, if an applicant considers that they satisfy virtually every aspect of the Rules but they have an insuperable problem with meeting one provision, then it is probably best to say so in the application, and ask for discretion to be exercised. If no such request is made, the Home Office can hardly be expected to exercise discretion favourably.

You may have a case where the applicant cannot meet one modest requirement. If this is a technical rather than a substantive requirement, particularly where their inability to meet the requirement is down to some action of the Home Office or a third party, there is a basis to argue that that deficiency should be overlooked. You should step back from the application and identify the policy objective of the criterion in question. If that objective is not threatened by the requirement being waived, you have a potential argument.

Practitioners generally report that the Home Office are much less receptive to waiving requirements these days than they were some years ago.

Graduate Entrepreneurs

There is a special set of Rules for those applying under the Graduate Entrepreneur route. As is usual those Rules are glossed by policy material – the Tier 1 (Graduate entrepreneur) of the Points Based System – Policy Guidance (version 04/17 for applications made on or after 06 April 2017). However the Graduate Entrepreneur guidance adds much less of note to the Route than does the mainstream Entrepreneur guidance for general applicants.

The route is for

- UK graduates identified as having developed **genuine and credible business ideas and Entrepreneurial skills** to justify their stay in the UK after completing their studies

- Graduates identified by the Dept for International Trade as **elite global graduate Entrepreneurs** to establish businesses here

The business may be as a sole trader, partnership or registered company. Those applying from abroad must have entry clearance before travelling. We have set out the conditions for graduate Entrepreneurs to switch into the Entrepreneur route above. One extra point to make regarding such applications is that they need not provide documentary evidence of their immigration history as the Home Office will note their current status from their passport and their own records ([Entrepreneur] Guidance page 57).

The route operates by giving an opportunity for individuals who demonstrate the entrepreneurial initiative just mentioned to obtain leave. This requires the recent backing of a higher education institute in the UK – either the institution must have the appropriate status which shows it is competent to assess such applications amongst its student population (basically being one of the authorised endorsing bodies listed on the Home Office website) or the Department for International Trade must have backed the application. The DIT does so via the Sirius Programme, which it runs in partnership with a consortium of private companies and charities on a "not for profit" basis.

The applicant must also establish their academic credentials by proving that they have a degree level qualification via tightly specified documents. They have to demonstrate a certain level of English language proficiency and show they can maintain themselves (as summarised below; we also address these requirements generally in Chapter 1: *General Themes in PBS Cases*). There are a finite number of applications which will be granted annually.

An in-country applicant can switch into the route only if they have leave as a student, or from Tier 2 General if they are a post-doctoral researcher whose place of study is endorsing their entrepreneurialism. There is the possibility of a single extension under the route. There is no provision for indefinite leave to remain under the route, and whilst they may switch into the mainstream Entrepreneur route, they will not accumulate residence for the purposes of settlement under that route whilst a Graduate Entrepreneur. They may have their leave curtailed if the institution endorsing them loses its status or stops backing them.

They enjoy certain benefits as against other applicants joining the Tier 1 Entrepreneur route: for example, an enterprise may qualify as a "new business" so long as it is established in the 24 months before first joining the route, and the investment may have been made within 24 months of the application to join the main route; whereas for other applicants, the corresponding periods are 12 months. An employer is exempt from carrying out the resident labour market test under the post-study work exemption for those switching into Tier 2.

Requirements under the core Rules

The requirements are

- Not falling under the general grounds for refusal or being an illegal entrant

- Having 75 points under Appendix A, 10 points under Appendix B, 10 points under Appendix C
- For those applying to switch into the route, last having had leave as
  - a Tier 4 student sponsored by a UK recognised body, one in receipt of public funding as a higher education institution (HEI), or an overseas HEI to undertake a short course of study abroad programme in the UK
  - A Tier 1 Graduate Entrepreneur
  - A Tier 2 (General) Migrant (though only if granted leave to work as a post-doctoral researcher for the same institution now endorsing the present application)
- They must not previously have been present in these categories: Tier 1 (Post-Study Work) Migrant; a participant in the Fresh Talent: Working in Scotland Scheme; or a participant in the International Graduates Scheme (or its predecessor, the Science and Engineering Graduates Scheme)
- They may not have more than one extension of leave in this category – as a consequence they cannot stay in the route for more than two years (e.g. Guidance para 1.6)
- An applicant presently not in the Entrepreneur category must have the unconditional written consent of the Government or Agency that is presently or has previously sponsored them (within the last year if the latter)
- The usual prohibition on overstaying applies, subject to Rule 39E (i.e. up to 14 days of overstaying is permitted where the application follows an immediately prior refusal; otherwise, up to 14 days overstaying may be condoned, but only if a good reason is supplied)
- The same English language requirements apply as for Tier 1 Entrepreneurs, set out above
  - With the addition (B9) that there is no need to provide such evidence of a qualification taught in English if their UK HEI provides the specified details of the qualification
  - And there are further dispensations than those available to Tier 1 Entrepreneurs regarding having previously been granted leave, going beyond the business categories to a prior grant of leave as a Minister of Religion under Tier 2 or Tier 4 (General) Student after 21 April 2011 based on a qualification of degree level plus (B12); or in a prior grant as a Graduate Entrepreneur or under Tier 2 General from that April date
  - Possession of funds of £1,890 (entry clearance) or £945 (leave to remain) for their maintenance (Appendix C), to qualify for the necessary 10 points – this will be satisfied either if the applicant proves they hold the funds, or if the Dept of International Trade confirms their award included such a sum (C2(c))

The detailed criteria in Appendix A
They must then meet the relevant Appendix A criteria, set out in Box 10:

- **Endorsement by a UK HEI** (Row 1):
  - Which must have a Tier 4 Sponsor status, or A-rated Sponsorship if it has a Tier 2 or Tier 5 licence

- Has degree-awarding powers

- Either the institute has established processes and competence for identifying, nurturing and developing entrepreneurs among its undergraduate and postgraduate population; or

- The applicant has been endorsed by the Department for International Trade

➢ **A degree** (not a mere equivalent) exceeding a UK Bachelor's degree (Row 2)

➢ **An endorsement** (Row 3) confirming the intended business sector/intention, outside of property development/management

  - Stating that the applicant has a genuine and credible business idea, will spend the majority of his working time developing business ventures, and if applying for an extension within the Graduate Entrepreneur category, has made satisfactory progress since leave was first granted

Limit on Graduate Entrepreneur Visas
There is a limit on the number of Graduate Entrepreneur applications that will be granted in any year:

➢ 2,000 at present in the year from 6 April to 5 April

➢ 1,900 allocated to qualifying HEIs: via an annual allocation round in which all eligible institutions will be invited to indicate the allocation sought, and allocated the smaller of 20 places or the number requested or the number available

➢ 100 allocated to Dept of International Trade

Endorsement
The endorsement will receive points only where it is

➢ Issued within three months before the application

➢ Had not been withdrawn at the time the application is considered

➢ Provided from the relevant endorsing body, showing the applicant's name, birth date, nationality, passport number, details of present or intended dependents, the name date and level of award unless provided on an earlier application, the endorsement reference number, name of endorsing body and contact details for an authorised official and an administrator, its reasoning for the endorsement, confirmation that the business idea is considered genuine and credible and that the applicant will spend the majority of their time working on it, and confirmation of satisfactory progress if leave was previously granted in this category

Qualifications
Points will be awarded for a degree level qualification

➢ If the endorsement is by the UKHEI which awarded it, and it has provided the details of the qualification in the endorsement

➢ Otherwise, only if these specified documents are provided: the dated award certificate, showing applicant's name, award title, and name of awarding institution; if awaiting graduation or the applicant no longer has the certificate and a replacement is not available, an academic reference from the awarding institution, plus an academic transcript

- An academic reference must be on headed paper and show the applicant's name, award title and date, and the date the certificate will be issued or confirmation no replacement can be awarded

- An academic transcript must be on official paper and show the applicant's and institution's name, course title, and confirmation of the award: no transcript is required if the award includes a significant research bias and the academic reference provides the required information

- For degrees outside the UK, a letter or certificate from UK NARIC must be provided demonstrating the equivalence to the relevant UK qualification

Conditions of grant
Entry clearance or leave is granted for one year, subject to conditions:

- No recourse to public funds

- Police registration if Rule 326 requires it

- No employment as a Doctor or Dentist in Training, or as a professional sportsperson/ coach

- A person may study subject to the conditions in Part 15 of the Rules

There is no provision for indefinite leave to remain under the route, and whilst they may switch into the mainstream Entrepreneur route, they will not accumulate residence for the purposes of settlement under that route whilst a Graduate Entrepreneur (Table 6 Row 4).

The general grounds of refusal
Graduate Entrepreneur applicants may be refused under the general rules just as they may be refused under the specific rules. We have discussed the ways in which this might happen for Entrepreneurs generally above. However Graduate Entrepreneurs also have their very own *General refusal reason*: Rule 323C. This provides for *curtailment* of leave where their endorsing body for their present grant of leave:

- Loses its status as an endorsing institution for Tier 1 (Graduate Entrepreneur) Migrants

- Ceases to be a sponsor with Tier 4 Sponsor status

- Ceases to be an A-rated Sponsor under Tier 2 or Tier 5 of the Points-Based System because its Tier 2 or Tier 5 Sponsor licence is downgraded or revoked by the UK Border Agency, or

- Withdraws its endorsement of the migrant.

The Rule states that leave *may* be curtailed – so this is a discretionary rather than a mandatory ground of refusal. Where the Graduate Entrepreneur is innocent of wrongdoing, the Guidance states that leave will be curtailed such as to end in 60 days (presumably from notification of the decision) (Guidance para 3.13).

Chapter 3: Tier 1 Exceptional Talent Migrants

As always with Points Based System cases, we see two forms of Guidance: that for applicants (Version 7/2018), and that for Home Office staff (Version 15.0; published 6 July 2018). We generally refer to the latter unless we expressly state the contrary.

Introduction and overview of the route

This route is for exceptionally talented individuals wishing to work in the UK within their chosen field of excellence: they will either already be recognised world leaders or have been identified as showing exceptional promise such as they are likely to become such (r245B). As the Guidance puts it, the route is

> for exceptionally talented individuals in the fields of science, humanities, engineering, the arts and digital technology to enrich the United Kingdom's knowledge economy and cultural life

As always with Points Based System cases, we see two forms of Guidance: that for applicants (Version 11/2018), and that for Home Office staff (Version 16.0; published 5 November 2018). We generally refer to the latter unless we expressly state the contrary.

The application has two stages (the Guidance styles these as Stage 1 and Stage 2 applications, making the point that one should not apply for the second until one has succeeded in the first):

(1) An application for an endorsement by a relevant institution (which may be made from abroad – generally speaking copies of qualifications are not required at this stage, though they are required for the next stage, the immigration application itself made direct to the Home Office)

(2) An application for entry clearance or leave to remain to the Home Office (which must be applied for within three months of the endorsement being granted)

There is no English language requirement within the route until the settlement stage is reached.

Applicants may apply for entry clearance from locations other than their home country: i.e. from entry clearance posts where they are situated at the time of the application, provided that the post in question has been designated as appropriate for this route, they are present there for a similar purpose to the activity proposed for their UK stay, and they are living their lawfully (r28A).

Key immigration requirements for Tier 1 Exceptional Talent migrants

There are a number of requirements under the entry clearance route:

- They must have entry clearance before travelling if applying from abroad (r245BA);
- They must not fall foul of the general refusal reasons or be an illegal entrant (r245BB(a));
- They must have 75 points under Appendix A (r245BB(c));
- They must have the appropriate consent from a government sponsor or international sponsorship agency (r245BB(d));

If switching into the route or extending leave thereunder:

- They must not fall foul of the general refusal reasons or be an illegal entrant (r245BD(a));

- They must have 75 points under Appendix A (r245BD(c));

- They must have last held leave under Tier 1 or Tier 2, or as a Tier 5 (Temporary Worker) Migrant, sponsored in the Government Authorised Exchange sub-category in an exchange scheme for sponsored researchers (r245BD(d));

- They must not be in the UK in breach of immigration laws, save as permitted by Rule 39E (r245BD(e))

Points criteria for Tier 1 under Appendix A

Points are set out in Table 1 of Appendix A (A1-A3), which provides for one of the simplest of all points-scoring provisos in the PBS: i.e. endorsement by a Designated Competent Body (DCB) according to its criteria is sufficient.

Before making their immigration application, applicants must apply for an endorsement on the specified form, identifying the relevant DCB and providing the relevant specified evidence.

If an endorsement application is refused, then a dissatisfied applicant can apply for an endorsement review, set out in Appendix C to the Guidance for applicants.

Those who can put a case for meeting the criteria may then go forward to assessment by the DCB in question: so just having a strong case under the criteria only takes the applicant so far. At the assessment stage the DCB will put forward relevant experts.

If the DCB identifies false or fraudulent information, they will inform the Home Office and the application will be ineligible to continue further (e.g. Guidance for applicants D4, A13).

The DCB criteria

The specified evidence by way of DCB criteria is set out in Appendix L. Letters of recommendation from a UK based individual or about holding a UK research-based fellowship may be provided from persons based in the Isle of Man (L1A).

Science Bodies – the British Academy, the Royal Academy of Engineering and the Royal Society

The Guidance to applicants contains very detailed lists of the precise disciplines covered by the various DCBs (for example, the Royal Society covers planetary science; The Royal Academy of Engineering deals with nanotechnology; The British Academy deals with the history of science and ideas).

This set of DCBs provide an accelerated endorsement process for two categories of applicant whose status is defined (by The Royal Society, The Royal Academy of Engineering or The British Academy) as follows:

- International awardees of specific peer-reviewed Research Councils UK (RCUK), Welcome Trust, British Heart Foundation, Cancer Research UK and UK National Academies research fellowships to apply with assurance once the recognised fellowship or award has been granted (there is a list of such fellowships linked from the Guidance to applicants at A4 showing those identified as suitable for the accelerated process) – these applicants must provide written confirmation of the award from the funding body in question

- Those with eligible senior academic or research positions – these applicants must provide a statement from the Director of Human Resources of the relevant establishment, confirming the name and senior position (i.e. Professor, Associate Professor, or Reader at a UK Higher Education Institute, or equivalent at a research institute) and that the role was advertised via an open competition that required and received at least three references, that the job has been offered and accepted following an interview process with at least four senior academic representatives and featuring a consultation with one senior external expert

The requirements are divided into those for leaders in the relevant field and those who show exceptional promise to become a leader in the relevant field. This definition of primacy is different from the one that preceded it in this particular sub-category of Exceptional Talent: previously the requirement was that the individual reach the "world leader" threshold. Applicants must meet (L1) the criteria set out in the Table (at L1), showing that they:

- Are an active researcher in a relevant field, typically within a university/industry or a research institute
- Hold a PhD or equivalent research experience
- Are backed by a dated letter of personal recommendation from a UK-resident eminent person qualified to make the assessment who supports the application and is familiar with their work and to the field
- Meet one of the qualifying criteria:
    - Being a member of their national academy or a foreign member of academies of other countries (including the UK national academies)
    - Have been awarded a prestigious internationally recognised prize
    - Provide a written recommendation from a reputable UK organisation concerned with research in his field. The dated letter must be written by an authorised senior member of the organisation, such as a Chief Executive, Vice-Chancellor or similar, on official paper

Potential leaders relying on endorsement by The Royal Society, The Royal Academy of Engineering or The British Academy must meet (L1) the criteria set out in the Table (at L1), showing that they:

- Meet the same requirements for world leaders as to active research and holding a PhD or equivalent experience, and have the personal recommendation letter
- Are at an early stage in their career
- Have been awarded, hold, or have held in the past five years, a prestigious UK-based Research Fellowship, or an international Fellowship or advanced research post judged by the competent bodies to be of equivalent standing

Their application (all documents being provided in hard copy, in printed not handwritten form and in English or backed by authorised English translations: L3) (L2):

- On the appropriate DCB application form supported by a CV of no more than three pages
- Supported by the recommendation letter, explaining how the eminent person knows the applicant and their familiarity with their work, their achievements and how they meet the exceptional criteria, how they would benefit from living in the UK and the contribution they would make to UK research excellence and wider society
- For (established) leaders, evidence showing they meet one of the qualifying criteria

Once applicants have established eligibility for assessment under the leader or potential leader in the relevant field category, the DCB will consider them according to these criteria (L4):

- Track record/career history (including his international standing, the significance of their publications, prizes and research funding awarded, patents, and the impact of past innovation activity, in a company, academia or as an individual);

- Strength of supporting statements in the letter of personal recommendation, and evidence in relation to qualifying criteria, including a written recommendation from a reputable UK organisation concerned with research in the applicant's field (if relevant)

- The expected benefits of the applicant's presence in the UK in terms of the contribution to UK research excellence and to wider society, including potential economic benefits from exploitation of intellectual capital

- For established leaders, whether they have won a prestigious international prize/award, secured significant funding in the last decade, and are regarded as a leader in their field

- For promising leaders, whether they have provided evidence sufficient to demonstrate their potential, the additional funding secured during or following tenure of a relevant fellowship, received a relevant prize/award for early career research, and have made a significant contribution to their field relative to their career stage

Having made this assessment, the DCB will award the endorsement if they meet the criteria, but not otherwise (L4A).

Example

Shirley is a US national with a PhD working in the UK for Cancer Research UK pursuing cutting edge medical research, presently with leave under Tier 2 General, whilst she pursues her research fellowship.

She qualifies under Appendix L without having to go through the various requirements for Exceptional Promise or Talent found in the Table L boxes: because simply holding such a position is sufficient. Of course she still has to make the "immigration" part of the application to the Home Office.

David is a US national working as an Associate Professor in astrophysics at the London School of Economics.

David may qualify under Appendix L without having to go through the various requirements for Exceptional Promise or Talent found in the Table L boxes: because this is potentially an eligible senior academic position at a UK Higher Education Institute. However this applies only if the stringent requirements for the recruitment process were satisfied, which include an external consultation with an expert outside the establishment, at least four senior academics interviewing him, and at least three references.

Arts Council England endorsements

Those relying on Arts Council England endorsement must be established as possessing Exceptional Talent as artists/experts within the fields of the arts (encompassing dance, music, theatre, combined arts, visual arts and literature), museums or galleries or within the film, television, animation, post-production and visual effects industry (L5). They must (L6)

- Be professionally engaged in producing work of outstanding quality published (other than exclusively in newspapers or magazines), performed, presented, distributed or exhibited internationally

- Provide evidence of regular professional engagement within the last five years

- Show **substantial** or **developing** track record in at least two countries, including their country of residence

- Those applying within the arts and culture fields must provide no more than 10 documents (and via hard copy or URL links, not DVDs or CDs) (L7) showing

  - For those with **established Exceptional Talent** (whose awards and appearances, etc. are to be adjudged by Arts Council England), evidence for at least two of these propositions:

    - **Two or more examples** (**within the last five years**) of **significant media recognition** critiquing their work **from at least two countries**

    - International award winning **within the last five years**: e.g. the Booker or a Grammy

    - Proof of appearances, performances, publications or exhibitions in the past **five years** in contexts which are recognised as **internationally significant** in the applicant's field or evidence of **extensive international distribution and audiences** for the applicant's work.

  - For those with Exceptional Promise within the relevant field, evidence for at least two of these propositions:

    - **Two or more** examples (**within the last five years**) of significant media recognition critiquing their work from at least at one country

    - Nomination for international award winning **within the last five years**: e.g. the Booker or a Grammy

    - Proof of appearances, performances, publications or exhibitions in the past **three years** in contexts which are **recognised internationally** in the applicant's field or evidence of **international distribution and audiences** for the applicant's work.

- Those applying within the film, television, animation, post-production and visual effects industry (L8) must have

  - **Won** (or made a **significant contribution** towards another person's win which was the result of their contribution or which they significantly influenced), or been **nominated within the last 10 years** for, an Academy Award, BAFTA, Golden Globe, Emmy, or been nominated for one of those at least twice in the last 15 years, providing full details of the production leading to the award and their involvement with it and the credit they received for it, or demonstrated **notable industry recognition** by providing evidence of: international distribution sales and recognition plus **winning** two (or winning one and **being nominated** for another one, or simply **being nominated** for at least three) out of a long list of film festivals and other awards **within the last 6 years** (or making a significant direct contribution to winning two or being nominated for three of those awards)

- These triumphs must be attested to via particular documentary evidence (L8A): full details of the award, evidence of their involvement within a group leading to the nomination or award, the credit they received, and of their significant and direct contribution to that achievement where relevant (applicants in the fashion business have a further raft of documents to produce: L8C-L8D)

➢ Letters of endorsement must be provided as specified (L9):

- Be written on headed paper, dated, and signed by the author who must be a senior member of the organisation, e.g. being on the senior management team or board as the Chief Executive, Artistic Director, Principal or Chair;
- Including details of the author's credentials (e.g. a CV/résumé) and how they know the applicant (whether through personal relationship or reputation);
- Detailing the applicant's achievements in their specialist field and how in the opinion of the author they have demonstrated that they are, or have the potential to become, a world leader in their field;
- Describing how the applicant would benefit from living in the UK and the contribution they could make to cultural life in the UK, including details of any future professional engagements in the UK that the author is aware of;
- Including full contact details of the author, including personal email address and direct telephone number so that personal contact can be made; and
- Be written specifically for the purpose of supporting the application, not as a general all-purpose reference letter

➢ Three letters of endorsement must be provided (see Table following L9), from each of

- A UK based arts or cultural organisation, institution or company which is well-established nationally and/or internationally and widely acknowledged as possessing expertise in its field
- A second such organisation, which may this time be UK or overseas based
- A third such organisation (UK or overseas based) or from an eminent individual with internationally recognised expertise in the applicant's specialist field

Example

Dmitri is a musician. He has a significant following online and sold records in his country of origin in his youth, around a decade ago. He has given several concerts in the UK which have been written up favourably in the national music press here.

Dmitri has some potential for making the "exceptional promise" route: for example he has some kind of reputation in more than one country. However, he is going to struggle to meet the fundamental requirement in Appendix L to produce two kinds of relevant evidence, bearing in mind he has apparently not won or been nominated for international awards, to show "(in the last five years) media recognition such as articles ... in at least two countries" or proof of "internationally recognised" performances given he only has evidence from his country of origin from more than five years ago and ostensibly no trans-national media reviews. He needs to focus on whether he can achieve this goal during his stay in the UK.

Tech Nation endorsements
Once again there is the distinction between the applicants who are established and those with potential, i.e. between Exceptional Talent and Exceptional Promise (L10).

The Guidance to decision makers explains that there is provision for fast-track applications under this sub-category, for those who are either working outside Greater London in a way that is relevant to their plans for employment or entrepreneurship, or able to demonstrate significant experience in upscaling under the "exceptional talent" or have been accepted onto a recognised UK accelerator programme as listed in the Guidance

- To establish **exceptional talent** it is necessary to show either (L10):

    - A proven track record of innovation in the digital technology sector as a director/founder of a digital technology sector company, or as an employee working in a new digital field or concept. This must be clearly evidenced (e.g. via a patent application), or

    - Proof of recognition for work outside the applicant's immediate occupation that has contributed to the advancement of the sector (e.g. via evidence that they have gone beyond their daily professional activities to contribute to advancing their sector – examples are given in the Guidance at A15, including a profile from Stack Overflow (an online resource by which software code developers learn, share their knowledge, and build their careers) showing a significant contribution to discussions around code, evidence of contributions to an Open Source project, or evidence of sharing or teaching skills, such as mentoring in the workplace)

    - Those criteria must be established via at least two of the following (the Guidance gives lengthy examples of each possibility):

        - Making significant technical, commercial or entrepreneurial contributions in the digital technology sector as either a director, founder, or entrepreneur of a digital technology sector company (the Guidance at A15 suggests examples including having led in the development of high-impact digital products or services)

- Being recognised as a world leading talent in the digital technology sector (e.g. authoring a well-reviewed book or leading the growth of a company or product)

- Having undergone continuous learning/mastery of new digital skills (commercial or technical) throughout their career (e.g. experimenting with new technologies, learning processes and tools)

- Having demonstrated exceptional ability in the field by making academic contributions through research published or otherwise endorsed by a research supervisor or other expert (e.g. publishing papers or receiving awards)

➢ To show **exceptional promise** one must show either (L10):

- Two or more examples of innovation as a director/founder of a digital technology sector company or an employee working in a new digital field or concept that must be clearly evidenced (e.g. via a patent application), or

- Proof of recognition for work outside the applicant's immediate occupation that has contributed to the advancement of the sector (e.g. via evidence that they have gone beyond their daily professional activities so to do)

- Those criteria must be established via at least two of largely the same criteria as for established exceptional talent applicants, but altered slightly:

  - Making significant technical, commercial or entrepreneurial contributions in the digital technology sector – though as a founder or entrepreneur rather than as a Director

  - Being recognised as a **potential** world leading talent

  - The same requirement for continuous learning/mastery of new digital skills (commercial or technical) throughout their career

  - Having demonstrated exceptional ability in the field by two or more examples of contributions through research published or otherwise endorsed by a research supervisor or other expert

The following documents must be provided:

➢ Completed Tech Nation (Tier 1 Exceptional Talent) application form, and CV

➢ Two letters of reference from senior members of two different established organisations who are familiar with their work and qualified to assess their contribution to the digital technology sector

- Including details of the author's credentials (a CV/résumé showing they are e.g. Chief Executive, Chief Operating Officer, Finance Director or Head of Course;) and how they know the applicant

- Detailing the applicant's achievements in his specialist field and how in the opinion of the author they have demonstrated that they are, or have the potential to show, exceptional talent in their field;

- Describing how the applicant would benefit from living in the UK and the contribution they could make to the UK the digital technology sector including details of any future professional engagements in the UK that the author is aware of

- Including full contact details of the author including personal email address and direct telephone number so that personal contact can be made; and

- Be written specifically for the purpose of supporting the application, not as a general all-purpose reference letter

➢ Evidence of any active businesses established or businesses that have been dissolved in the last five years in which the applicant has been a director, founder or entrepreneur, or evidence of share ownership through business in a digital technology sector company

➢ Evidence in relation to the relevant mandatory and qualifying criteria, via no more than 10 documents in total (not exceeding two A4 sides each), via paper documents provided in hard copy. Evidence provided in relation to continuous learning must not date back to more than a year before the date of application, in English or backed by authorised English translations (L12)

Tech Nation will consider the application with regard to the applicant's:

➢ Track record/career history (including their international standing, the significance of their work and the impact of their activity in a company or as an individual)

➢ The strength of the supporting statements in the letter of personal recommendation, and evidence in relation to qualifying criteria; and

➢ The expected benefits of the applicant's presence in the UK in terms of the contribution to the UK digital technology sector

Endorsements and their limitations

Presently endorsements are limited to 2,000 annually (doubled as from January 2018, and allocated via a year running from 6 April to 5 April). Those endorsements are of two kinds: allocated, and unallocated. There are 1,000 of each. If a DCB uses up its allocation for the year, it may dip into the unallocated pot, priority being given to the date of allocation (A5(b)(3)).

The allocation is split between (A4(b)) (and which are allocated in two six monthly tranches (A5(b)):

➢ 250 endorsements to The Arts Council for the purpose of endorsing applicants with exceptional talent in the fields of arts and culture;

➢ 250 endorsements to The Royal Society for the purpose of endorsing applicants with exceptional talent in the fields of natural sciences and medical science research;

➢ 150 endorsements to The Royal Academy of Engineering for the purpose of endorsing applicants with exceptional talent in the field of engineering;

- 150 endorsements to The British Academy for the purpose of endorsing applicants with exceptional talent in the fields of humanities and social sciences; and

- 200 endorsements to Tech Nation for the purpose of endorsing applicants with exceptional talent in the field of digital technology.

There are various provisos to the use of endorsements:

- DCBs may transfer unused endorsements, within the relevant year, between themselves, with mutual consent plus Home Office approval: A4(d) – but unused endorsements may not be carried over from one year to the next (A5(c))

- Applications will be refused once the allotted number has been used up (A5(e))

- An endorsement that supported a refused application may be re-used in the same year (A5(d))

The endorsement alone is not sufficient, because (A6)

- A valid approval letter from the Home Office must be provided with the endorsement within three months of the grant

- The endorsement must not have been withdrawn by the date of application

Proof of earnings
Points will be awarded only if pay is evidenced by the specified documents as set out in A6A, which must include (A6A(c)):

- A contract of service or work between the applicant and a UK employer/institution indicating the undertaken field of work; or

- A letter from a UK employer or UK institution on its official headed paper, confirming that the applicant has earned money in his expert field.

For salaried employees (A6A(a)):

- Formal payslips or a headed notepaper letter from the employer confirming the authenticity of copies plus a bank/building society statement, or

- Personal bank statements showing receipt of pay or electronic statements, with a headed covering letter from the institution or its official stamp, or

- Official tax documents from HMRC (e.g. tax refund letters or tax demands) or the employer (e.g. P60, official earnings return approved, registered or stamped by HMRC, showing earnings on which tax has or will be paid or dividend vouchers

For the self-employed (A6A(b)):

- Letter from an appropriately qualified accountant on headed paper breaking down gross and net earnings, or

- Company accounts showing net profit, profit and loss account, and a director-signed balance sheet, or

- If working as a sponsored researcher, a letter on official headed paper with name, identifying the sponsoring institution providing funding, the host institution's name where the research is based, funding details and post title

Period and conditions of entry clearance/leave for Tier 1 Exceptional Talent migrants

Where a person is granted entry clearance under this route, they will receive a period in line with the request they make in their application: either one, two, three or four years; or 5 years and 4 months (r245BC(a)).

Where they are granted leave to remain, they will receive a period in line with the request they make in their application: either one, two, three or four years; or five years (r245BE(a)).

- No recourse to public funds

- Police registration if Rule 326 requires it

- No employment as a Doctor or Dentist in Training, or as a professional sportsperson/ coach

- A person may study subject to the conditions in Part 15 of the Rules, which prevents certain forms of study unless a valid Academic Technology Approval Scheme clearance certificate from the Counter-Proliferation Department of the Foreign and Commonwealth Office is issued before studies begin

Indefinite leave to remain for Tier 1 Exceptional Talent migrants

The key requirements for settlement are:

- They must not fall foul of the general refusal reasons or be an illegal entrant (r245BF(b))

- They must have met the continuous residence requirements (r245BF(c)):

  - Five years within this category;

  - A five-year period where time has also been spent with leave as a Tier 1 Migrant (excluding Graduate Entrepreneurs or Post-Study Workers) or as a Tier 2 Migrant (excluding Intra-Company Transfers);

  - Absences of no more than 180 days in 12 calendar month period within the five years

- They must have 75 points under Appendix A (r245BF(d))

- They must have demonstrated sufficient knowledge of the English language and life in the UK, as per Appendix KoLL (r245BF(e))

- They must not be in the UK in breach of immigration laws, save as permitted by Rule 39E (r245BD(f))

Points are set out in Table 1 of Appendix A, which provides a route to settlement for a Tier 1 Exceptional Talent migrant who has

- Earned money working in the expert field for which they were endorsed by a DCB

- The DCB has not withdrawn its endorsement

Endorsement reviews

This is a special remedy available in this immigration route alone, and created and set out by Annex C of the Guidance for applicants.

The remedy is

- Free of charge; the form is available on the Tier 1 (Exceptional Talent) Endorsement Review Form
- Must be made within 28 days of the date of the refusal email, subject to exceptional circumstances
- Conducted by the DCB: the decision is made within 28 days of receipt of the form
- No new evidence will be considered: the process just reviews that previously submitted
- The endorsement reviewer may recommend that the refusal should be reconsidered if they find that the Home Office:

    - failed properly to pass on evidence submitted with the original application;
    - made a mistake in processing the application;
    - failed to pass on correctly the reasons for refusing the endorsement.

  Refusal may still follow the identification of flaws such as these, but new refusal reasons would be supplied.

- The result of the application comes by email, and will either be upholding the original decision, reversing the decision, or providing an amended refusal letter with improved reasoning

Chapter 4: Tier 1 Representing Investors

Introduction

The general purpose of this route is to allow generous immigration consequences for people with a high net worth who make a substantial financial investment in the UK. They enjoy certain benefits seldom available to other migrants: for example, there is no English language requirement in this route, the rationale being that they will not need to work in order to support themselves. The financial firepower they need to evidence in order to be granted a visa is such that there are no separate maintenance requirements: it is simply presumed that they will be able to look after themselves given their overall wealth. The relative shortness of the provisions in Part 6A of the Rules pays testimony to the ease with which the route may be satisfied.

There was a change in the route from 6 November 2014, when the overall investment required was doubled. Previously, the requirement was for £1 million to be available for investment, of which at least £750,000 was invested in UK government bonds, or in share or loan capital in actively trading UK companies, and the remaining £250,000 had to be held in assets or money on deposit. Thereafter, the requirement changed to simply having appropriately invested £2 million.

Applicants entering in the pre-November 2014 route may still extend their leave, so long as they can show that they made and maintained the appropriate investment. To do so they must show £1 million of funds under their control of which three quarters has been invested in qualifying investments, within three months of arriving in the UK or being granted an entry clearance.

There are controls on the source of the investment monies: the decision maker must be confident that they are truly at liberty to invest the money said to be under their control, and that the money has not been acquired unlawfully, and that any third party providing funds is of good character.

The investment may have been made before the application is made, though not more than a year previously. If the investment has not yet been made, then the money that underlies it must be shown to be available to the applicant for UK investment: either because it is held in an institution here, or freely transferable to the UK and convertible to sterling.

Money for these purposes can include funds held by the person's spouse, civil partner or unmarried or same-sex partner, so long as they are under the applicant's control and are free to invest them. Certain documents have to be produced to demonstrate that the relationship is a genuine one, and that the funds are truly available to the applicant: so their partner has to demonstrate their intention by evidencing a gift of beneficial ownership, backed up by a legal advisor's letter confirming the gift is valid and enforceable in the country where it is made.

Those newly entering the route must have held the investment monies for 90 days before applying (ending no more than a month before the application is made). The money has to be evidenced via portfolio reports from the institution holding it where an investment professional is in charge of the investment, or, for those managing their own investments, official company accounts or statements showing the value of holdings in shares/bonds/trust funds and so forth, or via bank statements or a letter from a regulated bank confirming the funds are found in the relevant bank balance. If the investment monies have not been held for 90 days, then there is a very long set of criteria for every imaginable source of funds, specifying the documents needed to back up their heritage: gifts, asset sales, business accounts, inheritances, divorce settlements, prize winnings, and any other source.

The investment in question must be in UK government bonds, or in share or loan capital in actively trading UK companies.

When applying for an extension of leave or settlement, there are specific limitations on the available investments which qualify: money held offshore is generally excluded, as is investment in open-ended investment companies, investment trust companies, investment syndicate companies or pooled investment vehicles, and leveraged investment funds; investment in property investment, management and development companies; bank, building society and other funds held on deposit, ISAs, premium bonds and national saving certificates.

Those seeking extensions of leave must demonstrate that they maintained their investment throughout their residence. If investments within the portfolio are sold, they must be replaced ("topped up") within six months or before the next reporting period (if sooner). Fees must be paid from surplus funds over and above the requisite investment: it is perfectly permissible to pay them from the investment funds, but only where those funds have contained a consistent surplus so that fee payments do not cause dips below the relevant threshold.

Leave may be curtailed if the appropriate investment has not been maintained throughout their stay. There are subtly different wordings for those who entered the route before and after November 2014, and at the time of writing we are yet to see the approach taken to extension applications. Time will tell as to the precise extent to which the Home Office expects the capital to remain tied up in the original investment for these modern entrants to the route.

The general guidance on the Home Office website states that an application should not be made more than three months before travelling: decisions should be made within three weeks of the application. Those wishing to speed things along may always use the Super Premium Service to do so.

Our methodology in this Guide is to first set out concepts which recur throughout the Investors route, then to explain the introductory Immigration Rules, before going on to address the detailed criteria set out in Appendix A for each stage of the process: initial applications, extensions and applying for indefinite leave to remain. We give examples along the way to bring the commentary alive.

There are various aspects of the PBS which are essentially generic in nature, and which we deal with in Chapter 1: *General Themes in PBS Cases.*

As always with Points Based System cases, we see two forms of Guidance: that for applicants (Version 11/2018), and that for Home Office staff (Version 16.0; published 5 November 2018). We generally refer to the latter unless we expressly state the contrary.

Generic concepts

Regulated financial institutions

Money will only be considered as eligible for investment if it is maintained in an appropriate institution. This requires that it be regulated by the appropriate regulatory body for the country in which the financial institution operates (A43, A62).

Genuineness: Liberty to Invest

Investors may be vetted as to the genuineness of their investment activities. As it happens, the Rules resist the temptation to expressly refer to the term *genuine*, which litters the rest of Part 6A. Slightly different terminology is used, but the aim is still to give leeway to a decision-maker to question whether the individual in question is truly at liberty to invest the funds. There are also constraints on the *origin* of funds – so points will not be awarded where a decision-maker considers there are reasonable grounds to suspect that they are derived from unlawful activities or emanate from a third party of dubious character, conduct or associations (r245EB(e), r245ED(g)).

The Guidance explains that reasonable doubts might arise from scenarios such as these, where the applicant:

- Has been gifted funds by a third party who has been accused of serious fraud in their home country

- Is currently a domestic worker for a third party where the latter plans to base themselves in the UK with the applicant remaining in their employment if they are approved under the Tier 1 (Investor) category

- Holds funds which checks have shown are likely to be the proceeds of criminal activities

Criteria for the Investor route under the Rules

There are broadly similar requirements for entry clearance and leave to remain. You can find them in 245EB for entry clearance applicants, 245ED for those seeking leave to remain. These are

- Not falling foul of the general refusal reasons (r245EB(a), r245ED(a))

- Acquiring the relevant points under Appendix A (A54-A65-SD) (r245EB(b), r245EB(d))

- Being at least 18 years old and the assets/investment underlying the application must be completely under their control (r245EB(d), r245ED(e))

- Having the consent of any sponsoring Government or Agency if they have Tier 4 leave, or were last granted leave under Tier 4 – i.e. as a student (r245EB(c)/r245ED(d))

- Satisfying a "genuineness" test, which encompasses several dimensions (r245EB(e)/r245ED(g)), posing the question whether the applicant:

    - Is truly at liberty to freely invest the money

    - Acquired the money by means of conduct which is unlawful in the UK, or would constitute unlawful conduct if it occurred in the UK

    - If relying on funds made available by another party, the character, conduct or associations of that party are such that approval of the application would not be conducive to the public good

- Providing a criminal record certificate if aged over 18 (entry clearance only) for countries in which they have been present for 12 months or more in the last decade (r245EB(f)-(g))

Particular requirements for applications switching into the category/extending leave

- Must not be in breach of immigration law save for under the r39E proviso (r245ED(f))

- May switch from certain categories (r245ED(c)):

    - The rest of Tier 1 (save for Graduate Entrepreneur) and HSMP

    - Tier 2

    - Tier 4 (Child) students

    - Suitably sponsored Tier 4 (General) students

Period and conditions of grant of leave

The pattern of grants of leave is as follows:

- Entry clearance is granted for three years and four months (r245EC)

- Leave to remain will be granted for two years for those previously in the Investor route, for three years for those switching into it (245EE(a))

Accordingly the normal sequence of decisions for an investor who enters the route via entry clearance will be a three year grant of leave following by a two year extension, at which point they can apply for settlement. Those who first obtain leave to remain having previously been present in another route must build up five years of leave as an investor, which will involve an initial grant of three years followed by a further grant of two years (or its equivalent in the islands) (Tables 9A and B, Rows 2 and 3 respectively).

However, there are possibilities for accelerated access to settlement depending on the scale of the sums invested: after two years for a £10 million investment, and after three years for a £5 million investment.

Example

Midas plans to enter the UK as an investor relying on £2 million. He does not expect to increase his investment significantly during his time here.

If his application succeeds, Midas will be granted entry clearance for three years and four months. He will then have to apply for leave to remain, which should be granted for two years. Once he has achieved five years of relevant continuous residence (he may include time after the grant of entry clearance but before arriving in the UK as part of that period, although of course it will be counted towards the maximum 180 days abroad), he can apply for settlement.

Leave is granted subject to conditions:

- No recourse to public funds
- Police registration if r326 requires it
- No employment as a Doctor or Dentist in Training unless holding the appropriate listed qualification, or as a professional sportsperson/coach (at the entry clearance stage, the restriction is in r245EC(iii); the requirements are different for those applying for leave to remain, when a person who has been working in such a capacity without any restriction may continue to do so, if their application is backed by a letter from a Postgraduate Deanery or NHS Trust stating they have been working in a post or programme that has been approved by the General Medical Council or Joint Committee for Postgraduate Training in Dentistry as a training programme or post: r245EE(iii))
- A person may study subject to the conditions in Part 15 of the Rules

The Appendix A requirements

As usual the route-specific requirements are mostly located in Appendix A. There was a significant change in the investment levels required in November 2014 which means that there have to be different requirements for those who had previously entered the route than for those entering thereafter. The core criteria are found in three Tables, which are introduced by the opening paragraphs of Appendix A (A54-A56):

- Table 7 addresses the finances required to enter the route for modern applicants: essentially holding a set sum of money and having documented plans for investing it

- Table 8A addresses further leave for those who entered the route under the Rules in force from 6 November 2014 in the 12 months before the application is made; and for those now applying for an extension of leave in the investor category granted under those Rules

- Table 8B addresses further leave for those who entered the route under the Rules in force before 6 November 2014 in the 12 months before the application is made; and for those now applying for an extension of leave in the investor category granted under those Rules

As elsewhere within the PBS, the requirements are essentially binary: either you are awarded the criteria or you not are not. Partial point scoring gets an outright refusal.

New entrants to the route – the Table 7 requirements
New entrants are classed as those who have not had leave in the category within the last 12 months and whose previous grant of leave was not as a Tier 1 Investor or an investor under the pre-PBS rules (i.e. under the rules in force before 30 June 2008 – see Guidance).

The core investment requirements for those now joining the route are that the applicant has

- Money under their control in a regulated financial institution of not less than £2 million

- Opened an account with a UK regulated bank for the purposes of investing not less than £2 million

There are some constraints on the holding of money and timing of investment:

- If not already invested, the money must have been held for a consecutive 90-day period ending no more than one calendar month before the application – unless the source of the funds is a gift between spouses/partners, an asset sale, funds from a business, an inheritance, divorce settlement, financial award or winnings, or some other source: each source must be evidenced by tightly defined criteria for the specified documents, set out in A64A-SD (A64(a))

- Whilst an investment may have already been made at the date of application, any such investment must have taken place no more than 12 months before the application date (A63) (this is styled the "fresh investment" criteria in the Guidance)

- However, where the investment has been made pre-application, it is necessary to demonstrate its reality via a distinct set of specified documents (A64(b), A64A-SD)

The specified evidence required to show that the bank account is available is

- A bank letter from a UK-regulated bank dated within three months of the application, giving their account number and name, and confirming that the account has been opened for the purposes of investing £2 million and is FCA-regulated for accepting deposits (A59)

- The Guidance explains that if the applicant has opened an account with a body that is FCA regulated but which does not accept deposits, such as a wealth management organisation, the body in question may still provide admissible evidence to back the application, by way of a letter confirming that it applies the applicable FCA/PRA due diligence standards and is authorised to make investments and hold/control client money (e.g. there is an underlying regulated custodian bank working with the wealth management organisation)

- If the FCA-regulated investment firm is not itself authorised to hold/control client monies then it should have an agreement in place with a deposit holding institution upon whose due diligence it can rely (such as the underlying regulated custodian bank) and whose records it can obtain on request

- If the account is with an institution that accepts deposits but does not make investments, the institution may provide a letter confirming they are satisfied an account has been open for the relevant investment purposes albeit that the investment will not be made from the account

There are some further requirements before the money and assets are established as eligible for investment purposes:

- Money is classed as disposable in the UK if the money is held here or freely transferable here and convertible to sterling (A60) – the Guidance explains that international financial sanctions are a potential barrier. Thus, where necessary, it is important to show that any necessary approval has been obtained: if the applicant is individually subject to some restriction then proof from the relevant official body such as HM Treasury is necessary. The HM Treasury website sets out the sanctions regime to which the UK is party; equally, many countries have currency controls which may prevent the transfer of money

- Conversion calculations will be made via the www.oanda.com facility as at the application date (A60)

- Funds can include money or assets belonging to the applicant's spouse or civil/unmarried/same-sex partner, provided that partner meets the requirements of the PBS dependent route, so long as the relevant specified evidence is provided (A61)

- Funds may not include money against which a loan is secured, where another party would have a claim on the money were the loan repayments not met (A61A), except where

  - The applicant has a pending application, or had one granted application, in this route, which was made before 13 December 2012

  - They have not since had leave in another category

  - The money is otherwise under their control, save for the loan secured upon it

Examples

Beatrice wishes to enter the Investor route. She holds funds of £2 million. Half is held in a UK bank account. Half is held in a bank account in her country of origin, Canada.

These funds would qualify as money that is "disposable in the UK" so long as

- **The money held in the UK is with a regulated financial institution**
- **The money held in Canada can be freely transferred here (one should always check the value of funds at www.oanda.com but this is especially important if the applicant is aiming to provide the bare minimum). Canada is not a regime where one would expect financial sanctions to bite. Where money is coming from abroad, a UK bank**

account must already be open to receive it, though that is no problem here as the UK element of the funds is presumably held in such an account

Ranjiv wishes to extend leave in the investor route. The funds on which he wants to rely include a significant loan of money from a UK institution.

Ranjiv will only be able to rely on that loan if he entered the route before 6 November 2014 and so is claiming points under Table 9B. In that scenario he may rely on Row 1(b)(ii), which permits reliance on loan funds of £1 million as an alternative to relying on money of one's own.

Where the money comes from a partner, the specified evidence required to show that money/assets are under the applicant's control and they are free to invest them in the UK is

- Marriage certificate confirming the relationship showing the parties' names (A61-SD(a)(i))
- Evidence of cohabitation for at least two years, via at least three forms of evidence from this list: bank statement; official document such as a mortgage agreement or an agreement showing a joint investment in business or property, tenancy agreement, council tax/utility bills, life insurance policy naming the other as beneficiary, birth certificates of children from the relationship, any other evidence adequately demonstrating long-term commitment names (A61-SD(a)(ii))
- A dated declaration from the partner that they will permit all joint or personal money to be used to claim points as being under the applicant's control "known as a gift of beneficial ownership of the money while retaining the legal title", showing the sum in question, the names of the applicant and partner and signed by them both, and stating that the applicant has sole control over the sum (A61-SD(a)(iii)) – note that there is a template in the Home Office investor guidance *Declaration for joint funding for Investors* (Annex G document 3)
- A dated letter from a legal adviser authorised to practice in the country where the third party or the money is located, confirming that the declaration is signed and valid in the country in which it is made, naming the legal representative, identifying their registration/authority to practice in the relevant country, and naming the applicant and partner (A61-SD(a)(iv))

Example

Liu Wei wishes to enter the investment route. He has funds of £1 million. His long-term girlfriend Li Min has funds of £1 million. She is willing to support his investment plans.

Liu may rely on the funds of his unmarried partner which count as "money of his own". However their relationship must be extant at the date of application and they must have cohabited for two years for her to meet the definition. There will then be a further tranche of "specified documents" to be provided, as set out in A61-SD, proving the relationship, the fact of cohabitation, and a declaration confirming Liu has beneficial ownership of the money such that he can freely dispose of it for himself, and the validity of that declaration must be backed up by a lawyer's letter

The specified documents for demonstrating that the money has been held over the relevant period are at least one of the following (A64-SD(a)):

- **Where the investment is managed by a regulated institution, a portfolio report or breakdown of investments letter**, in either case from a UK regulated financial institution, confirming (A46-SD(a)(i)):

  - The amount of money invested
  - The beneficial owner of the funds
  - The date of the investment period covered by the report
  - The author's registration as a regulated financial institution and
  - That the money can be transferred into the UK if it is held abroad, or that the money has already been invested in the UK via UK Government bonds, share capital or loan capital in active and trading UK registered companies, and the dates of these investments

- **For a person who manages their own investments**, or has a **portfolio manager who does not operate in the UK** and so is not FCA/PRA-regulated, *one or more* of these documents must be provided covering a consecutive 90-day period of time, ending no earlier than one calendar month before the date of application (A64-SD(a)(ii)):

  - *Certified copies of bond documents* showing the value of the bonds, the date of purchase and the owner
  - *Share documents* showing the value of the shares, the date of purchase and the owner
  - The *latest audited annual accounts* of the organisation in which the investment has been made, showing the amount of money held in the investments, the applicant's name or that of their partner, the date of investment, or, if no accounts have been produced, a certificate from an accountant showing the amount of money held in the investments
  - *Trust fund documents* from a legal adviser showing the amount of money in the fund, the date that the money is available and the beneficial owner, and including the name and contact details of the legal adviser and at least one of the trustees

- **Personal bank statements** on official bank stationery from a bank regulated by the official regulatory body for the country in which the institution operates and the funds are located, showing the account number and the amount of money available in the name of the applicant or their partner's name, covering a consecutive 90-day period of time, ending no earlier than one calendar month before the application date, the most recent statement being no more than one calendar month old at the application date; electronic bank statements to be accompanied by an authorised supporting letter from the bank on the institution's headed paper, confirming that the statements are accurate and genuine (A64-SD(a)(iii))

- **Where bank statements cannot be provided**, an authorised letter on headed paper from a bank regulated by the appropriate national regulatory body of the country where the funds are located, no earlier than one calendar month before the application date, confirming the account number, the applicant's name or their partner's, that the money is available in their name, the regulatory arrangements, the dates of the period covered showing the stated balance, over a period of at least three calendar months running up to the date of the letter (A64-SD(a)(iv))

- Where **funds are not held in the UK** then a further dated authorised headed letter from the bank/financial institution is required, confirming the amount of money to be transferred and that it can indeed be so transferred to the UK, details of the regulatory arrangements by the appropriate national body for the institution holding the money, the name of the beneficial owner (i.e. the applicant/their partner), account numbers, and that the institution will confirm the content of the letter to the Home Office on request (A64-SD(b)). Where bank statements are not able to be produced, then the letter (as described in the last paragraph) giving relevant details in their absence can serve both purposes

- Note that there is a template in the Home Office investor guidance *Letter for authorised financial institution* (Annex G document 1)

- If **accountants are providing the specified documents**, then their own bona fides must be established: confirming that they are a member of the appropriate professional body in the UK or, if based abroad, the appropriate national supervisory/regulatory body (A64-SD(c)).

Example

Crassus plans to use the investor route to enter the UK. He has slightly over £2 million of investments in UK shares in companies trading in the energy business. He wants to rely on this investment (which he manages himself) for his application.

You should check whether he has made the investment in the last 12 months; otherwise it is ineligible. So long as that requirement is satisfied, then the investments may be relied upon. As he self-manages his investment, he will need to provide evidence himself of the investment via share documents showing the value of the shares, the date of purchase and the owner.

Evidencing funds held for more than 90 days

These are the further documents required in order to establish that the investment money is under the applicant's control, where that money was not under the applicant's control in the sense of being held for 90 days in an investment portfolio or bank account (i.e. the proviso to A64(b)). They are set out at A64A-SD(a). It will quickly be seen that these provisions effectively operate in pairs, firstly identifying the source of the money, secondly giving the specified documents. The relevant supporting documents must be provided as follows, always with verifiable contact details.

- **Money given** in the three months before the application date must be supported by **an irrevocable dated memorandum of gift** (described as such), showing its amount and that the legal value is being transferred, the name and signature of donor and recipient, their relationship (A64A-SD(a)(i)) – note that there is a template in the Home Office investor guidance (Annex G document 2): *Memorandum of deed of gift for Investors*

- Where an irrevocable dated memorandum of gift is provided, alongside it must be a named legal advisor's dated letter confirming the arrangements and showing that they are entitled to practise in the country in which the gift was made, confirming the amount, donor and recipient, their relationship, date of transfer of the money, that the memorandum is indeed irrevocable, signed, valid and legally binding in the relevant country (A64A-SD(a)(ii))

- **Money generated by asset sale** in the three months before the application date must be backed by **a deed of sale** showing the name of the applicant/partner and the date of sale and the amount of money raised (A64A-SD(a)(iii))

- Where such a deed of sale is provided, alongside it must be a named legal advisor's dated letter confirming the arrangements and showing that they can practise in the country in which the gift was made, confirming what was sold, for what amount, the name of the person receiving money from the sale, their relationship, dates of sale and of transfer of the money, and that the sale was valid and legally binding in the relevant country (A64A-SD(a)(iv))

- Where the **funds are presently held in a business** of applicant/partner, profit and loss accounts (or income and expenditure accounts for an organisation not trading for profit) showing the amount of money available for investment, prepared and signed off as per the appropriate statutory requirements (A64A-SD(a)(v))

- Where such accounts are provided, alongside them must be a named legal advisor's dated letter confirming that they can lawfully extract the money in question, showing that they can practise in the country where the business operates, and confirming that the money in question can indeed be lawfully extracted as claimed (A64A-SD(a)(vi))

- Where the money comes via the applicant being the **beneficiary of a will**, a notarised copy must be provided (assets may not be valued and monetarised, only money may be relied on). The will must be dated, show that the applicant/partner is the beneficiary, the amount of the inheritance, and the names of any executors, plus any codicils (additions) to the will that affect the amount of money that was received (A64A-SD(a)(vii))

- Where such a notified copy will is provided, alongside it must be a named legal advisor's dated letter showing that they can practise in the country where the business operates, confirming the date and amount of money received, the name of the person making the will and the beneficiary, their relationship, and that the will was signed and valid according to the laws of the country in which it was made (A64A-SD(a)(viii))

- Where the money comes from a **financial agreement pursuant to a divorce settlement** (non-money assets from the divorce may not be valued for these purposes), a notarised copy of a financial agreement must be provided (A64A-SD(a)(ix))

- Where a notarised copy of a financial agreement is provided, alongside it must be a named legal advisor's dated letter showing that they can practise in the country where the divorce took place, confirming the details of the parties to the divorce, the date and amount of money received by the applicant/partner, and that the divorce settlement is complete and valid according to the laws of the country in which it was made (A64A-SD(a)(x))

- Where the money comes from a **financial award or winnings**, a letter from the organisation from which the funds came giving its contact details, confirming the date and amount of money received by the applicant/partner, and that the winnings are genuine (A64A-SD(a)(xi))

- Where a letter confirming that the money comes from a **financial award or winnings** is supplied, alongside it must be a named legal advisor's dated letter showing that they can practise in the country where the award was made, confirming the details of the funds' source and recipient, and the date and amount of money received by the applicant/partner including the date funds were transferred to them (A64A-SD(a)(xii))

- Where the money emanates from another source than those just named, relevant documentation must be provided evidencing the source of the money, together with independent supporting evidence, which both clearly confirm the source, amount and date, and the fact that the applicant/partner was the legal recipient of the money them (A64A-SD(a)(xiii))

Example

Jermaine, a US citizen, wants to make an investment having just received a significant inheritance of several million. He has held the money for a week, but wants to enter the Tier 1 Investor route as soon as possible.
Jermaine must hurdle the requirement to have held the money in Table 7 (ie £2 million) for 90 days. For a person who has not held the funds for 90 days in a bank account or within investments backed up by portfolio report from an investment manager or other admissible evidence, they need to provide the further specified evidence in A64A-SD: inheritances are dealt with expressly therein at (vii)-(viii).

Extending leave to remain

Tables 8A and 8B provide the detailed criteria for extending leave. They contain specified dates by which the investment must have been made. The requirements differ depending on whether or not the applicant first entered the route via an application made before, or from, 6 November 2014.

Where the investment is in institutions that produce portfolio report, then a series of portfolio reports must be provided, running through the investment period, from the specified date given in the table, until the last reporting date of the most recent reporting period. If the investment is into an organisation, then its scale must be shown via accounts, audited or unaudited.

Extension of leave – applications from 6 November 2014

Table 8A addresses the requirements for individuals who applied to enter the route **from 6 November 2014**. Table 8A contains a single requirement, satisfaction of which brings the award of 75 points, which is that the money was invested:

- Within three months of entry if granted entry clearance in the Investor category where the date of entry is ascertainable, or otherwise within three months of the grant of entry clearance/leave to remain unless there are exceptionally compelling reasons justifying the delay – any such exceptionally compelling reasons must be unforeseeable and outside of the applicant's control, delays caused by the applicant failing to take timely action will not be accepted, and where possible, reasonable steps to mitigate such delay should have been taken (Table 8A(1-2))

- Where the investment was made prior to the application leading to the first grant of leave, no earlier than 12 months before the date of application (Table 8A(3))

- So long as the investment has been maintained for the whole of the remaining period of such leave

Individuals who applied to enter the route before 6 November 2014
Table 8B addresses the requirements for individuals who applied to enter the route **before 6 November 2014**. The Table 8B requirements are threefold:

- **Holding money or assets** (Table 8B row 1: 30 points) by way of

    - Money under their control of not less than £1 million, or

    - Personal assets with a value of not less than £2 million, having regard to any liabilities to which they are subject, plus money under their control of not less than £1 million which been loaned to them by a UK regulated financial institution

- **Completion of investment activity** (Table 8B row 2: 30 points)

    - Not less than £750,000 of their capital being invested in the UK by way of UK Government bonds, share capital or loan capital in active and trading UK registered companies

    - Where the remaining balance (i.e. of up to £250,000, such as to make up the £1 million) in the UK is invested by the purchase of assets or by maintaining the money on deposit in a UK regulated financial institution

- **Timing of investment** (Table 8B row 3: 15 points)

    - Within three months of entry if granted entry clearance in the linvestor category where the date of entry is ascertainable, or otherwise within three months of the grant of entry clearance/leave to remain unless there are exceptionally compelling reasons justifying the delay (as already glossed above)

    - Where the investment was made prior to the application leading to the first grant of leave, no earlier than 12 months before the date of application

    - So long as the investment has been maintained for the whole of the remaining period of such leave; any shortfall in the investment element must be made good within six months of the sale or before the next reporting period

Example

Khalid entered the investor route three years ago having been granted entry clearance to do so. He is planning an extension of leave. He entered the UK around three months after the entry clearance grant (he cannot recall the precise date) and put his funds into UK government bonds 14 weeks after he arrived.

As he entered the route three years ago, he must have done so before November 2014. So it is Table 8B which applies. The period within which he needed to have made his investment depends on whether there is concrete proof of the date of entry; if his passport is not stamped and he has no other evidence, the entry clearance grant will be taken as the relevant date. Accordingly he had three months from then to make his investment. In fact, even if he can prove the date of entry, he will still have invested late.

He will need to show that there are *exceptionally compelling reasons for* the delay in investing. This is a very high test, of course, and must be based on circumstances beyond his control.

Qualifying investments

The definition of active and trading UK companies are those with a registered office or head office in the UK, a UK bank account showing current business transactions, and are subject to UK taxation (A65A).

Funds held in one of the institutions listed as unreliable in Appendix P do not qualify (A65B).

A65 addresses investment for individuals applying for an extension of leave or settlement, creating specific limitations on the available investments which qualify, excluding the following:

- By way of sums held in an offshore company or trust, or held in offshore custody (unless the application was made before 13 December 2012 and the applicant succeeded in entering the route, or an application made before that date remains undecided)
- Open-ended investment companies, investment trust companies, investment syndicate companies or pooled investment vehicles
- Companies mainly engaged in property investment, property management or property development: the policy being that investment should be in activities other than investing in property for resale or rental
- Deposits with a bank, building society or other enterprise whose normal course of business includes the acceptance of deposits
- ISAs, premium bonds and saving certificates issued by the National Savings and Investment Agency (NS&I), for an applicant who has, or last had leave as an Investor
- Leveraged investment funds, except where the leverage in question is the security against those loans which are expressly permitted in some of the Tables. There is a transitional arrangement in place for those who applied under older Rules (see Guidance A14)

There are some further restrictions:

For those entering the route from 6 November 2014, points will be scored for maintaining the investment funds (A65C(a)) only if

- The applicant has purchased a portfolio of qualifying investments for a price of at least £2 million

- ➢ Where any part of the qualifying investments in the portfolio is sold (whether at a gain or at a loss) during the specified continuous period of leave, their gross proceeds are re-invested in qualifying investments before the end of the next reporting period, or within six months of the date of completion of the sale, whichever is sooner

For those entering the route before 6 November 2014, points will be scored for maintaining the investment funds (A65C(b)) only if

- ➢ The applicant has maintained a portfolio of qualifying investments with a market value of at least £750,000;
- ➢ Any fall in the market value of the portfolio below that amount is corrected before the end of the next reporting period, or within six months of the date of completion of the sale, whichever is sooner, by the purchase of further qualifying investments with a market value equal to the amount of any such fall; and
- ➢ The applicant has maintained a total level of investment, aggregating the qualifying investments with other investments, of £1,000,000

Example

Lydia is present as an Investor. She entered the route in October 2014. Her assets comprise an investment fund of £750,000 and a share in the family home of £300,000. She wishes to extend her leave. She is worried that her investment will not qualify because the fund fell to a value of £745,000 for a 30- day period.

The difficulty this poses will depend on when that fall occurred and what action she took to rectify matters. She has to make good the fall in value within six months of a sale of the investment, but there is no indication of a sale here. So she would have had to do so by the end of the next reporting period for the fund. If that is not yet due, she may still take remedial action; if it has passed without action, then she is in difficulties on an extension application.

There are specific provisions relevant to the withdrawal of investment proceeds and payment of fees (A65C(c))

- ➢ The applicant may withdraw interest and dividend payments generated by the qualifying investments from the portfolio
- ➢ Fees (e.g. those charged by institutions managing the portfolio), and transaction costs and tax incurred through buying and selling investments cannot be paid for from the investment funds for which the applicant scores points; and
- ➢ If the applicant has invested more than the required level in qualifying investments, the fees, transaction costs and tax just mentioned may be paid from the surplus investment, providing the surplus investment was made at the same time or before the fees, transaction costs and tax were incurred

There are then some specified documents which must be provided as evidence of investment (A65-SD):

- A series of investment portfolio reports (to prove the reality of the investment and of the period of maintenance (A65-SD(a), (e)))

    - Certified as correct by a UK regulated (FCA/PRA-regulated) financial institution which provides its name, contact details and date of certification, from no later than the beginning of the relevant three-month period set out in the appropriate Table, continuing up to the last reporting date of the most recent reporting period, including the price, date and destination of investments, certifying that the total investment was maintained as required and that it was made in the name of the applicant/partner and not in the name of an offshore company/trust even if wholly owned by the applicant and that the institution will confirm the content of the letter to the Home Office on request (A65-SD(a))

    - If these investments were made as loan funds to companies, be accompanied by audited accounts or unaudited accounts with an accounts compilation report for the investments made, giving the full details of the applicant's investment, from an appropriately qualified accountant (A65-SD(a)(vii)) – the guidance notes that the statutory requirements for overseas applications may be difficult to assess but as a minimum, the accounts must be signed by the company's directors and the accountants

- Where the investment relates to an application made pre-November 2014 on the basis that 75% of the investment has been made in qualifying assets, proof of investment of the remainder in UK assets or holding the money on UK deposit must be provided (A65-SD(c)):

    - Documents confirming **the assets purchased**, their value and the date of purchase: when using property it must be owned by the applicant/partner, and only the unmortgaged portion of the applicant's own home can be considered, excluding any share of the property held as tenants in common with another person save for their partner, and the valuation must be provided by a surveyor who is a member of the RCIS (A65-SD(c)(i)) dated within the last 6 months

    - For **money on deposit**, statements or statements of account on official stationery if the fundholding institution, in the name of the applicant/partner, confirming the dates and amount of money held; and a letter from the financial institution on official headed paper confirming the dates and amount of money held and that the institution will confirm the content of the letter to the Home Office on request (A65-SD(c)(ii)-(iii))

- If the three-month period within which the investment was made is based on a known date of entry to the UK, evidence proving this date such as a passport or airline boarding card

Example

Croesus has invested £2.2 million in shares in active trading UK companies. He accordingly scores points for £2 million of qualifying investments.

Croesus may pay up to £200,000 in fees, transaction costs and tax out of the investment funds. He has already invested sums including a significant surplus before the sums in question became due. However, he would not be entitled to run a bare £2 million fund and then top it up subsequently with further sums in order to compensate for monies paid out for those purposes.

Indefinite leave to remain

Under Part 6A, the applicant must meet these requirements:

- Not falling foul of the general refusal reasons, and must not be an illegal entrant (245EF(b))
- Obtaining 75 points under Appendix A – there is no requirement under Appendices B or C to meet (245EF(c))
- However that does not mean there is no English language requirement: instead, the requirements of Appendix KoLL must be met (245EF(d))
- Not being in breach of immigration laws save for the usual proviso that overstaying within the ambit of Rule 39E will be disregarded (245EF(e))
- Having resided in the UK for five years (or for a shorter period where access to ILR is accelerated) – during which time the applicant has not been absent from the UK for more than 180 days during any 12 month period within the continuous period in question (r245AAA) – note that we deal with r245AAA in detail, which applies generally in PBS cases, in Chapter 1: *General Themes in PBS Cases* – of course, investors are likely to be especially globally mobile individuals, and so the residence requirement needs to be flagged up to them early in their planning process

Appendix A introduces the two tables for indefinite leave to remain (para 57): Table 9A for those last granted leave under the **post**-November 2014 route, Table 9B for those last granted leave under **pre**-November 2014 route. The Tables are then explained by accompanying notes (para 58).

For those entering the route from 6 November 2014, there are three requirements set out in Table 9A:

- **Completed investment in the UK** by way of UK Government bonds, share capital or loan capital in active and trading UK registered companies, of the sum in question: £2 million, £5 million or £10 million (Table 9A Row 1)
- **A period of continuous residence** (with absences from the UK of no more than 180 days in any 12 calendar months during that period) dependent on the scale of investment ("the continuous specified period"), being five years, three years or two years (so long as the most recent leave is as a Tier 1 Investor in the UK, time spent in Jersey, Guernsey or the Isle of Man in an equivalent immigration category may count (Table 9A Row 2)
- **Time restrictions on the investment**, which must (Table 9A Row 3)
    - Have been made no earlier than 12 months before the grant of leave by which the applicant entered the Investor route,
    - Have been maintained throughout the relevant continuous residence period from Row 2 (excluding the first three months)
    - The continuous residence period will be taken as the later of these dates:

- o The date of entry clearance, or of first entry to UK, as a Tier 1 Investor (or date of entry to one of the islands where there was equivalent residence where this is earlier)

- o A date three months before the full specified amount was invested in the UK (or three months before the full required amount was invested in one of islands where there was equivalent residence)

For those entering the route before 6 November 2014, there are three requirements set out in Table 9B:

- ➢ **Money and asset holding requirements** (Table 9B Row 1):

  - Holding money of their own under their control of not less than £10 million, or owning personal assets net of liabilities of not less than £20 million including £10 million of money loaned to them by a UK financial institution under their control and disposable in the UK (Table 9B Row 1(a))

  - Holding money of their own under their control of not less than £5 million, or owning personal assets net of liabilities of not less than £10 million including £5 million of money loaned to them by a UK financial institution under their control and disposable in the UK (Table 9B Row 1(b))

  - Holding money of their own under their control of not less than £1 million, or owning personal assets net of liabilities of not less than £2 million including £1 million of money loaned to them by a UK financial institution under their control and disposable in the UK (Table 9B Row 1(c))

- ➢ **A specified investment amount**, of which 75% must be invested in UK Government bonds, or in share capital or loan capital in active and trading UK registered companies, the remaining balance of the specified invested amount in the UK being held via the purchase of assets or by maintaining the money on deposit in a UK regulated financial institution (Table 9B Row 2), depending on whether points are claimed for the figure in Row 1(a)), 1(b)) or 1(c)): the respective thresholds are

  - £10 million
  - £5 million
  - £1 million

- ➢ **A period of continuous residence** as a Tier 1 Investor (with absences from the UK of no more than 180 days in any 12 calendar months during that period) dependent on the scale of investment ("the continuous specified period"), being five years, three years or two years (so long as the most recent leave is as a Tier 1 Investor in the UK, time spent in Jersey, Guernsey or the Isle of Man in an equivalent immigration category may count (Table 9B Row 3):

  - 2 years
  - 3 years
  - 5 years

For those entering the route from 6 November 2014, points will be scored for maintaining the investment funds (A65C(a)) only if

- ➢ The applicant has purchased a portfolio of qualifying investments for a price of at least the specified amount

For those entering the route before 6 November 2014, points will be scored for maintaining the investment funds (A65C(b)) only if

- The applicant has maintained a portfolio of qualifying investments with a market value of at least the specified amount

There are some very specific provisions, which are especially heavy-going, regarding how the *source of the additional money* that underlies an accelerated settlement application is to be evidenced (i.e. the £5 million or £10 million for post-November 2014 applicants, or the similar sums of available money for pre-November 2014 subject to the permitted alternative of providing double those sums via more general assets or borrowed money):

- Possession of available monies must be shown for 90 days before the relevant investment was made (A64B-SD(a)) and

- Either

  - The documents required to evidence possession of money (at A64B-SD(i): i.e. bank statements showing the money, or portfolio accounts where the money comprises an investment which is professionally managed, or for a self-managing investor certified copy bond documents/documents showing share values/annual accounts from businesses/trust fund documents) or

  - The documents showing the source of the money where it has not been held for 90 days: i.e. the admissible evidence of sale of assets, business funds, inheritances, divorce settlements, prize winnings (A64B-SD(ii))

- Where loaned money is being relied on for the additional money, then it is necessary to provide an authorised letter on headed paper from a UK regulated financial institution, confirming the amount of money loaned, the date the loan was taken which must be no later than the date of investment of the additional capital, and confirming that the applicant has personal assets of the appropriate net value and that the institution will confirm this information to the Home Office if required via direct request (A64C-SD)

Curtailment of leave

There are specific provisions for leave to be curtailed if certain actions critical to the investor route have not been taken, regarding the volume and timing of investment (r245EE(c)):

- The investment must have been made and maintained thereafter within three months of a specified date (r245EE(c)(i)): the funds must be at least £2 million if last granted leave under the Rules from 6 November 2014 and granted points under Table 8A, or £750,000 if last granted leave under the Rules before that date and scoring points under Table 8B (r245EE(e))

- The specified date is the date of entry if granted entry clearance as an investor and the date of entry is ascertainable, or the date of entry clearance itself if entry is not ascertainable, otherwise within six months of the date of grant of leave to remain (r245EE(d))

- However this possibility of curtailment does not apply where the applicant has had two prior grants of entry clearance as an investor (r245EE(f))

Chapter 5: Tier 2 Sponsored Workers

Introduction

This chapter we provide:

- A practical explanation of the way the Tier 2 route for skilled workers operates, explaining the major concepts underpinning the route before presenting the detailed requirements in a user-friendly format

- Highlights of the most useful parts of the Home Office Guidance

- Practical examples and casework tips showing the common pitfalls of the route

- Strategies for avoiding genuineness refusals in advance; and for managing, and challenging, such refusals when they arise

Our methodology

Our objective in this Chapter is not to reproduce the rules verbatim. Although we deal with everything in the Rules that seems significant, we aim to simplify and shorten the material to make it digestible. First we explain the recurring concepts within the Rule before going on to the detailed substantive criteria, with a view to making the latter more intelligible once the reader gets to them.

Now, we should emphasise that any practitioner advising on a live case should always read the Rules in full, and not on any surrogate for them, be it training notes or the Home Office's own Guidance. As usual in PBS routes, there are two overlapping sets of Guidance relevant to the route:

- *Tier 2 of the Points Based System – Policy Guidance*, Version 11/18 (which we call *Guidance for Applicants*)

- Tier 2 of the points-based system (Version 31; 12 November 2018) (we reference this as *Guidance for decision makers*)

The Guidance is undoubtedly very helpful – but it can be misleading, and it is the Rules which will be used by judges to resolve disputes when things go wrong. Our ebooks should help the reader to get a much better understanding of the Rules, by providing a practical guide to read alongside them, which makes their contents more palatable, by using bullet points within a logical structure, giving examples and practical tips as we go along.

We have other guides to Tier 2 which are written from the perspective of Sponsors, in this manual.

Overview of Tier 2

These routes enable UK employers to recruit workers from outside the EEA to fill a particular skilled vacancy that cannot be filled by a British or EEA worker (r245H). They are entry clearance only routes (r245HA) with limited opportunities to switch into them, usually from other business categories. The general policy is that migration under this route should not displace settled workers suitable for the role in question.

There are four sub-categories:

- **Tier 2 (General)** – for those with offers of skilled work that cannot be filled by a resident worker, including shortage occupations

- **Tier 2 (Intra-Company Transfer)** (ICT) – for existing employees of multinationals who need to be transferred to the UK for training purposes or because a settled/EEA worker cannot fulfil the role: the overseas employer must be linked to the UK branch by common ownership or control. There are three sub-categories:

    - **Long Term Staff**: for postings up to five years, for individuals who have been working for the firm for at least 12 months

    - **Short Term Staff**: for postings of at least 12 months, for individuals who have been working for the firm for at least 12 months: the route closed on 6 April 2017, so it is a legacy route, though practitioners may still come across people last granted leave in this capacity

    - **Graduate Trainee**: for recent graduate recruits being transferred to the UK for training as part of a structured graduate training programme with clearly defined progression towards a managerial or specialist role within the organisation for a maximum period of 12 months

- **Tier 2 Minister of Religion** – for a Minister of Religion undertaking preaching and pastoral work, Missionary, or Member of a Religious Order, taking up employment or a post/role within their faith community

- **Tier 2 Sportsperson** – for elite sportspersons or coaches whose employment will make a significant contribution to the development of their sport at the highest level in the UK

Central concepts are the **Certificate of Sponsorship** (CoS) and the **CoS Checking** Service (CoSCS). The former is the means by which the Sponsor records all relevant criteria for the job in question; the latter is the central record maintained by the Home Office on which these are registered. The CoS has a unique reference number, and contains information about the job in question and the applicant's personal details (the *Guidance for Applicants* in Part 8 gives more information). A multiple entry CoS may be issued for a person who travels significantly (*Guidance for Applicants* A5). The Sponsor has duties including the requirement to report not turning up for work on the first day, unreasonable absence (e.g. beyond 10 days), significant changes of employment circumstances and information suggesting an employee is breaching the terms of their leave. A CoS must be assigned within six months of the job vacancy first being advertised subject to certain exceptions for university milkround recruitment, PhDs, barristers and orchestral musicians.

It is not the physical CoS which lies at the system's heart, because applications are checked against the CoSCS, which you will see many references to the Rules. So if relevant information is missing from the electronic version, or were the existence of the hard copy not to be verifiable in the Home Office sponsor system virtual world, a paper hard copy would be useless.

Unlike most routes found in the Rules, there are limitations as to the numbers of applicants under Tier 2 according to the **Tier 2 (General) Limit** (often called the "cap"). It bites on entry clearance applicants only, not those applying to switch into the category or extend their leave (save for those in-country applicants who have previously been a dependent of a Tier 2 (General) migrant).

So a person who applies at the wrong time may in theory get caught out, either because the cap bites or because their intended Sponsor lacks a sufficient allocation of CoSs to back their application at the relevant moment– because Tier 2 Sponsors have to bid for CoSs which they can then allocate to migrant workers. The more high-powered the job, the greater the chance of the Sponsor striking lucky in the monthly allocation, as jobs themselves are allocated via a Points Based System for competing employers.

However, there is a get-out clause for some skilled jobs under the Tier 2 (General) entry clearance route, which can thereby swerve the cap: these include jobs where the salary exceeds the upper target, or whose work is pursuant to a large relocation or inward investment project involving significant job creation. The jobs not subject to the limit are the subject of **unrestricted** CoSs.

The route requires entry clearance to be obtained before travelling for those applying from abroad, and there are tight controls on switching into the route for in-country applicants: the ICT route essentially only permits those in the route already (who have resided here already under ICT for some years; and sole representatives of overseas businesses) to join; whereas the other three routes may be joined by sole representatives, students, migrants in Tier 1 and those already within another route in Tier 2. Students must leap various hurdles, such as obtaining the consent of their educational Sponsor, if backed by a government or international scholarship agency.

All Tier 2 migrants (save for ICT in-country applicants) face a "cooling off" period whereby a previous beneficiary of the route must have been abroad for at least a year before returning under it.

Tier 2 (General) is not routinely intended to be a way for small business owners to enter the UK, and so there is a prohibition for those who own more than 10% of the shares of the Sponsor business: unless they are really high earners (though an ICT is not caught by this proviso).

Tier 2 (General)

Once we reach the sub-routes within Tier 2, there are particularised criteria that the CoS must satisfy. There are substantive requirements for the CoS, regarding the quality of work (or working history) which it espouses: points are only awarded where the work is in Table 2 of Appendix J (i.e. it is at RQF level 6 of the national qualification rankings – or for people present in the route before 13 June 2012, at RQF level 4, via the cross-reference to Table 3 of Appendix J), or in certain specified jobs in the creative sector, or in a shortage occupation (or was a shortage occupation when leave was last granted and the application is to continue that job for the same or a different employer). Innocent victims of a downwards reclassification of a job category by the National Audit Office since their last application was granted are let off the hook. People also avoid the requirement for meeting the skills thresholds where they are working for the same employer in the same occupation as previously.

Then the CoS has to hurdle some more barriers: the Sponsor must not be hiring the worker out to a third party for routine contract work, and applicants must survive a genuineness audit in case the job or the advertising for it have been tailored to rule out resident workers. Nurses and midwives must be fully registered with the appropriate Council (the Nursing and Midwifery Council: NMC), or have passed its computer based competence test (or will be sitting for it soon after starting work), or obtained its permission before the end of April 2015 to join the Overseas Nursing Programme (ONP).

Another feature of the route is the Resident Labour Market Test (RLMT). This requires appropriately detailed adverts to have been placed in one or more general or specialist publications, for set periods (or to have participated in the university milkround). Alternatively the RLMT may be swerved for shortage occupations, for certain doctors and dentists in training, in research positions, or where the job is post-study work for certain classes of switcher; students can do so only where they have passed the student switching controls on level and place of study, and have to provide extensive evidence of their qualifications. Finally, it is possible to avoid the RLMT by continuing to work for the same Sponsor in the same occupation, so long as there is no associated move within the occupation from a job inside, to outside, the shortage occupation list.

Once we reach the issue of salary, then there are precise criteria by which it is to be calculated, essentially aiming to include only guaranteed earnings and allowances that would be received by a settled worker in the same line of work, and limiting the earnings to those gained in a 48-hour week. There are precise minimum acceptable salaries set out in a Table, being the higher of the Appendix J figure for the work in question, or the figure given in the Table.

Tier 2 (General) Migrants may apply for indefinite leave to remain once they have five years' continuous residence in various combinations of leave in different work routes, and their Sponsor must back their application by certifying that they are still needed in the role and will be for the foreseeable future, also providing their record of absence including any excess absences for serious and compelling reasons, and confirming that their salary meets Appendix J requirements and will continue to do so (and this may be audited subsequently). Their salary from guaranteed sources must reach certain levels, specified for now in Table 11C (and rising in the years to come), evidenced by recent payslips and matching bank statements/building society passbooks. They must meet the knowledge of life and language in the UK requirements and must not have committed any overstaying beyond that which the Home Office condones (i.e. the 14 days permitted under Rule 39E).

Tier 2 ICT

As already mentioned, there are now only two extant sub-categories under this route, for Graduate Trainees and Long Term Staff.

There is no cooling-off period for in-country applicants; entry clearance applicants must not have been present in Tier 2 for the last 12 months, with certain exceptions, or paid in excess of the upper target. Extensions of leave are only available from the same sub-category: so a Graduate Trainee can only extend leave if they remain working for the same employer, whilst Long Term Staff must have entered the UK as such, or as a sole representative.

Once one reaches the Appendix A requirements, they are similar to Tier 2 (General), featuring the usual restrictions on the validity of a CoS, and then constraints on points scoring. The occupation must be within the creative sector, or listed in Table 2 at RQF level 6 and above (or for RQF level 4 if leave was previously held under the Rules before 13 June 2012); an application may also succeed where a reduction in the RQF level is down to an internal reclassification of the RQF system.

Generally speaking the salary must exceed £73,900 unless the applicant has been working outside the UK for a linked business or in the same occupation for the 12 months before the application (a longer period is permitted if they have been on leave for child-related reasons or on long-term sick leave). Salary must be evidenced by a very particular set of documents: pay slips for the relevant period backed by bank statements or a building society passbook with matching entries for the salary. The basis for permitted absences that trigger the longer period in which the person has been the same occupation must be established by documents proving the underlying birth/adoption; sick leave needs to be evidenced via a letter from the sponsor employer or via pay records, otherwise by medical evidence attesting to the health problems in question.

Graduate Trainees must demonstrate that they were previously working for the Sponsor outside the UK for three months before the application, and that they are on a structured graduate training programme, with clearly defined progression towards a managerial or specialist role, and that their Sponsor has assigned no more than 20 CoSs within the sub-category in the last year. They may be asked to prove their working history via payslips and matching bank statements.

There are set levels of minimum salary for Long Term Staff and Graduate Trainees.

The settlement route for ICTs who have arrived in recent times is now shut. They may apply for indefinite leave to remain once they have accumulated five years' leave only if they held leave as ICTs prior to 6 April 2010, or were previously work permit holders on an ICT basis. The Sponsor must certify they are still needed for the job in question, and that pay is in line with the Codes of Practice; the records of pay must be evidenced via painstakingly detailed requirements. They must meet the knowledge of life and language in the UK requirements and not have overstayed beyond the tolerated period.

Minister of Religion
Ministers are subject to Part 6A requirements that are very similar to those for Tier 2 (General). They must provide a CoS satisfying the usual validity requirements, and must be employed mainly for preaching and pastoral duties (unless in a senior position), with pay and conditions in line with the equivalent for settled workers, living within a religious order or apart from society for religious reasons. They may be employed only after a RLMT has shown that a national hunt for settled workers via the appropriate media is fruitless.

They may settle in the UK if they meet the same requirements as for Tier 2 (General), and if their Sponsor confirms they are still needed for the role, and absences are fully explained.

Sportspersons
Sportspersons must meet specific Appendix A requirements showing that their Governing Body has endorsed them and that they will be UK-based and will comply with conditions of leave. They must supply the letter containing that endorsement, confirming that they are internationally established at the highest level, will make a significant contribution to the sport's development at the highest level in the UK, and showing that the post could not be filled by a suitable settled worker.

Practical operation of the Tier 2 Rules

The Rules are structured in a distinct way throughout the Points Based System. The Tier 2 routes are set out in Part 6A of the Rules. These usually concentrate on what we might call the "immigration" dimension of the application: who can switch into the route for leave to remain applications, cross-references to other relevant parts of the Rules that relate to misconduct (overstaying, or refusals for past misbehaviour, or curtailment for losing one's Sponsor or impermissibly changing job), and general restrictions on students and youngsters entering the route.

However, the detailed provisions by which the working, maintenance and English language requirements are to be satisfied are laid out in Appendices A–C. Appendices B–C simply set out the English language and Maintenance requirements – we address them in Chapter 1: *General Themes in PBS Cases* as their operation is generic across the PBS rather than bespoke to the individual routes.

Each of the above routes has its own provisions in the Rules and the Appendices. However, some Rules cater for more than route: thus the provisions for leave to remain are found in r245HD for Tier 2 (General), Ministers of Religion, and Sportspersons, whilst ICTs have their own provisions in r245GD.

Like some other aspects of the Points Based System, the reality is that usually one either satisfies a particular requirement, or one does not. If one satisfies it, then one gets full points for that aspect of the Rules. There are no silver or bronze medals for attaining lower levels of points: one is either granted leave, or one's application is refused. And if one satisfies each of the requirements of the Table under which one is applying, then one gets the necessary 50 points to qualify for the targeted form of entry clearance or leave to remain.

The real detail of the route lies within Appendix A. Applicants must obtain 50 points for whichever stage of the process they are applying under: (see, for example for Tier 2 (General), Table 11A). There is only a single table for each class of Tier 2 applicant, whether their application is to join the route at the entry clearance stage or to extend their leave. However, the indefinite leave to remain criteria for Tier 2 are found wholly in the Part 6A Rules, unlike (for example) for Entrepreneurs (for whom Box 6 addresses the settlement criteria).

The points are either awarded for simply satisfying the requirements for the CoS (Ministers and Sportspersons) or for meeting the requirements both for the CoS and for salary (Tier 2 (General) and ICTs). However, there are then a large number of subsidiary requirements that gloss the manner in which those requirements are met. These are found in very dense criteria in Appendix A, which could quite readily drive the reader to distraction.

There are formalities regarding the CoS: it has to be allocated within a few months of its own allocation and before the job starts; it must stay valid up to the date of decision without having been cancelled by the Sponsor or the Home Office; and the Immigration Skills Charge must have been paid in full.

All the routes are subject to a genuineness test that measures the credibility of the application. Its precise scope varies: sometimes it is only the question as to whether the vacancy is a genuine one for which no resident worker is available which is assessed, sometimes the intentions and qualifications of the applicant will also be scrutinised.

Recurring concepts

Consent of educational Sponsor

Part 6A of the Rules cross references to Rule 245A, which is the general provision in the Rules addressing this issue (245HB(h); those switching from Tier 4 must satisfy this requirement too, 245HD(ii) and (vi)). Rule 245A is cross-referenced from any route which permits students to enter it, and requires

- Unconditional written consent
- In the form of a letter on official headed notepaper bearing the official stamp of the organisation and issued by an authorised official
- Confirming that the organisation gives its unconditional consent to the applicant remaining in the UK for an unlimited time

Criminal record certificate (CRC)

The CRC is only required for adults applying under the Tier 2 (General) entry clearance route who are coming to work in the health, education and social care sectors (r245HB(q)). Relevant features are:

- A CRC must be obtained from the relevant authority in any country in which they have been present for 12 months or more, whether continuously or in total, in the last decade, whilst aged 18 plus (245HB(q))
- If no CRC is provided, then the decision maker may contact the applicant or their representative in writing, seeking a CRC, or explanation of one's absence (245HB(r)). The response must be received within 28 calendar days
- There is no proviso in the Tier 2 Rules for a person who cannot provide a CRC to seek exemption from the requirement (contrast the Entrepreneur route)
- The Guidance explains how to obtain such certificates (*Guidance for Applicants* paras 69ff) and the required information that must be provided in a translation of any such document, which will be necessary when the original is not in English. CRCs are only valid if dated within six months of the Tier 2 application date (*Guidance for Applicants* para 77). Failure to provide a valid CRC without good reason will lead to a general refusal reason

Student switching controls

There are controls on switching into Tier 2 (General) from Tier 4: essentially a student must have

- Completed and passed a UK-recognised bachelor's or master's degree (not an equivalent non-degree), or a UK Postgraduate Certificate in Education or Professional Graduate Diploma of Education (not a mere equivalent), or completed a minimum of 12 months study in the UK towards a UK PhD – and done so whilst present under Tier 4 with that Sponsor, not via supplementary study (r245HD(d)(i), (v)) – the Guidance sets out the requirements for a degree to be recognised (*Guidance for Applicants* paras 108ff)

- Studyied throughout at an institution that is UK recognised or listed, or which is a licensed Tier 4 Sponsor, with leave that was not subject to any restriction inconsistent with such study (r245HD(d)(ii), (iv))

- Such study must have been within their last grant of leave, or within a period of continuous leave (being leave which is unbroken having regard to the statutory extension of leave under section 3C NIAA 2002: see e.g. *Guidance for Applicants* para 17) which included the last grant, allowing for these purposes a period in Jersey, Guernsey or the Isle of Man with leave for an equivalent kind of study (r245HD(d)(iii))

The qualification must be proved via the dated award certificate, showing applicant's name, award title and length, or an academic reference or an academic transcript from the awarding institution (though for PhD studies they need only evidence a minimum of 12 months' study towards the qualification, not its completion).

Switching controls beyond those for Students
There are relatively complex Rules explaining who can join the route from within the UK. As usual, the controls appear early on in the substantive rule addressing leave to remain (i.e. they appear in the destination route rather than the route being exited): thus the limitation on who can switch into Tier 2 is found within Tier 2, in r245HD(b) in Part 6A.

To switch into the Tier 2 (General), Minister of Religion or Sportsperson routes, a person must have last had leave:

- As a Tier 1 Migrant, Tier 2 Migrant, Representative of an Overseas Business, or as the partner of a Tier 4 Migrant (r245HD(b)(i))

- As a Tier 4 Migrant, sponsored by a UK recognised body or a body in receipt of public funding as a higher education institution (HEI) from one of the UK home countries, or by an overseas HEI to undertake a short-term study abroad programme in the United Kingdom (r245HD(b)(ii))

- And, if a Tier 4 Migrant (r245HD(d)), they must have satisfied the Tier 4 switching controls

- If the applicant to switch into one of the non-ICT routes is presently a Tier 2 ICT (r245HD(c)) then they must

    - Have been granted leave under the Rules in place before 6 April 2010, or in the Established Staff sub-category under the Rules in place before 6 April 2011

    - Not have been granted entry clearance under Tier 2 or otherwise since that original grant

    - Not be applying to work for the same Sponsor as last time

The cap: that 2 (General) limit
Even satisfying all the requirements of Part 6A and the Appendices does not guarantee success, because there are only a limited number of visas available. The Home Office *Guidance on Allocations of restricted certificates of sponsorship* shows the number available each month: usually some are carried over as not every restricted CoS is taken up.

- The limit is specified in Appendix A: 20,700 presently

- A Sponsor must apply for a CoS to the Secretary of State

- To obtain a CoS, they must score points under Table D: at least 20 points for the nature of the job and at least 1 point for salary – the idea is that the more valuable the job, the more points are scored; and the higher the salary, the more points are awarded

- Table 11D sets out various jobs and salaries by which points are scored

Once the Sponsor has scored sufficient points, they are eligible for inclusion in the allocation of CoSs via the process set out in the Monthly allocations provisions of Appendix A (A82 onwards). These are of more significance to Sponsors than they are to applicants, and we deal with the subject in detail in Chapter 7: *Representing Tier 2 and Tier 5 Sponsors*, so we do not deal with them further here, save to say that the monthly allocation runs from 6 April to 5 April, with more (2,200) at the start of that year than at the end (1,000).

Relocation of high value business/significant new inward investment project
There are certain benefits accruing where the applicant will be working in support of a posting from an overseas firm to the Sponsor in connection with the relocation of a high value business to the UK or a significant new inward investment project: Tier 2 (General) Migrants who have such an employer are exempt from the RLMT (A78(c)) and are not subject to the cap.

Eligible investment projects exclude those where the project includes the supply of services to a third party client.

Applications under this proviso will succeed only where the CoSCS explains clearly why these criteria are satisfied (A78C(f)):

- The sponsor was registered in the UK with Companies House no earlier than three years before the date the Certificate of Sponsorship was assigned;

- The sponsor is the registered branch or wholly owned subsidiary of a business which has its headquarters and principal place of business outside the United Kingdom;

- The relocation or inward investment involves new capital expenditure of £27 million or the creation of at least 21 new UK jobs

Overstaying
The general scheme of the Rules is that "where paragraph 39E of these Rules applies, any current period of overstaying will be disregarded".

Rule 39E provides that

- Where an application is made following the refusal of another application (made in time, or within 14 days of leave expiring) and any subsequent section 3C leave, administrative review or appeal application has ended, the relevant period is within 14 days of leave expiring – to put it another way, where the second application follows on from a recent refusal which it aims to rectify, one is permitted 14 days overstaying as of right

- Where an application is made in other circumstances, the period is within 14 days of leave expiring but *only where the Secretary of State is satisfied* that there was a good reason beyond the applicant's control (or their representative's): such reason must be supplied with the application

Upper salary target
Earning a certain figure (which for convenience we call the upper salary target) brings certain benefits: this refers to the total stated in Part 6A from time to time, presently a gross annual salary (as recorded by the CoSCS including specified acceptable allowances) of £159,600 per year (for the last year's applicants, the figure is slightly lower, see for example A77D(ii)). That salary buys the applicant certain dispensations: for example, exemption from the cooling-off period, from the restriction on owning no more than 10% of the sponsoring company, and from recruiting only after a RLMT exercise.

For ICTs, the salary is £120,000: that level of remuneration buys one out of the cooling-off period, and permits a length of leave of up to nine years.

Standard occupational classification: the SOC Code system
Appendix A to the Rules contains criteria by which to measure the quality of job on offer. It does so via the codes of practice for skilled work found in Appendix J, which set out the skill level and appropriate salary level for Tier 2 Sponsors.

These are defined by reference to the Regulated Qualifications Framework, which is a national governmental scheme for identifying the difficulty level of an occupation or qualification. For example, an honours degree is at RQF Level 6, and a Masters at Level 7. Level 4 equates to qualifications such as a certificate of higher education, or higher apprenticeship.

In times past, when the skilled migration tranche of the Points Based System permitted less skilled migrants to come to the UK, the threshold for skills fell as low as RQF Level 3: the transitional arrangements for that category closed on 6 April 2017, save for the creative sector. Level 4 transitional arrangements ended on 6 April 2018. The objective was for any workers still in those categories to have extended their leave sufficiently to apply for settlement by the time the route closed. However, those applying to continue working for the same employer may continue to extend their leave in that category (see Table 11 which makes this one of the three routes for acquiring points under Tier 2 (General), and A78D), as may individuals who fall foul of a skills reclassification by the Office for National Statistics (ONS) (i.e. workers whose *role* remains the same but its *classification* by the ONS has altered).

The standard occupational classification (SOC) codes are devised by the ONS, and are aimed to cover all possible jobs. The Tables therein give both the occupation description and the SOC code assigned to it, examples of typical job tasks, related job titles, and salary rates, both for new entrants and experienced workers. J14 provides set weekly hours for various classes of occupation and explains that

> Rates will be pro-rated based on the number of working hours stated on the Certificate of Sponsorship.

Casework Tip

The salary for jobs in Appendix J are assessed on the basis of a set amount of working hours: generally 40 hours a week, but sometimes lesser amounts, e.g. for nurses or teachers (J14(f)). This is a pitfall for the unwary: because if the hours in the CoS for the salary given exceed the J14 threshold, then the Home Office decision maker will recalculate the salary downwards to reflect the difference in hours. There is a UT decision which shows the way this works in practice: Tukhas [2016] UKUT 183 (IAC).

However, as explained in J14(d), the **new entrant** rate applies only in specific scenarios, where:

- A Tier 2 (General) applicant under the Post-Study Work provisions
- A Tier 2 (General) applicant whose Sponsor carried out a university milkround
- An ICT applying under Graduate Trainee
- They are aged under 26 when the application is made

Examples

An employer may be interested in bidding for a CoS on the basis that they want to recruit a university maths lecturer, which they believe means they have a PhD-level job to fill. A81C provides that the job must therefore appear in Table 1 of Appendix J: and indeed we find at Code 2311, "Higher education teaching professionals". However, they will only be awarded points if the salary is at the appropriate level (A81F) so it is necessary to check the rates in Table 1, an enquiry which comes with £25,700 (new entrants) or £32,300 (experienced workers).

A Tier 2 (General) migrant wants to extend their leave. They have a job offer lined up as an engineering manager and want to make sure it will qualify in terms of the calibre of work. They are not working in the creative sector, and the job is for a new employer; it is not a shortage occupation, and they arrived in the UK in 2014. In these circumstances the only sub-category for an acceptable CoS that is open to them is A77E(a): the job must appear on "the list of occupations shown in Table 2 of the codes of practice in Appendix J". So we look in Appendix J at Table 2 which is headed *Occupations skilled to Regulated Qualifications Framework (RQF) level 6 and above* and we see that this job title is one listed as related to SOC Code 1121 *Production managers and directors in manufacturing*. Jackpot!

Legacy routes and sub-categories

We have already mentioned some dispensations to individuals who have entered in the past under particular criteria who may have their ability to remain in the route preserved. Thus Appendix A sometimes mentions dates, usually 6 April of a particular year, from when a route closed. Sometimes these dispensations give benefits to individuals who entered the pre-PBS routes.

- ICTs who were in the UK under that route under the Rules, or as Highly Skilled Migrants, before 6 April 2011 are one category: they may qualify for points under Table 11AA where their pay is at the Appendix J rate
- ICTs may apply for indefinite leave to remain where present under the Rules in place before 6 April 2010 or as Highly Skilled Migrants (r245GF(d)(i))
- Transitional arrangements for workers sponsored at RQF level 3 closed on 6 April 2017, and closed for workers sponsored at RQF level 4 in July 2018 (unless within one of the listed creative sector

occupation codes); from these dates, individuals will no longer be able to apply to extend their leave in jobs at these skill levels

- Tier 2 General applicants recruited before 6 April 2017 enjoy a slightly lower salary for entering as Long Term Staff ICTs (Table 11B)

Shortage occupations list (SOL)
The jobs in the SOL are identified as such by the Migration Advisory Committee and are periodically revised. They appear in Appendix K to the Rules. As just mentioned when introducing the SOC code system, the general principle in the Rules is to only countenance jobs that are at RQF level 6 and above, with savings for people extending their leave in the same occupation (e.g. *Guidance for Applicants* para 22).

In general the RLMT need not be conducted for jobs in the SOL.

Calculating appropriate salary
Only guaranteed gross basic pay and guaranteed allowances are to be included which would be paid to settled workers, such as a London weighting (A75(a) for ICTs, A79(a) for Tier 2 (General)).

Generally speaking additional requirements are excluded:

- Overtime and bonus/incentive pay, pension contributions, medical benefits, tuition fees, travel and subsistence including any travel allowance to and from home country, and any shares received in exchange for UK employee rights (A75(b), A79(b))

- Where they are paid hourly, only earnings up to 48 hours a week will count, even if the applicant works longer hours (A75D, A79C)

- No salary points are awarded unless a valid CoS is produced (A75E, A79D)

For ICTs, the appropriate salary may have some additional components, by way of a mobility premium and a proportion of accommodation allowances:

- A mobility premium to cover the additional cost of living in the UK (A75(a))

- Allowances solely for accommodation will be included only up to a value of 30% of the total salary package for Long Term Staff or 40% for Graduate Trainees (A75(c)) (there are some examples of the calculations given in the *Guidance for Applicants* at para 45)

- However one-off payments, e.g. for relocation, are excluded, as are any payments for which the applicant would have to reimburse their employer or a linked overseas business (A75(b))

Funds in a foreign currency will be converted to pounds sterling (£) using the spot exchange rate which appeared on www.oanda.com on the date on which the application was made (Guidance para 46).

Creative sector occupations
There are a series of references in the Rules to creative sector occupations. These are a specific set of roles (essentially artists, authors, actors, dancers, designers, and related jobs), involvement in which provides a less taxing route to entry; because rather than having to show a salary level at Table 2 (i.e. RQF level 6), they must only need to demonstrate skills at RQF level 4.

You can see the full list in any of the routes where the dispensation applies: the ICT route (A74B(a)(ii)) and Tier 2 (General) (A77E(a)(ii)).

No "third party hire"

It is the Sponsor who is responsible for ensuring that Tier 2 migrants act consistently with the requirements of immigration control in their route. Accordingly no points will be awarded under Appendix A if the CoSCS records that the role amounts to the worker's hire to a third party who is not the Sponsor to fill a temporary or permanent position or for contract work to undertake an ongoing routine role or to provide an ongoing routine service for a third party of any nature or length; this applies to ICTs (A74G) and Tier 2 (General) Migrants (A77G).

There is more detail provided in the Guidance (para 37, 96). The Sponsor must have full responsibility for deciding the *duties, functions and outcomes or outputs* of the job on the CoSCS. It is possible to carry out a limited period of work for a third party, but it must be *a time-bound service or project on your Sponsor's behalf.* The secondment must not amount to agency work or an *ongoing role*.

Example

Ruby is present in the UK as a Tier 2 ICT working in the IT business. Her Sponsor has received two requests from other businesses wishing to make the most of her potential:

(a) From a neighbouring IT business which has lost a key staff member with an identical skill set to Ruby, due to an accident at work which will take them two months to recover from. In return the neighbouring business will meet her wages and will additionally share some of its future research results with her Sponsor.

(b) From another neighbouring IT business which wants to use Ruby to cover for a number of its staff from time to time over the next year.

Option (a) would seem compatible with the Guidance at para 37, being a time-bound service which is on the Sponsor's behalf. However option (b) seems to amount to little more than agency work, where the neighbouring business will have control over her duties and functions.

The cooling-off period

In general, an applicant may not return under Tier 2 if they have recently been present in the Tier 2 category. They must not have held entry clearance or leave to remain as a Tier 2 migrant in the 12 months before the application, unless

- The period of engagement for said leave was three months or less (the Guidance para 24 explains that this is intended to give employers the flexibility of bringing in staff for short spells in the UK without risking the "cooling-off" proviso biting; thus one or more Tier 2 CoSs each of less than three months in a calendar year avoid its bite) or

- The applicant can prove they were not in the UK with leave over the period in question (the Guidance at para 135 posits non-exhaustive examples of the relevant evidence: travel tickets/stubs plus a UK employer's letter confirming their engagement had ended, passport stamps, a letter from an employer abroad confirming work starting there: the cooling-off period will be calculated from the earliest date proven by such evidence)

- Their gross annual salary exceeds the upper target

You can see the cooling-off Rule for the non-ICT categories both for entry clearance and leave to remain applicants (245HB(g), 245HD(k)), and for ICTs in the entry clearance route (245GB(d)) (ICTs are not subject to the restriction if applying for leave to remain).

There are exceptions for ICTs now applying to be Long Term Staff who were previously here as Short Term Staff or Graduate Trainees/Skills Transfer sub-categories: R245GB(e).

Genuineness

The Points Based System was originally seen as an opportunity to end the era of subjective evaluation by decision makers in return for objective precision. However, the Home Office's enthusiasm for this approach waned after a few years of experience. Tier 2, like other routes, now contains various provisions for measuring the genuineness of an application. At first sight, one might think these bite only on Ministers of Religion, as Part 6A of the Rules only singles them out for a genuineness assessment: however, once one reads on into Appendix A, we find that it is replete with tests as to an application's genuineness.

There is a distinct procedure for Ministers for Religion (r245HB(m) onwards). Taking the entry clearance route as an example (the leave to remain route is the same, r245HD(q) onwards):

- The ECO must be satisfied that they
  - genuinely intend to take up the role, and
  - are capable of so doing, and
  - will not take other work other than as permitted under the Rules
- The ECO may request further information which must be provided within 28 days of the request, or request attendance at an interview; failure to comply may lead to a refusal (r245HB(n))
- The genuineness assessment may be skipped if the application fails on some other ground; but if this happens, decision makers reserve the right to apply it next time round (r245HB(p))

A similar process is found in Appendix A for Tier 2 (General) applicants (A77H): here, however, the job itself as well as the applicant may be targeted, as the scope of enquiry covers whether

- The job is a genuine vacancy, and that the relevant advertising has not been tailored to exclude domestic workers
- The applicant is appropriately qualified/registered (by the time they begin the job: thus a person who does not yet quite fit the bill needs to provide evidence with their application that they have the requisite exams lined up before they start, A77I)
- The decision maker may again request further information, with a 10-day turnaround (A77J) (there is no provision for an interview in Appendix A, which appears to rule one out in the normal course of events for applicants outside the Minister of Religion route – nevertheless, fundamental principles of fairness may well require that an adverse case is put to a decision maker before a decision is made based on suspicion)

Example

Mithras applies for leave as a Marketing Director for one-branch outfit Harry's Hair Salon having been assigned a CoS with the appropriate salary.

A Marketing Director is a level 6 job under the RQF system set out in Appendix J; however, the Home Office would be entitled to question whether a small firm really needs a full–time person in this role. A very thorough business case would need to be established.

The general grounds of refusal, including curtailment

Any of the general grounds for refusal are in theory available for Tier 2 applicants. They are found in Part 9 of the Rules. HJT has an ebook addressing this subject in detail, *The General Refusal Reasons*; here so for now we just make a few general points.

There are a few Points Based System-specific refusal grounds found in Part 9, which focus on the kind of mishap that tends to undo sponsored workers. These permit the curtailment of leave:

➢ On a mandatory basis ("*is to be curtailed*"), for failing to commence the job, or ceasing the job before the end date in the CoS (already, or in the future) (r323A(a)) – note there are some potential let-offs where the individual is young, has childcare responsibilities, or has a pending application, etc., set out below

➢ On a discretionary basis ("*may be curtailed*")

- If the Sponsor ceases to hold a Sponsor licence for whatever reason, or if they transfer their business to another person who lacks one and fails to apply for one within 28 days of transfer, or applies for one and is refused, or receives a licence that does not cover the relevant class of migrant (r323A(b)(i)-(ii))

- If the employment recorded as permitted by the CoSCS undergoes one of the prohibited changes (r323A(b)(iii): see *Prohibited changes* below)

- For failing to commence the job or premature cessation (i.e. the r323A(a) misdemeanours) in one of these scenarios (r323A(b)(iv)): where the person in question

  - is aged under 18,
  - has a dependent child under 18,
  - has received a curtailment of leave because their Sponsor lost their licence under the Home Office policy to give a brief opportunity to find a new Sponsor,
  - has been granted leave in another category
  - has a pending application with the Home Office, or a pending appeal or administrative review application

Leave will be curtailed to 60 days from the date the curtailment decision is made, unless the migrant is considered complicit in the actions leading to the licence's withdrawal (*Guidance for Applicants* para 242) – the expectation is that the person will leave the country absent making a successful application to change Sponsor or obtaining leave in another route (para 244). A person will be notified in writing of the immigration decision that curtails their leave (para 249). In the case of Islam and Pathan [2017] UKUT 369 (IAC), the UT found there was no legal obligation on the Home Office to provide the opportunity to obtain another Sponsor by providing a 60-day "grace period". The decision does not, however, refer to the fact that present Home Office Guidance *does* provide for that very safeguard.

Mere *suspension* of a Sponsor's licence does not trigger these provisions: sponsored workers can continue working (para 306). However the Sponsor will be unable to issue more CoSs and any pending applications will be suspended – a decision may be made, however, if the application falls for refusal for other reasons, such as a non-genuine vacancy (para 307).

Possible "general refusal" mishaps that may befall Tier 2 applicants are:

- An allegation that English language skills are based on dubious test results (Rule 320(7A))

- An entry clearance application might be refused because of suspicions of dishonesty in the present application or due to past immigration misdemeanours during a previous sojourn in the UK – these include the mandatory bans under Rule 320(7A) and the provisions for previously contriving in a significant way to frustrate the purposes of the Rules (320(11))

The prohibited changes in employment
Rule 323AA **prohibits certain job changes**, unless leave is granted that expressly permits the change:

- Absence from work without pay for four weeks plus (whether over one or more periods), according to the person's normal working pattern during any calendar year (1 January to 31 December), unless the absence from work is due solely to maternity/paternity/adoption/shared parental leave, or a one-off period of long term sick leave of one calendar month or more during any one period (r323AA(a))

- The employment changes such that the migrant is working for a different employer or Sponsor (r323AA(b)), unless this is due to arrangements covered by the TUPE Regulations or similar protection, or

- The employment changes to a job in a different SOC code to that recorded by the CoSCS (unless the individual is sponsored to undertake a graduate training programme covering multiple roles within the organisation and the change is within that programme or due to appointment to a permanent role at the programme's end, and the Sponsor has notified the Home Office of the change including salary) (r323AA(c))

    - For ICTs and Tier 2 (General), the employment changes to a different job in the same SOC recorded by the CoSCS, and the gross annual salary (including permissible allowances: see Appendix A) is below the appropriate salary rate for that new job as specified in Appendix J (r323AA(d))

    - If previously sponsored at a minimum NQF level in the last application leading to entry clearance/leave, and the employment changes to a lower level job under Appendix J (r323AA(e))

    - For Tier 2 (General) applicants previously scoring points for working in a shortage occupation and the employment changes to a job which does not appear in Appendix K (r323AA(f))

    - Except for certain exceptions, where the gross annual salary (including permissible allowances: see Appendix A) reduces below (r323AA(g)):

- any minimum salary threshold specified in Appendix A relied on for the last grant of entry clearance/leave
- the appropriate salary rate for the job as specified in the Codes of Practice in Appendix J, or
- in cases where there is no applicable threshold in Appendix A and no applicable salary rate in Appendix J, the salary recorded by the Certificate of Sponsorship Checking Service

- The exceptions to the gross annual salary falls just mentioned are where due solely to maternity/paternity/adoption/shared parental leave, or a one-off period of long term sick leave of one calendar month or more during any one period, or studying for professional examinations during the sponsorship period which are essential for regulatory reasons, or where ICTs work abroad

Parental consent for youngsters
An application must be supported by both parents, or parent with sole legal responsibility, or legal guardian, and they must also confirm that they consent to the proposed care arrangements for the child during their time in the UK (245HB(i)-(k)/245HD(l)-(n)).

The full details for such a letter appear in the *Guidance for Applicants* (paras 10-15), which adds that if the child is to live with someone who is not their parent or a close relative as defined in the Guidance, the accommodation will count as a private fostering arrangement such that the local authority must be notified and must give their approval to the care being adequate.

Criteria for the Tier 2 route under Part 6A: the non-ICT Routes (Tier 2 (General), Ministers of Religion, and Sportspersons)

There are broadly similar requirements for entry clearance and leave to remain. You can find them in 245HB for entry clearance applicants, 245HD for those seeking leave to remain. These are

- Acquiring the relevant **points under the Appendices A-C** (the precise paragraphs addressing Tier 2 are identified: for Tier 2 (General) 76-84A; for Ministers of Religion 85-92A; for sportspersons 93-100 of Appendix A, 1-18 of Appendix B, 4-5 of Appendix C) (245HB(b)-(f)/245HD(e)-(j))

- The **cooling-off period** must have been completed (245HB(g), 245HD(k))

- A genuineness test, which checks both intention and capability for the role recorded in the CoSCS, and checks that there is no intention to work outside of the Tier 2 scheme (245HB(m), 245HD(q)-(u))

- Students who are, or were, **sponsored by a government or international scholarship agency, must obtain that body's consent** to an immigration route that implies long term stay in the UK such as Tier 2 (245HB(h), 245HD(ii) and (vi))

- The applicant must be **at least 16 years old**: however where they are under 18, there must be **appropriate support and consent** from parents/guardians (245HB(i)-(k)/245HD(l)-(n))

- If the Sponsor is a limited company, **the applicant must not own more than 10% of its shares directly or indirectly**, unless the gross annual salary (as recorded by the CoSCS including specified acceptable allowances) is £159,600 or higher (245HB(l), 245HD(o))

- Providing a **criminal record certificate** where aged over 18 and the occupation is in the list stated in the Rule (245HB(q)): an entry clearance only requirement

- Not falling foul of the general refusal reasons or being an illegal entrant (245HB(a), 245HD(a))

Tier 2 (General) – the Appendix A requirements

The core requirements under Table 11A which deals with points-scoring for Tier 2 General applicants are the acquisition of 50 points, thus:

- 30 points for one of three possibilities related to the CoS (Table 11A, A77):

    - the job offer passes the Resident Labour Market Test
    - the RLMT exemption applies
    - the applicant still works in the same occupation for the same Sponsor

- 20 points for salary level

The CoS

A valid CoS number must be supplied (A77A).

The only Certificates of Sponsorship to be allocated to Sponsors for applicants to be sponsored as Tier 2 (General) Migrants are those:

- **Allocated under the Tier 2 (General) limit** (A77B(a)) (which must accordingly match a CoSCS entry under the Tier 2 (General) limit (A77B(a), A77D(a))

- However **not all entrants are subject to the limit** (which applies principally to entry clearance cases), given the following exceptions (A77B(b)):

    - **Applicants applying for leave to remain generally** (unless they have previously been granted leave as the partner of a Relevant PBS Migrant) (A77B(b), A77D(b)(i)) or

    - Entry clearance applicants whose gross annual salary as shown by the CoSCS **exceeds the upper target** (A77B(b), A77D(b)(ii))

    - Medical practitioners and nurses A77D(b)(iv))

- The gross annual salary as shown by the CoSCS exceeds the upper target (A77B(c))

- The CoS links to a posting from an overseas firm as above (A77B(d))

The CoS must satisfy certain requirements in order to be valid (A77C). It must:

- Match a CoSCS entry naming the applicant and confirms the Sponsor is sponsoring them under Tier 2 (General) (A77C(a))

- Be assigned to the applicant no more than three months after it was allocated to the Sponsor under the Tier 2 (General) limit (A77C(b))

- Be assigned to the applicant no more than three months before the application for entry clearance/leave (A77C(c)) and no more than three months before the job start date given by the CoS (A77C(d))

- Not have been previously used in an application that was approved or refused (i.e. not rejected as invalid, declared void or withdrawn) (A77C(e))

- Not have been withdrawn or cancelled by the Sponsor or Home Office since assignment (including where the Home Office cancelled it due to it being used in a previous application) (A77C(f))

- Relate to an A-rated Sponsor unless the application is for leave to remain and the applicant has Tier 2 (General) leave and the current application is for the same employer named in the CoS leading to the last grant of leave (A77C(g))

- Relate to a Sponsor who has paid any applicable Immigration Skills Charge in full (A77C(h))

Example

Olowulu entered the UK as a student and subsequently varied her leave to that of Post-Study Worker. Her next application for an extension of leave on human rights grounds was turned down and she lodged an appeal within the deadline; her leave was accordingly extended under section 3C of the Immigration Act 1971 during the currency of the appeal. She was consistently working as an administrator in the health sector over this period.

She decided to try to switch from her Post-Study Work leave into Tier 2 (General) as her employer is willing to sponsor her and obtained a suitable CoS for her. She makes the application to switch into Tier 2 a few months before the human rights appeal hearing.

She decides to save money and not pursue the appeal, and withdraws it a few weeks before the hearing. The Home Office notify her Sponsor which realises that she may no longer work and notifies the Home Office, who cancel her CoS.
When her application is decided by the Home Office, they refuse it.

The Home Office decision is correct: the CoS is invalid under A77C(f) as whilst it was valid at the date of application, it has been cancelled and so fails under this provision: "that reference number must not have been withdrawn or cancelled by the Sponsor or by the Home Office since it was assigned". You can see this problem in practice in this unreported decision of the UT.

Points will only be awarded for the CoS where:

- It appears in Table 2 of Appendix J or is a creative sector occupation (A77E(a)(i)); or

- The CoSCS records the job as a shortage occupation (A77E(b)); or

- It is for a person previously holding Tier 2 (General) leave and not having been granted leave in another route since, whose previous CoS was issued at a time the job was in list of shortage occupations and whose present CoS is for the same role for the same or a different employer (A77E(c))

- The applicant was last granted leave in Tier 2 (General), and they are now applying for leave to remain in the same occupation for the same Sponsor but the occupation has been reclassified by the Office for National Statistics so that it no longer meets the skill level required (A77E(f))

Points will not be awarded for a CoS where

- The role amounts to third party hire (A77G)

- There are genuineness suspicions (A77H)

- The work is as a nurse/midwife SOC code (A77K), unless

  - The applicant provides evidence that they have obtained full registration with the Nursing and Midwifery Council, or passed the NMC's Computer Based Test of competence (CBT), or obtained a NMC permission before 30 April 2015 to undertake the Overseas Nursing Programme and be sponsored to undertake supervised practice as part of the programme in a placement approved by the NMC, or are undertaking an approved programme with a view to returning to practice

  - For evidence relating to passing the CBT or a pre-April 2015 permission under the ONP in an approved placement, the NMC must confirm it will continue to sponsor them as a nurse or midwife and will pay the applicant at least the appropriate rate for a Band 5 and equivalent nurse or midwife, as stated in Appendix J

  - For evidence relating to passing the CBT, the Sponsor confirms that the applicant will sit an Observed Structured Clinical Examination (OSCE) to obtain NMC registration no later than three months after the stated employment start date and will cease to be NMC sponsored if full registration is not achieved within eight months of the stated employment start date (or, if the applicant is applying for leave to remain and was last granted leave as a Tier 2 Migrant to work as a nurse or midwife, within eight months of the start date of that previous employment)

  - Where a person in the Nurses and Midwives sub-category fails to pass the test within the specified period, their leave will be curtailed in line with the process for so doing set out in the *Guidance for Applicants* (paras 63ff)

  - Additionally, the Tier 2 and 5 Sponsor guidance points out that it is necessary to give the start date as the earlier of (1) the beginning of familiarisation training, (2) starting work as a full NMC registered nurse/midwife having passed the OSCE exam, or (3) the date they are sitting that exam

A CoS must be assigned within six months of the job vacancy first being advertised, subject to certain exceptions (see generally Chapter 29 of the *Tiers 2 and 5: Guidance for Sponsors*):

- For university milkround recruitment (within 48 months of the milkround so long as the job was offered to the migrant within 12 months of the recruitment campaign)

- PhD level SOC Codes (within 12 months of the recruitment campaign)

- Trainee barristers Codes (within 12 months of the pupillage position first being advertised) and

- Orchestral musicians (within 12 months of the date the job was first advertised)

The Resident Labour Market Test
In order to score points for RLMT,

- Jobs must be advertised in line with Appendix A and Tables 11B and 11C in order to score points (A78(a)): Table 11B sets out the necessary methods and duration of advertising for various jobs, Table 11C specifies the required medium

- The advertisements must be published in English (or Welsh for a job in Wales) (A78(c)) and state (A78(b)):

    - The job title, location, main duties and responsibilities

    - Salary range/package/terms on offer

    - Skills, qualifications and experience required

    - Closing date for applications; unless a rolling recruitment in which case the period of the programme should be stated

- The RLMT must be satisfied unless the job is in a PhD-level occupation shown in Table 1 of the codes of practice in Appendix J. Settled workers will not be considered unsuitable on the basis that they lack qualifications, experience or skills (including language skills) that were not specifically requested in the job advertisement (A78(d))

- The CoSCS must show full details of when and where the job was advertised, any advertisement reference numbers, and the appropriate Find a Job/Jobcentre reference number (A78(e))

- Table 11B sets out

    - A series of occupations (new graduate jobs/internships, trainee barrister pupillages, Ph-D level occupations, jobs where the appropriate salary is £73,900, creative sector jobs, orchestral musicians and everything else) and

    - The method of recruitment for each

        - usually two of the media identified in Table 11C

        - for new graduate jobs, university milkround visits at least three universities or all the universities that offer the course if fewer than three, plus at least one prominent graduate recruitment website that is free to view and apply under, plus one of the media identified in Table 11C

  - for the creative sector jobs, those set out in Table 8 to Appendix J

  - Find a Job for orchestral musicians and everything else

- The duration of recruitment: the advert must have been out for a set number of days within a time frame: e.g. for PhD level jobs, for 28 days within the year immediately before the CoS was assigned

➢ Table 11C sets out the advertising media that satisfy the RLMT:

- Newspapers marketed through the UK or devolved nation in which job is located (e.g. Wales) published at least weekly

- Professional journals published at least monthly, available nationally via retail or subscription, and related to the job's nature, e.g. a trade journal

- Websites: though they must be either Find a Job, JobCentre Online, an online version of a newspaper/professional journal meeting the criteria above, the firm's own website if it is a multinational or has more than 250 permanent UK employees, or a prominent professional recruitment website that is free to view and apply under

Example

AlphaBeta, a large computer company with 220 employees, wishes to recruit two new operatives at NQF level 6 in the Tier 2 (General) category, each earning £80k. The firm is in a hurry to get people into posts and so simply advertised on its own website, via adverts which show job title, job description, salary package, and the required skills, qualifications and experience. The Board has now come to you for advice as to whether this exercise was adequate to satisfy the RLMT.

The RLMT seems inadequate: there is missing information from the adverts (which did not specify place of work or the closing date for applications), and for jobs at this level (Row 4 of Table 11B) there must be *two* kinds of advert as shown in Table 11C: so just advertising on the firm's website does not suffice. Furthermore, a firm may only rely on advertising on its own website if it is a multinational (we would need to seek instructions on this) or if it has more than 250 employees in the UK.

Jobs exempt from the Resident Labour Market Test
A job will be exempt from the RLMT so long as the CoSCS provides full details of why an exemption applies, in one of the following nine scenarios:

➢ It is a shortage occupation (A78(a)), where

- At the time the CoS was assigned the job appeared on the SOL in Appendix K

- Working hours are no more than 30 hours weekly

- If the Home Office list of shortage occupations designates it as "Scotland only", in which case of course the job must relate to employment in Scotland

➢ It is for post-study work (A78(b)), where

- The applicant is applying for leave to remain and last had leave as a Tier 1 Graduate Entrepreneur, Tier 1 Post-Study Worker, or Tier 4 Migrant

- The requirements set out above for the Tier 4 switching controls are satisfied

➢ The CoSCS shows that gross annual salary exceeds the upper target (A78C(a)); or

➢ The job offer is in a supernumerary research position where the applicant has been issued a non-transferable scientific research Award or Fellowship, either

- by an external organisation which is not the Sponsor, or

- by the Sponsor through a competitive process based on the applicant's own research proposal and where the funding is secured via objectively justified requirements that effectively prohibit a settled worker from taking the role – this exemption from the RLMT may continue after the third party funding ends for so long as the research is sponsored (A78C(b)); or

➢ The job offer is to continue working as a doctor or dentist in training, under the same NHS Training Number which was assigned to the applicant for previous lawful employment as a doctor or dentist in training in the UK (A78C(c)); or

➢ The job offer is as a Doctor in Speciality Training where the applicant's salary and the costs of his training are being met by the government of another country under an agreement with that country and the United Kingdom Government (A78C(d)); or

➢ The job offer is to resume a post in a Higher Education Institution, working for the same Sponsor as in a previous grant of entry clearance or leave to remain as a Tier 2 (General) Migrant, where the break in employment is due solely to a period of academic leave (A78C(e)); or

➢ The job offer is to continue working as a member of an existing research team, so long as the Sponsor is a Higher Education Institution or a Research Council, and the applicant has previously worked with the lead researcher as part of their team for a continuous 12 month period immediately before the application (or for 12 months during the 24 months immediately before the application if the applicant has been on child-related or long-term sick leave during that time) (A78C(f)); or

➢ The job offer is for the applicant to work in support of a posting from an overseas firm to the Sponsor in connection with the relocation of a high value business to the UK or a significant new inward investment project (see above) (A78C(g))

Example

Arabella entered the UK as a student and subsequently varied her leave to that of Post-Study Worker. She then switched successfully into Tier 2 (General) to work as a marketing officer for a university. There was no need to satisfy the RLMT as she was exempt, having previously been a Post-Study Worker (A78B(b)). The university loses its Sponsor licence and she finds an alternative employer who will sponsor her and issues her with a CoS; she applies for further leave, on the basis that she remains exempt from the RLMT.

Her application should be refused. The phrase in A78(b) is that "the applicant must have, or have last been granted ..." one of the types of leave that exempts one from the RLMT under the post study work proviso, and Tier 2 (General) is not one of them

Continuing to work for the same Sponsor in the same occupation

The third of the ways in which the Table 11 criteria may be met is where the applicant is applying to work in the same occupation for the same Sponsor. The requirements are (A78D):

- They are applying for leave to remain having last been granted entry clearance/leave under Tier 2 (General)
- The Sponsor is the same employer as on the last application that was granted
- The CoSCS must record the applicant as being engaged in the same occupation as last time, unless there has been a reclassification solely due to the ONS moving things round
- There must not be a change of jobs within an occupation from a SOL job to a non-SOL job

Example

Bernard is present in the UK as a Tier 2 General Migrant working for an IT company. He was granted entry clearance on the basis of working for Manhattan Bank as a financial director, a job at RQF level 6. He wishes to extend his leave in the same occupation for the bank.

Bernard can rely on points for continuing to work for the same employer, rather than having to pass the RLMT or demonstrate an exemption to the route: see Table 11A and A77D.

Appropriate salary

Table 11 requires points to be scored both via the nature of the work and by reference to the salary. Points are scored only if a valid CoS is provided (A79D). In order to accumulate the necessary 20 points for salary, the calculation must only include

- Guaranteed gross basic pay, and guaranteed allowances which would be paid to a settled worker in the same circumstances, e.g. a London weighting (A79(a))

- Where they are paid hourly, only earnings up to 48 hours a week will count, even if the applicant works longer hours (A79C)

The calculation must exclude (A79(b))

- Any other allowances than guaranteed ones

- One-off payments, e.g for relocation

- Overtime and bonus/incentive pay, pension contributions, medical benefits, tuition fees, travel and subsistence including any travel allowance to and from home country, and any shares received in exchange for UK employee rights

- Any payments for which the Applicant would have to reimburse their employer or a linked overseas business

Table CA then specifies minimum salary levels, according to the nature of the job. For each category, the level is the higher of the figure specified below or the rate provided in Appendix J (earnings will be assessed on a pro-rated basis, derived from their annual earnings for periods of work less than 12 months: *Guidance for Applicants* para 38, 84):

- £20,800 for **new entrants** who are not applying for leave that would take their total stay under Tier 2 or as a work permit holder beyond 3 years and 1 month: "new entrants" are those who

    - Satisfy the post-study work provisions for entering the route (ie having previously been a Graduate Entrepreneur, Post Study Worker, or Tier 4 student) above, or

    - Their vacancy was advertised for RLMT purposes under the "new graduate jobs and internships" box in Table 11B, or

    - Are under 26 at the application date

- £20,800 for certain public service occupations in health and science/language teaching

- £20,800 for those who last had leave under Tier 2 (General) based on a CoS issued before 24 November 2016 without having been granted leave in any other category since

- £30,000 if none of these exceptions apply. There are no transitional arrangements for individuals who have to meet this threshold who were previously granted leave after the announcement of its introduction on 24 November 2016; they will simply have to meet the higher threshold for any application made after 6 April 2017

Examples

Katy, a nurse, applies for entry clearance under Tier 2 (General) as a nurse, the SOC code provided being 2231. This requires Band 5 salary (see Appendix J), presently £21,909. Her CoS states she will be working for a 39-hour week, earning £21,909.

The application is refused because the hours for a nurse are calculated for a 37.5-hour week: the decision maker says that the extra hours to which she is contracted means there will be a shortfall in earnings once the excess hours are ruled out.

The refusal is correct: the earnings in Appendix J are tied to particular hours, see J14(f). This was precisely the misfortune that befell the Appellant in KG (India) [2016] EWCA Civ 477, who lost her case in the Court of Appeal.

Pablo, present with Tier 1 leave as a Graduate Entrepreneur, is applying to switch into the Tier 2 (General) category, to work as an arts officer. He is aged 27. He is worried that his £27,000 starting salary is insufficient to make the grade for an experienced worker, as he considers himself to be experienced having been involved in theatre design in his Entrepreneur activities.

Although he is aged over 26, he still qualifies for salary assessment under the "new entrant" provision: under Table CA, there are four rows setting out the classes of possible points-scoring for salary, and one addresses new entrant. Being a Graduate Entrepreneur puts him into that category: the second row addresses new entrants thus. Accordingly he must establish earnings which are the higher of £20,800 (the Table CA figure) or the Appendix J figure for new entrants in SOC code 3416 for arts officers, £25,000: as his salary exceeds the latter figure, he is home and dry.

Tier 2 Intra-Company Transfer

R245 explains that this route enables multinational employers to transfer existing employees from outside the EEA to their UK branch for training purposes or to fill a specific vacancy that cannot be filled by a British or EEA worker. There are two sub-categories:

(i) **Long Term staff**: for established employees of multinational companies who are being transferred to a skilled job in the UK which could not be carried out by a new recruit from the resident workforce (the business helpdesk has previously indicated that consultants who could evidence a real relationship with the company might also qualify)

(ii) **Graduate Trainee**: for recent graduate recruits of multinational companies who are being transferred to the UK branch of the same organisation as part of a structured graduate training programme, which clearly defines progression towards a managerial or specialist role.

The requirements are split between Part 6A of the main Rules and the Appendices, particularly Appendix A, as per the usual scheme of the Rules.

There are broadly similar requirements for entry clearance and leave to remain. You can find them in 245GB for entry clearance applicants, 245GD for those seeking leave to remain. These are

- Not failing under the general grounds for refusal (245GB(a), 245GD(a))

- Acquiring the relevant **points under the Appendices A and C** (there is no Appendix B requirement for ICTs – the precise paragraphs addressing Tier 2 ICT are identified: 73-75E of Appendix A, 4-5 of Appendix C) (245GB(b)-(c)/245GD(f), (h))

- For entry clearance applicants, the **cooling-off period** must have been completed (245GB(d-e))

- Students who are, or were, **sponsored by a government or international scholarship agency, must obtain that body's consent** to an immigration route that implies long term stay in the UK such as Tier 2. The rule cross references to r245A, which is the general provision addressing the consent requirements (245GB(f))

- The **parental consent** provisions must be satisfied; as for Tier 2 General (245GB(g-i), 245GD(i-k))

There are some additional requirements for applicants switching into the ICT route:

  - For those applying for leave to remain under the Long Term Staff sub-category, they must have been granted entry clearance/leave in that route or as a representative of an overseas business, and still be working for the same employer (r245GD(b))

  - If applying under the Graduate Trainee sub-category, they must have been granted entry clearance/leave in that route, and still be working for the same employer (r245GD(d))

It will be seen that these two provisos mean that there are only very limited possibilities for switching into this route.

Appendix A requirements for ICTs
These follow the usual pattern. Table 11 provides that points may be scored for the CoS (30) and appropriate salary (20).

The CoS must satisfy certain requirements in order to be valid (A74-A74A). These are essentially equivalent to those set out above for the validity of a Tier 2 (General) CoS, in basic summary:

- Linkage to a CoSCS entry naming the applicant as an ICT and his ICT sub-category, the Sponsor being A-rated unless the application is for leave to remain to work for the same employer

- The CoS having been assigned no more than three months before the application was made or before the job's start date

- The CoS not previously having been used in an application that was granted or refused, and remaining uncancelled by Home Office or Sponsor, and

- Any Immigration Skills charge having been paid in full.

There are then similar constraints on points scoring for the CoS as for Tier 2 (General), regarding

- The need for the occupation to be listed in Table 2 of Appendix J, or creative sector (A74B(a)) or

- The last grant of leave being in ICT where the applicant is now applying for leave to remain in the same occupation for the same Sponsor but the occupation has been reclassified by the Office for National Statistics so that it no longer meets the skill level required (A74B(d))

Additional points scoring limitations on an ICT CoS are:

- If the salary is under £73,900, no points will be awarded for a CoS (A74C(a)) unless the applicant has been working

    - In the same occupation for the last 12 months, defined as

        - a continuous period of 12 months before the application date, or

        - an aggregated period of 12 months within the previous 24 months where the Applicant is on maternity/paternity/adoption or shared parental leave or long-term sick leave exceeding a month (A74C(a)(i), (A74C(c))

        - The Guidance for Applicants explains that the 12 months period of work for Long Term Staff need not necessarily be immediately before the application (para 28)

    - Outside the UK for a business established outside UK territory linked by common ownership or control to the Sponsor (A74C(b))

    - These criteria must be proved by specified documents:

        - Pay slips and bank/building society stamps meeting the usual requirements and showing matching transactions from the Sponsor for the period in question (A74C-SD(a)-(b))

        - The most recent pay slip must be within 31 days of the application date: so if the 12 month period ends more than 31 days before the date of application, it will be necessary to provide further evidence within the 31-day period (Guidance for Applicants para 46ff)

        - Where there has been leave for the specific purposes identified, full birth/adoption certificates, confirming the name of the parents for whom the leave was taken, and then one of the following, unless that certificate is unavailable in which case both are required: a letter from the Applicant and the Sponsor confirming the start and end dates of leave, and pay slips or bank statements showing the payments over the entire period of leave (A74C-SD(c))

        - For long-term sick leave, a letter from the Sponsor, on headed paper, confirming the start and end dates of leave, if available, or payslips/bank or building society statements/passbook showing the statutory sick pay or health insurance sick pay, or a full explanation of why these documents are not available, backed by medical documents, from an official source which are independently verifiable (A74C-SD(d))

        - Those specified documents must be provided *if requested*: an application may be refused if they are not received within 10 business days of request

Examples

Andrew wishes to come to the UK as an ICT. He joined the US-based firm which would be his Sponsor here (at its national UK office) 2½ years ago. He has been on paternity leave for a

period from six months ago to 15 months ago. He is worried that this has broken his necessary period of continuous work.

Andrew is in the clear: under A74C(c) he may rely on an aggregate period of 12 months from the periods of work before and after his paternity leave.

Jackie wishes to obtain entry clearance under the ICT category. She worked in Canada for a multinational for six months before joining them in the UK for two years, whilst she was present as the spouse of her Canadian husband, who is now working abroad once again. Then she returned to Canada with him and resumed work there for another six months.
Jackie may aggregate her two periods of time abroad: see for example *Guidance for Applicants* para 27ff.

- A Graduate Trainee must show that (A74D):

  - The CoSCS entry records they are sponsored for a structured graduate training programme, with clearly defined progression towards a managerial or specialist role within the organisation

  - The Sponsor has assigned 20 or fewer CoSs (including the Applicant) in this category for the year from 6 April to 5 April

  - The CoSCS confirms they have been working for the Sponsor outside the UK for a continuous period of three months immediately prior to the date of application: there are specified documents which must be produced on request to show this, again as a matter of discretion, with a right to refuse if they are not received within 10 business days – those documents are the bank statements/building society passbook/payslips or copies with an employer's letter

- No points will be awarded under ICT for a CoS that shows the job is for a Minister of Religion or Sportsperson (A74F)

- No third party hire (A74G)

- Points are awarded only where there are no reasonable grounds to suspect the job is not a genuine vacancy, if in the Long Term Staff category, or to suspect the applicant is not appropriately qualified for the job (A74H) – additional information may be requested to support this assessment which must be supplied within 10 working days (A74I)

ICT and appropriate salary
The calculation for assessing the eligible salary is set out above in the "recurring concept" section.

No points will be awarded if the salary is less than the figure in Table 11AA, which sets out three scenarios and the appropriate minimum salary:

- For Long Term Staff: £41,500 or the figure given for the role in question under Appendix J, if higher

- Long Term Staff who previously had leave under the rules in place before 6 April 2011 and have not since been granted entry clearance in any route: the Appendix J figure

- Graduate Trainees: £23,000

Leave to remain granted to ICTs
Leave to remain will be granted for the shortest of these periods (r245GE(a)):

- length of engagement plus 14 days, OR
- Five years, OR
- the difference between the continuous leave they have spent as an ICT (on the one hand) and a maximum time period (on the other) (leave will be refused if the calculation gives an answer of zero or a negative) (r245GE(a)(iii)): that maximum period is (r245GE(b))
    - 12 months for Graduate Trainees
    - Five years for Long Term Staff where the CoSCS records that they earn below £120,000, unless they fall within the class where there is no limit on the period of leave below
    - Nine years for Long Term Staff where the CoSCS records that they earn more than £120,000
    - Without limit, if applying as Long Term Staff and previously had ICT leave under the Rules in place before 6 April 2011 or as a work permit holder
- In addition to the period established by this assessment, additional days will be granted to equal the period between the job starting and the date of decision on the application (r245GE(c))

Settlement for ICTs
The criteria under the Part 6A rules provide that an Applicant must:

- Not fall foul of the general refusal reasons, and must not be an illegal entrant (245GF(b))
- Have accumulated five years continuous lawful residence in any combination of these categories:
    - Tier 2 ICT, but only if the period of five years residence includes ICT pre-6 April 2010 or as a work permit holder pursuant to ICT arrangements (245GF(d))
    - as a representative of an overseas business or as a work permit holder (245GF(c))
- The requirements of Appendix KoLL must be met (245GF(g))
- Must not be in breach of immigration laws save for the usual proviso that overstaying within the ambit of Rule 39E will be disregarded (245HF(h))
- The Sponsor backing the last grant of leave must still hold an ICT Sponsor licence or have a renewal application pending, and certify in writing that the applicant remains required for the role in question (though there is no statement required that this will remain the case for the foreseeable future), confirming that pay is in line with the Appendix J Codes of Practice, and if they are on maternity/paternity/adoption or shared parental leave confirming the start date and that they were paid that salary immediately before the break began (245GF(e) read with 245GF-SD)
- Pay must be evidenced by the specified documents as set out in para 245GF-SD – these reflect the requirements in para 245HH for Tier 2 (General) settlement set out below, though additionally where maternity, paternity, shared parental or adoption leave underlies the difference, documents are

required confirming the underlying event, i.e. birth/adoption certificate or explanation for its absence from an independent officially verifiable source 245GF-SD C(c)

Period and conditions of grant across Tier 2

When is entry clearance granted from?

Entry clearance will be granted with effect from **the latest** of these three possibilities (Tier 2 (General): r245HC(a); Tier 2 ICTs r245GC(a)):

- 14 days before the *start date of the applicant's employment* in the UK, as recorded by the CoSCS
- Seven days before the *intended date of travel* recorded by the applicant either through the relevant online application process or in the specified application form, providing this is not more than 14 days after the start date of the applicant's employment in the UK, as recorded by the CoSCS, or
- The *date entry clearance is granted.*

Length of visa

Entry clearance will be granted for a **period ending at the earliest** of these two possibilities (Tier 2 (General) (r245HC(b)-(c)); Tier 2 ICTs (r245GC(b))):

- 14 days after the end date of the applicant's employment in the UK, as recorded by the CoSCS, or
- at the end of the maximum time available for the applicable Tier 2 sub-route:
    - 5 years and 1 month for Tier 2 (General)
    - 3 years and 1 month for Ministers of Religion or Sportspersons
    - For ICTs: 12 months in the Graduate sub-category, 5 years and 1 month for Long Term Staff (r245GC(b))

Conditions of leave

The conditions are (245HC for Tier 2 (General), 245GC for ICTs):

- no recourse to public funds
- registration with the police, if this is required by Rule 326 (essentially where a person is a national of one of the countries listed in Appendix 2 of the Rules and is given leave for more than six months)
- no employment except (245HC(d)(iii), 245GC(d)(iii) for ICTs)
    - The sponsored work and any permitted change to it: Rule 323AA **prohibits certain changes**, unless leave is granted that expressly permits the change; we have addressed prohibited changes in our recurring concepts section above above (r323AA(a)-(g))
    - Supplementary employment (defined in the Guidance for Applicants para 226 as within a shortage occupation list job found in Appendix K or at the same level as the job as described in the CoS, for no more than 20 working hours a week outside the normal working hours for the role for which the CoS was issued)

- Voluntary work (receiving no pay beyond expenses authorised in s44 of the National Minimum Wage Act 1998)

- A person may study subject to the conditions in Part 15 of the Rules, which sets out that if a person is studying one of the courses listed in para 1 of Appendix 6 of the Rules (for example Biology), then they may not do so via undergraduate or postgraduate research leading to a Doctorate/Masters, or via a Taught Masters in certain other subjects (listed in para 2 of Appendix 6, for example Physics), or a period of study or research exceeding six months at an HEI as part of an overseas postgraduate qualification, unless they have obtained a valid Academic Technology Approval Scheme clearance Certificate from the Counter-Proliferation Department of the Foreign and Commonwealth Office issued before their studies began

Starting work before the Biometric Residence Permit is issued
The Guidance recommends that applicants do not start work before receipt of the BRP; however they may do so, though at their own risk (for both employee and employer) of losing the statutory protection against civil penalties for working without permission if the BRP is incorrect or withdrawn (para 219).

Secondary employment
There is scope to take on further employment than that in the CoS and other permitted (e.g. supplementary) work: however this must be the subject of a new application under Tier 2 made only after starting work in the primary position (*Guidance for Applicants* para 228ff). A new BRP will be issued if the application is granted and there will now be two named Sponsors. It is not possible to start work in the second role pending the application's approval.

Changing employer or job; notifying change of circumstances

The *Guidance for Applicants* (para 215ff) addresses the issue of changing employer. It is necessary to make a change of employment application, with a new CoS from the new Sponsor. It is also necessary to make such an application when remaining with the same employer in circumstances where:

- Core duties change such as to move SOC code

- Core duties change such that the role is no longer in the shortage occupation list

- A person earning the target salary threshold suffers a salary reduction to beneath that level

A new RLMT will be required unless the change is within the same company under the ICT route, for a shortage occupation list job or where the salary is above the upper target (para 224).

However, other changes to the job do not require a change of employment application, as where (para 223):

- A job change (or change of duties within a job) with the same employer remains within the same SOC code, or

- A change takes place with TUPE protection due to a takeover or merger;

- Professional exams are undertaken for regulatory requirements that are necessary before the job starts, or where salary reduces due to child-related leave or long-term sick leave;

- Graduate Trainees under the ICT route change occupation at the programme's end so long as their employer notifies the Home Office of the role and any salary change

Changes of circumstance must be notified by via the *change of circumstances* form and procedure (para 239).

Indefinite leave to remain (settlement) for Tier 2 (General) and Tier 2 (Sportsperson)

The criteria under the Part 6A rules provide that an Applicant must:

- Not fall foul of the general refusal reasons, and must not be an illegal entrant (245HF(a))

- Have accumulated five years continuous lawful residence in any combination of these categories (245HF(b)): Tier 1 (though not Graduate Entrepreneur or Post-Study Worker), Tier 2 (though ICT only if the period of five years residence includes ICT pre-6 April 2010 or as a work permit holder pursuant to ICT arrangements), as a representative of an overseas business, a Highly Skilled Migrant, or as a work permit holder

- Continuous residence is defined by r245AAA: the qualifying period may run from the approval of entry clearance (*Guidance for Applicants* para 253): we address this in more detail in Chapter 1: *General Themes in PBS Cases*

- The requirements of Appendix KoLL must be met (245HF(i))

- Must not be in breach of immigration laws save for the usual proviso that overstaying within the ambit of Rule 39E will be disregarded (245HF(j))

- The Sponsor backing the last grant of leave must still hold a Sponsor licence or have a renewal application pending, and certify in writing that the applicant remains required for the role in question for the foreseeable future, confirming the gross annual salary and that it will be paid for the foreseeable future, if they are on maternity/paternity/adoption or shared parental leave (start date and salary on return), and if paid hourly, the number of hours a week that the salary is based upon (245HF(c))

- The certified pay must be equal to the appropriate rate specified in the Codes of Practice under Appendix J (245HF(d)), and the calculation must

    - exclude overtime and bonus/incentive pay, pension contributions, travel and subsistence including any travel allowance to and from home country, and share value

    - include only such allowances as are guaranteed and would be paid to a settled worker in similar circumstances

    - where they are paid hourly, only earnings up to 48 hours a week will count, even if the applicant works longer hours

    - be at least the figure specified (via earnings only from the main sponsored employment, *Guidance for Applicants* para 266): £35,500 for applications before 6 April 2018 and then subject to increments annually thereafter as set out in the Rule, unless

- the five years' continuous residence includes a period of Tier 2 leave under the Rules in place before 6 April 2011 or as a work permit holder,

- the job specified in the CoS leading to the most recent leave appears on the list of PhD-level occupations in Appendix J, or the Shortage Occupation List in Appendix K, or

- previously appeared on the SOL during a period in which the applicant received a CoS founding Tier 2 (General) leave sponsored by the same or a different Sponsor in the six-year period leading up to the ILR application

➢ Pay must be evidenced by the specified documents as set out in Para 245HH:

- A payslip plus a bank/building society statement:

  - which must be the most recent payslip (bearing the applicant's name) dated no more than a calendar month before the application, on company-headed paper or with a letter on company headed paper signed by a senior official, confirming the payslip's authenticity

  - and the most recent statement dated no more than a calendar month before the application, showing name, account number, date, financial institution's name and logo, showing the last month's transactions including one matching the figure in the payslip; they must be on the institution's letterhead or, if they are electronic statements, with a headed covering letter from the institution or its official stamp and they must not be from ATM mini-statements

  - or Building Society passbook, either the original or a copy with a certified letter from the institution confirming it is genuine, showing the same information as for a bank statement

- An employer's letter, detailing period and purpose of absence, including annual leave, and where any absence was due to serious and compelling reasons, providing a letter from the applicant fully detailing the reasons and with any relevant supporting documents

- If the applicant is not being paid the appropriate salary in Appendix J due to maternity/paternity/adoption/shared parental leave, payslips and bank statements for the month preceding that leave commencing, and for every month of the last grant of leave

Ministers of Religion

In some respects the provisions for Ministers of Religion are the same as for Tier 2 (General); however, they have their own Appendix A criteria to meet.

There are some differences under Part 6A of the Rules:

➢ They face a genuineness testing process within Part 6A itself (245HB(m)-(p)), 245HD(q)-(u)), though this does not put them in a very different position from other Tier 2 applicants, who face genuineness testing under Appendix A

➢ Leave to remain will be granted for the shortest of these periods (r245E(a)):

- length of engagement plus 14 days, or

- three years, or

- the difference between the continuous leave they have spent in the Tier 2 category (on the one hand) and six years (on the other): unless

    - o the applicant previously had leave under the Rules in place before 6 April 2011, under Tier 2 (except ICT), Minister of Religion or various other categories identified in the Rule (r245E(b)(i));

    - o has not been granted leave under Tier 2 under the Rules in place since 6 April 2011 since then, and has not been granted any other leave or entry clearance since then (r245E(b)(ii)-(iii));

- In addition to the period established by this assessment, additional days will be granted to equal the period between the job starting and the date of decision on the application (r245E(c))

➢ There is a bespoke settlement Rule, 245HG:

- The criteria are essentially the same as for Tier 2 (General) under 245HF regarding the general refusal reasons, the ability to combine various kinds of Tier 1 and Tier 2 leave, meeting Appendix KoLL requirements, not being in breach of immigration laws save so far as Rule 39E applies, and ability to rely on residence in Jersey and Guernsey in categories akin to aspects of Tier 1, Tier 2 and their predecessor rules

- The requirements for the Sponsor to remain recognised as such remain, but they only need to certify that they require the applicant for the foreseeable future, and do not have to provide the plethora of details regarding earnings that are set out above for Tier 2 generally; however they do have to provide an employer's letter certifying their absences and their own evidence-backed explanation of any serious and compelling reasons justifying excess absence ((r245HG(c)-(d), 245HH)

Ministers of Religion: Appendix A requirements
The sole Table requirement is that in Table 12: a Certificate of Sponsorship brings 50 points.

The CoS must satisfy certain requirements in order to be valid (A88-A91). These are essentially equivalent to those set out above for the validity of a Tier 2 (General) CoS, as to linkage to a CoSCS entry, the Sponsor being A-rated unless the application is for leave to remain to work for the same employer as a Minister, the CoS having been assigned no more than three months before the application was made or before the job's start date, not previously having been used in an application that was granted or refused, and remaining uncancelled by Home Office or Sponsor.

There are then the route-specific requirements, by which the CoSCS must confirm that:

➢ The applicant is being sponsored for religious duties, which are outlined within the CoSCS, within or directed by the Sponsor's organisation, which may include preaching, pastoral, and non-pastoral work, but must not involve mainly non-pastoral ones (e.g. schoolteaching, media production, domestic work, administrative or clerical work – unless the role is a senior one) (A92(a)-(b))

➢ The applicant is a member of the Sponsor's religious order, if the Sponsor is such an order (A92(c))

➢ Pay and conditions are at least equal to those of settled workers in the same role, detailing the remuneration and showing that it complies with or is exempt from the National Minimum Wage requirements (A92(d)

- The RLMT specific to the Minister of Religion route has been met (A92(e))

- The applicant is qualified to do the job in question, intends to base themselves in the UK and will comply with the conditions of their leave (A92(f))

- Maintenance and accommodation will be met by the Sponsor (A92(g))

-

The RLMT must be met, and for points to be awarded (A92A), it is necessary that the CoSCS shows

- The role is supernumerary, in that is over and above the normal staffing requirements and if the person was not there, it would not be needed to be filled by someone else

- The role involves living mainly within and being a member of a religious order, i.e. a lineage of communities or people living apart from society on account of their religious devotion

- The Sponsor holds detailed records of all available individuals nationally who could fulfil the role, confirming that no resident worker could fulfil the role

- A national recruitment search was undertaken:

    - Where advertised, the reference number and period of advertising (to include 28 days during the six months before the CoS was assigned) must be provided, for at least one of (A92A(d)):

        - A national form of media appropriate to the religion/denomination, or

        - The Sponsor's own website if that is how the Sponsor usually reaches out to its community nationally and where adverts normally appear, and the advert is free to view

        - Jobcentre Plus/Online, or in the employment section of a national newspaper, if there is no suitable national form of media appropriate to the religion/denomination

    - Confirmation that no suitable settled workers were appropriate, or that the Applicant is applying for leave to remain for the same Sponsor as in their last grant of leave

Tier 2 (Sportsperson)

In some respects the provisions for Sportspersons are the same as for Tier 2 (General); however, they have their own Appendix A criteria to meet.

These are the main differences:

- As to their conditions of leave, there is the usual restriction for work, with a twist in their favour:

    - no employment except that authorised by the CoS for the Sponsor (r245HC(d)(iii), supplementary employment and voluntary work, however there is a specific relaxation for employment as a sportsperson for his national team while his national team is in the UK, playing in British University and College Sport (BUCS) competitions and Temporary Engagement as a Sports Broadcaster (r245HC(d)(4), r245HE(d)(5))

- There is an additional route by which they may switch into the category, having previously been a Tier 5 (Temporary Worker) Migrant (though only if last granted leave as a professional footballer within the Creative and Sporting sub-category and where now applying as a Sportsperson: r245HD(e))

- They will be subject to the same conditions and duration of leave as for Ministers of Religion (r245HE(i)), and enjoy a similar relaxation of the "no more than six years leave in this route" bar if they held leave in the category before 6 April 2011 (r245HE(b))

- The same access to indefinite leave to remain as for Tier 2 (General) (r245HF), including a proviso that they may count time spent in Jersey or Guernsey towards their continuous residence so long as it was as a professional sportsperson

- Within the general refusal reasons, there is a general ban on changing employer without making a fresh application (R323AA). However, there is a get-out within R323AA for sportspersons, where the Sponsor is a sports club, and they are being temporarily loaned as a player to another sports club and will return to working for the Sponsor at the end of the loan, where the governing body listed in Appendix M permits this, and arrangements have been made by the Sponsor with the loan club to enable the Sponsor to continue to meet its Sponsor duties

Tier 2 Sportsperson: Appendix A requirements
The sole Table requirement is that in Table 12: a Certificate of Sponsorship brings 50 points.

The requirements for validity of the CoS apply as for Ministers of Religion, already summarised above, including the relaxation of the A-rated Sponsor requirement where the application is for leave to remain to work for the same employer within the Sportsperson route (A97).

The route specific requirements for Sportsperson within Appendix A are that the CoSCS confirms:

- The migrant is qualified for the job, has been issued with a unique endorsement number confirming endorsement in line with the Governing Body for the sport in question, intends to base themselves in the UK, and will comply with conditions of leave (A100(a))

- The letter is provided containing that endorsement, confirming that they are internationally established at the highest level, will make a significant contribution to the sport's development at the highest level in the UK, and that the post could not be filled by a suitable settled worker (A100(b))

Chapter 6: Tier 4 Students

Introduction

We start by identifying the main concepts that are repeated throughout the Rules, before going on to describe the various features of each stage of the student route, including the distinct rules for child students. We deal with student maintenance briefly in this chapter, covering the more general requirements (aspects of which are generic across PBS routes) in Chapter 1: *General Themes in PBS Cases*.

There are two sets of Guidance:

- Tier 4 of the Points Based System Guidance (Version 45.0; published for Home Office staff on 1 November 2018) (which we reference as *Guidance to decision makers* para ...)

- The Tier 4 of the Points Based System – Policy Guidance that helps applicants complete the application form (Version 11/2018; to be used for applications made on or after 1 November 2018) (which we refer to as *Guidance to applicants* para ...)

Overview of Tier 4 General and Child Routes

There are two types of student visas:

- General student visas; and

- Child student visas

We will first deal with general student visas, and then turn to child student visas. There are similarities between the routes (for example, needing to demonstrate maintenance funds). However, there are various differences.

Key to the system's operation is the need for a Sponsor, who issues a Certificate of Acceptance for Studies (CAS). Numerous aspects of immigration control are essentially devolved downwards to the Sponsor, who is under significant record-keeping and reporting duties in order to earn the trust that the award of a Sponsor licence implies. A CAS has to comply with numerous formalities, including the provision of information about every aspect of the proposed studies, including whether or not the course chosen demonstrates academic progression where leave is being extended.

Tier 4 allows students to come to the UK to pursue studies at various levels as defined by the Regulated Qualifications Framework (RQF – previously the NQF and QCF). In England, Wales or Northern Ireland, studies at Tier 4 Sponsors may be at Level 3 and with Probationary Sponsors at Level 4 or above. In Scotland, the Scottish Credit and Qualifications Framework (SCQF) applies, and studies must be at Level 6 or Level 7 thereof for full Tier 4 Sponsors and Probationary ones respectively. The ultimate award must be an "approved qualification", i.e. one found on the Register of Regulated Qualifications or validated by Royal Charter, or awarded by a body recognised by the Department for Business, Innovation and Skills, or recognised otherwise through a formal articulation agreement with the awarding body or covered by a formal legal agreement between a UK recognised body and another education provider, or awarding body, signed by an authorised signatory for institutional agreements (or be an aviation qualification issued by the Civil Aviation Authority).

The CAS must be for a single course of study unless it is for a permissible pre-sessional course (including an English language primer to reach B2 level proficiency) which precedes degree-level studies. Studies must be full-time, either at degree level or involving at least 15 hours weekly organised daytime study (though there is an exception for an overseas course of degree level study recognised as equivalent to a UK degree and provided by an overseas Higher Education Institute).

There is some provision for a single resit or repeating of a particular module.

Those studying at a publicly funded Sponsor or one which is a "recognised body" get a better deal generally, as we discuss below.

Students wishing to pursue certain courses in the sciences must obtain an ATAS certificate to ensure that their studies do not risk contributing to the proliferation of weapons of mass destruction. Postgraduate doctors and dentists must have completed a UK degree in the relevant field and previously been granted leave as a student for the final academic year of that course, and may not remain in the route for more than three years.

There are limitations on permissible periods of study, essentially preventing a student from remaining in the UK for a period beyond two years for studies below degree level, and for five years for studies at degree level or above. The period is calculated by reference to the period of leave granted, not by the length of course or the actual time spent studying.

A person may switch into Tier 4 General from the Tier 2 or Tier 4 child routes, and may extend their student leave so long as their Sponsor is a publicly funded/recognised body (or they are at an "Embedded College" which has strong links with one), where they are pursuing short-term studies abroad in the UK for an overseas higher education institution, or where they are studying at an independent school. Academic progression must be shown where extending leave as a student, subject to various exceptions including resits, completing a PhD or certain doctorate, medical or dentistry courses of study, and moving to a new Sponsor following the former Sponsor losing its licence.

Under Tier 4, English language proficiency may be shown by any one of the usual methods: in summary, essentially holding the nationality of a majority English speaking country or having studied there for a qualification deemed by UK NARIC as "degree level plus", or having studied at "degree level plus" with an educational establishment in the UK, or providing an English language test result (the latter being an option where the studies are not with a UK recognised body or one in receipt of relevant funding as a higher education institution). There are also dispensations for those who are pursuing studies on a short-term basis as part of a USA-based course which is deemed by UK NARIC as "degree level plus", or for those who completed a course over six months long as a Tier 4 (Child) Student or its antecedent rules, and were granted permission to stay whilst under the age of 18.

Degree level studies require B2 proficiency whereas those below degree level require language skills at level B1. Consistently with the scheme of the system, the Sponsor is often responsible for satisfying themselves that the student's language skills are adequate for the course, recording the basis for such a conclusion in the CAS. UK-recognised and publicly funded bodies may certify the student's aptitude for themselves; other institutions must confirm that one of the modes of showing proficiency is established, including suitable test results from an approved English language test provider. Although an applicant may have demonstrated English proficiency to their Sponsor's satisfaction, they are still liable to having their language skills tested as part of the immigration application itself. These impromptu assessments are not via a formal test but are simply based on the impression given at interview with the relevant Home Office decision maker.

The leave granted depends on the length of the course. There are five bands of course identified by the Rules and periods of entry clearance and leave will be granted so as to cover short periods before and after the course ends (known as "wrap-up" leave). Students may have no recourse to public funds and must register with the police.

Students who are still minors require the consent of their parents or legal guardian to their proposed study, reception and care arrangements. Specified documents are required to establish the parental relationship.

Tier 4 students can only work subject to strict conditions: for 20 or 10 hours a week during term-time where they have a publicly funded/recognised body Sponsor for studies respectively above/below degree level, or for more hours where the employment is for a course-related work placement for up to a third of the course, or on such a placement for up to half the course, where they have a publicly funded/recognised body Sponsor. Additionally there are provisos for working as a student union sabbatical officer, postgraduate doctor or dentist under a recognised foundation course, and for Tier 4 students who have pending applications to switch to the Tier 2 sponsored worker route or into the Graduate Entrepreneur category.

There is limited provision for further studies beyond those for which the CAS was issued: some supplementary study is permitted, a student may study at an institution which is a partner institution of the Sponsor, they may study pending the final resolution of a Tier 4 extension application and any subsequent administrative review proceedings. They may also swap to a new course capable of completion within their leave (which must be degree-level plus, and at the same academic level as the previous course, and be related to the previous course or otherwise credibly shown to support the applicant's career goals) where their publicly funded/recognised body Sponsor permits them to do so; and they may study on a programme abroad with a partner institution where the studies are integral to the primary course, and are formally assessed. There may be no study at academies or local authority-maintained schools unless their present institution of study converts to such status within their period of leave.

The Tier 4 child route is for children aged from four years to 18 years, who seek to be educated in the UK at an independent school (thus only CASs issued by such schools with a Tier 4 (Child) Student sponsor licence are valid). Academies and schools maintained by a local authority cannot sponsor students under this route (though there is an exception for voluntary grammar schools with boarding in Northern Ireland). If a foster carer or a relative (not a parent or guardian) of the applicant will be responsible for the care of the applicant then there are detailed arrangements for their welfare, which must be evidenced via confirmation that the accommodation is a private address, the intended care arrangements and the availability of adequate funds for maintenance.

The conditions of stay include a bar on working under the age of 16; thereafter child students may work as they wish in the holidays and for up to 10 hours weekly in term-time. Work placements which are part of the assessed element of their course and employment as a Student Union Sabbatical Officer are also permitted.

Central and recurring concepts within Tier 4

Certificate of Acceptance for Studies (CAS)

This is the record of the student's sponsorship by a college or university. Although paper copies are likely to be obtained and retained by the student, the true CAS is simply the electronic record on the database (the Certificate of Acceptance for Studies Checking Service: CASCS) held by the Home Office and accessed whenever they assess a person's application.

If by the time an application is considered the CAS has been withdrawn or the sponsoring institution has lost its licence and thus its ability to issue CASs, the application will be automatically refused.

Tier 4 Sponsors

A student must study at an institution which possesses and retains a Sponsor licence. Sponsors must satisfy both the relevant educational regulator and UKVI of their ability to meet academic and immigration control standards.

If the institution fails an audit by the relevant educational supervisory body then it will be labelled a "Legacy Sponsor", unable to issue new CASs and simply permitted to continue teaching whilst its current student population completes the last course of study they embarked upon there.

A more common problem is that an audit by UKVI lead to a licence's suspension or revocation. Tier 4 Sponsors must apply to the Home Office annually for a basic compliance assessment, via which they demonstrate that most of the students issued with CASs receive entry clearance or leave, enrol on and complete their course, and that decent record-keeping and reporting arrangements are in place.

Where a Sponsor licence expires, is revoked (usually for breach of the arduous record-keeping and reporting regime imposed) or is surrendered (or where a Legacy Sponsor ends it teaching operations before its students have all completed their studies), the student's leave will be curtailed to end 60 days from the date of the letter from the Home Office notifying them of this development. That of course is presuming they are deemed innocent of any complicity in wrongdoing by a Sponsor: if they are suspected of collusion, their leave will be curtailed to end at once (*Guidance to Applicants* Annex 1, *Guidance* to *decision makers* under heading *if a Tier 4 Sponsor is removed from the Tier 4 Register of Sponsors*).

A student in this situation has potential options: transferring their studies to another institution willing to be their new Tier 4 Sponsor, making an immigration application in another route from which Tier 4 students can switch, or leaving the UK, perhaps to return subject to identifying a suitable immigration category. Generally speaking, remaining in the UK after the 60-day window is a bad idea, as it will mean they become an overstayer and subject to the various mandatory bans that may then kick in.

There is a good guide to the various possibilities on the UKCISA website here.

Examples

Daniel is a Tier 4 student at Bethlehem College studying a three year degree in hotel management; he has entry clearance due to expire after that course ends, in six months time. The College's star wanes with the Home Office and it loses its licence.

Presuming there is no evidence that Daniel was complicit in wrongdoing by the Sponsor, his leave will be curtailed to end in 60 days from the date of the Home Office letter so notifying him. If he manages to find a new Sponsor in that period, then he can use a CAS from them as the basis of an application for an extension of leave.

Probationary Sponsors
When an institution first obtains a Tier 4 licence it will be listed as a Probationary Sponsor on the Tier 4 sponsor register. This is a transitional status by which the Sponsor must earn their spurs relatively quickly, for it can last for no more than 12 months, at which point the institution must apply to obtain full Tier 4 Sponsor status. Probationary Sponsors can only sponsor students at RQF level 4 or above, whereas full Sponsors may offer courses at RQF level 3 too. Students cannot commence their studies with Probationary Sponsors until their latest Tier 4 application has been granted.

Legacy Sponsors
In some circumstances, a sponsor may be made a Legacy Sponsor – usually where a publicly funded institution fails a statutory education inspection by the educational oversight body which has responsibility for it. A Legacy Sponsor is not permitted to sponsor any new students, but can continue to sponsor students who are already studying with it. Thus the CAS will only be acceptable where emanating from a Legacy Sponsor where the relevant studies are for completion of a course already commenced, by way of resitting examinations or repeating a module of a course, this being the same course and Sponsor for which leave was previously granted.

If a Legacy Sponsor decides not to renew its licence at a time when there are still students seeking to complete courses with it, their leave will be curtailed to 60 days to give them an opportunity to find a new Sponsor.

The Academic Technology Approval Scheme (ATAS)

For certain courses (defined by Appendix 6 of the Rules), the putative student must obtain an ATAS certificate so that the UK authorities and international community can be assured that they will not misuse their learning experience to become involved with weapons of mass destruction. These courses are generally research orientated, e.g. mathematical and computer sciences, biological sciences, etc. (r245ZV(da)).

The Counter-Proliferation Department of the Foreign and Commonwealth Office issues ATAS clearance certificates, and applicants will need to have a print-out of their ATAS to demonstrate that this condition is satisfied.

Applicants will need to apply for a new ATAS if there are changes (even minor ones) to their proposed research, or to the content of their course (*Guidance to Applicants*, para 171ff).

In practice, if the issue of an ATAS certificate is delayed, then the Home Office are known to allow the certificate to follow the remainder of the application. An applicant wishing to take this route can provide their ATAS application reference number and explain the situation in their covering letter, promising to forward the certificate as soon as it is received. UKVI will usually keep such applications on hold pending an ATAS decision. This means an applicant can pursue an application without becoming an overstayer. During the summer, the ATAS team within the FCO is inundated with applications and struggles to turn its work around.

Example

Emma, a visa national, plans to apply for entry clearance as a Tier 4 student. She will be studying for a research Masters in Chemistry.

A Chemistry Masters is a qualification listed in Appendix 6 to the Rules at para 1, and therefore it is necessary to hold a valid ATAS certificate (this being a postgraduate qualification in a sensitive subject identified as one from which knowledge could be used in programmes to develop weapons of mass destruction) from the FCO.

The Regulated Qualifications Framework

The level of a particular qualification is defined by reference to the Regulated Qualifications Framework, which is a national governmental scheme for identifying the difficulty level of an occupation or qualification. For example, an honours degree is at RQF Level 6, and a Masters at Level 7. Level 4 equates to qualifications such as a certificate of higher education, or higher apprenticeship.

UK recognised bodies and those in receipt of public funding; and UK listed bodies

Students whose studies are at institutions of this nature get numerous perks. Bodies in receipt of public funding for these purposes are those in receipt of public funding as a higher education institution from the Department of Employment and Learning in Northern Ireland, the Office for Students, the Higher Education Funding Council for Wales, the Scottish Funding Council or any other provider registered with the Office for

Students. Rule 6 defines *UK recognised bodies* as those granted degree awarding powers by either a Royal Charter, an Act of Parliament or the Privy Council.

These students may study for up to six years in the UK if there is a Masters component to their course, and they have advantageous access to work:

- For up to 20 hours weekly in term time if their course is at degree level and otherwise for 10 hours weekly
- On placements for up to half their study period
- If they have completed degree level studies they can work for a Tier 2 Sponsor pending the final decision on the application and any administrative review of a refusal
- On a self-employed basis pending the decision on a Graduate Entrepreneur application

Furthermore, they can swap to a new degree level course (other than that in their CAS) so long as it can be completed within their grant of entry clearance/leave, and they are able to apply to extend their leave.

A UK listed body is an institution that is not a UK recognised body but which provides full courses that lead to the award of a degree by a UK recognised body.

You can see the list of recognised bodies at the *Check if a university or college is officially recognised* web page.

Studies which are above and below degree level
There is frequent reference in the Rules to various limitations and opportunities available because of the level of a course.

For example, there are limitations on the ability to study "below degree level" courses for more than two years, or on studying courses "above degree level" for more than five years (always in the sense of the total leave granted, not merely the period spent studying or the length of courses).

There are some exceptions to the bar on more than five years studies above degree level:

- The limit goes up to six years where the course of studies culminates with a Masters or to eight years with a PhD so long as there is a UK recognised or publicly funded Sponsor

Subject areas where the professional dimension requires longer study are architecture, medicine, dentistry, law, veterinary studies and music at a college that is part of Conservatoires UK (r245ZV(ga)-(gb).

There are also certain advantages as identified in the last paragraph regarding working limits and study opportunities.

It may well be obvious whether a particular qualification is below or above degree level, but if in doubt, you may find that the government resource *What qualification levels mean* is helpful.

UK NARIC
UK NARIC is the designated United Kingdom national agency for the recognition and comparison of international qualifications and skills, an official function which it performs on behalf of the UK Government. Where an academic qualification is awarded by an educational establishment outside the UK the applicant must provide a letter or certificate from UK NARIC confirming that the level of the award is equivalent to a relevant UK qualification. It can grade academic, vocational and professional qualifications.

For example, qualifications that are deemed by UK NARIC to meet or exceed the recognised standard of a Bachelor's or Master's degree or a PhD in the UK from an educational establishment in a majority English speaking country may be relied on as evidence of English language proficiency.

Maritime and Coastguard Agency courses
Where there is a regulatory requirement from this Agency that the applicant must spend at least 12 months as sea during the course, the normal limitation of two years for "below degree level" studies is lifted to three years (r245ZV(gaa), r245ZX(haa)).

Overseas higher education institution
A person may be sponsored by an overseas higher education institution to undertake a short-term study abroad programme in the United Kingdom. These individuals get certain advantages under the Rules – they can work on placements for up to half their study period, they can work for up to 20 hours weekly in term-time, and they are able to apply for further leave to remain. They need not demonstrate academic progression, and must apply no more than three months before the start date (*Guidance for decision makers*).

Embedded College offering Pathway Courses
Some colleges that are not themselves recognised bodies or in receipt of public funding nevertheless have relationships with such institutions. Embedded Colleges offering Pathway Courses are Sponsors recognised by the Home Office as a private provider, and are usually part of a network and operating within or near to the premises of a higher education institution, delivering pathway (but not pre-sessional) courses which prepare students for entry to higher education programmes at that institution. A Pathway Course is defined (Rule 6) as a course preparing a student to another course at a publicly funded or specific UK recognised body.

Students who have studied at such an institution may apply to extend their leave in the Tier 4 category, and indeed they may also access the Investor and Entrepreneur routes under Tier 1.

Part time studies
Part-time studies are permitted from 11 January 2018. These must be at RQF level 7 (i.e. Masters) or above. Students in this sub-route may not work: thus r245ZY(c)(iii) has been amended to refer only to full-time students being able to work.

Student Union Sabbatical Officer
Although generally Tier 4 migrants will be studying, there is a dispensation for Student Union Sabbatical Officers.

The post must be one to which they have been elected and based at the sponsoring institution, unless they are elected to a National Union of Students (NUS) position. They may either be in the course of their studies or be sponsored to fill the position for the academic year immediately following graduation. They may then work throughout the period of leave, for up to two years.

They may extend their leave thereafter, and are exempt from the need to show academic progress where they are applying to complete the course which was interrupted to take up this role.

State funded and independent schools
The policy of the Rules is to exclude studies at state funded schools and academies. If a Tier 4 Sponsor alters its status to one of these during the currency of their leave, they may complete the current course, but not embark on a new one (r245ZW(c)(vi)). Rule 6 defines these so as to include local authority maintained schools of all kinds including special schools and nursery schools, grant-aided schools, public schools and academies. Independent schools are defined as those which are not academies and where full time education is provided for five or more school-age pupils, or for one or more pupils under special arrangements such as those under special educational needs statements.

Genuineness assessment
As with most aspects of the PBS, merely satisfying the formal requirements of the route is not enough. The Home Office reserve the right to carry out a detailed assessment of a person's genuineness, for within Part

6A, the Rules stipulate that applicants must be "genuine students" (r245ZV(k)). The ECO should interview the applicant in accordance with their policy as laid out in the Entry Clearance Guidance (ECG). This basically says certain factors should be taken into account:

- All relevant evidence from both interview and application
- Immigration history and compliance in the UK and abroad (bearing in mind lengths of stay in other countries and their purpose)
- Education history and future study plans bearing in mind the time since they were last in education, whether they demonstrate *sufficient commitment* to the course, and whether it truly credibly represents academic progression (see further below)
- Their research into, and knowledge of, the place and course of study, bearing in mind its relevance to their post-study plans
- The circumstances of any dependent and the impact that might have on the applicant's ability or motivation to study; particularly where the purpose of studies is said to be related to a dependent's benefit by way of education, employment or health
- Their personal and financial circumstances bearing in mind any dependents in the UK and abroad, living costs in the UK and their ability to maintain themselves without working, how their funds for study have been acquired, the distance between their proposed accommodation and place of study
- Whether the application is to study at an institution that is under investigation or has been identified as of concern, or if the application is being managed by an agent as to whom there are concerns

The interview may be short and brutal. Some critics with experience of the system opine that the decision maker may well be looking for reasons to refuse the application and will take no prisoners. Any adviser must ensure their clients understand what may be expected from them at interview. Applicants should bear in mind that the interviewer may well look up the website of the institution and then expect the interviewee to be able to answer questions about information found there – right down to the library opening times.

However, ECO questioning must be fair, both exploring all material issues fully and giving an opportunity to respond to concerns in the mind of the potential decision maker: see Mushtaq IJR [2015] UKUT 224 (IAC).

Example

Xan is a citizen of China. He plans to come to the UK as a Tier 4 student. He wants to know what to expect at the interview which has been scheduled following his application.

You can see the approach of entry clearance officers in Mushtaq mentioned above: they may expect detailed knowledge of the course of studies and an explanation of how it fits into the individual's career plans, and that the costs are realistic given the circumstances of the applicant and their family. Failure to attend an interview without a reasonable explanation is a mandatory ground of refusal (r320(7D)). It is therefore key to advise clients of the potential for an interview at the earliest opportunity.

Furthermore, if refused a visa or leave to remain, applicants now have to apply for administrative review of the decision. Applicants will not usually be able to rely on evidence not submitted with their application. It is therefore important to get the application right first time.

Maintenance and English language requirements
Generally speaking in the PBS, the requirements for maintenance and English language proficiency are addressed in Appendices B and C. However, under Tier 4, the English language requirements are actually dealt with under Appendix A which we address below

Consent of the government or agency that previously sponsored an applicant
Students who are, or were, sponsored by a government or international scholarship agency, must obtain that body's consent to an immigration route that implies long term stay in the UK. Part 6A of the Rules cross references to Rule 245A, which is the general provision in Rules addressing this issue.

Rule 245A requires

- Unconditional written consent
- In the form of a letter on official headed notepaper bearing the official stamp of the organisation and issued by an authorised official
- Confirming that the organisation gives its unconditional consent to the applicant remaining in the UK for an unlimited time

Parental or legal guardian's consent for minors
Where the applicant is under 18, applications will need to be supported by their parents or guardians, or one parent if that parent has sole legal responsibility (see r245ZV(j), r245ZZA(g) for the Tier 4 child category).

Evidence of the parent's relationship to the child will need to be provided (r245ZV(ja), r245ZZA(ha)). The evidence may include:

- A birth certificate showing the names of the applicant's parent(s);
- A certificate of adoption showing the names of the applicant's parent(s) or legal guardian; and
- A court document naming the applicant's legal guardian

Overstaying
The general scheme of the Rules is that "where paragraph 39E of these Rules applies, any current period of overstaying will be disregarded".

Rule 39E provides the following exceptions:

- Firstly, where the application is made within 14 days of the applicant's leave expiring, and the Secretary of State accepts that there is a good reason preventing the application from being made in time, the overstaying will be disregarded (the reason for overstaying should be provided in the application); and
- Secondly, where the application is made following a previous refusal (which was in-time) and within 14 days of (a) the previous refusal, (b) leave expiring under section 3C of the Immigration Act 1971,

or (c) the time limit for making an application for administrative review, the overstaying will similarly be disregarded

The general grounds of refusal

Any of the general grounds for refusal are in theory available for Tier 4 applicants (r320). They are found in Part 9 of the Rules. HJT has an ebook addressing this subject in detail, *The General Refusal Reasons*; we just make a few general points.

For Tier 4 applicants, the main issues to highlight relate to an applicant's intention to attend the proposed course of study, Sponsors and English language requirements. At r323A, there are specific grounds which '*will*' cause a Tier 4 applicant to have their leave curtailed, which include:

- Where an applicant fails to commence their studies;
- The Sponsor withdraws and excludes the applicant from the course; or
- An applicant does not obtain B2 English language proficiency after completing a pre-sessional course

There are also grounds which '*may*' cause a Tier 4 applicant to have their leave curtailed, which include:

- Where a Sponsor ceases to have a valid Sponsor licence

Scheme of the Tier 4 General rules

The provisions for entry clearance are found in Part 6A of the Immigration Rules (r245ZT and r245ZZA) as are the requirements for leave to remain applications (r245ZX and r245ZZC). Most of the requirements for entry clearance are simply replicated for leave to remain; however, where this is not the case, we address these specific requirements in the sub-section dedicated to "leave to remain" below.

For entry clearance as a Tier 4 (General) applicant r245ZT, which cross-references Appendices A and C, is the starting point. Appendix A deals with the CAS, for which applicants receive 30 points (Table 16). Appendix C addresses the maintenance funds which students need to evidence, which adds another 10 points, ensuring that the applicant reaches the required 40 points for entry clearance.

Appendix A also contains a great amount of detail on the requirements for the CAS. There are many formalities about what makes the CAS valid, for example, being issued a few months before the application is made.

General and Tier 4-specific refusal grounds are located in Part 9 of the Rules which we have addressed above.

Beginning at Part 6A, r245ZT sets out the route through which the majority of applications for the purpose of studying in the UK are made; r245ZU makes it clear that entry clearance is required for all routes. The general requirements for entry clearance are outlined under r245ZV.

An applicant must gain 40 points, made up of a minimum of 30 points for a valid sponsorship arrangement (i.e. the issue of a CAS to them by their Sponsor, see Tables 16 and 17 of Appendix A), and a minimum of 10 points for maintenance funds (r245ZV(c) and C10-14).

Those applying for general student visas will also need to meet English language requirements – which, unusually under the PBS, are found in Appendix A (generally PBS language standards are in Appendix B). It is for the Sponsor to assess that the English language requirements are met when issuing the CAS. Importantly, a failure by the Sponsor to properly do so could render the CAS invalid. This is therefore something to be aware of and check for on the CAS. As we mention below, however, an ECO or immigration officer can also check English language proficiency for themselves.

Requirements for entry clearance

Firstly, the applicant must be at least 16 years old. If under 18, the applicant must have the support and consent of their parent(s) (r245ZV(h)-(ja)).

As stated earlier, eligibility for Tier 4 (General) visas requires an applicant to obtain 40 points. The only way to receive 30 of these points is through possessing a CAS (r245ZV(b)). And, to achieve the further 10 points, an applicant must demonstrate that they have the requisite maintenance funds to support their studies (r245ZV(c)). The detailed requirements for the CAS and maintenance funds will be discussed when we address the substantive aspects of Appendix A and C respectively.

Tier 4 applicants must be able to demonstrate the relevant proficiency in English (without an interpreter) at interview (albeit not via a formal test at that level) (r245ZV(ca)). Further details on the English language requirements are explained when we address Appendix A.

Course specific requirements

- The Academic Technology Approval Scheme (ATAS) certificate described above
- Postgraduate Doctors and Dentists
- A specific point to consider in relation to doctors and dentists (applying for entry clearance to a Foundation Programme) is that their application must not be made more than three years from when they were first granted entry clearance (r245ZV(e)).

Time limitations

If studying *below* degree level, an applicant cannot spend more than two years in the UK once aged 18. The calculation is based on the *length of leave granted*, rather than the *time actually spent studying* (r245ZV(g)). This means that if a grant of leave was curtailed, the overall length of historic leave will decrease.

In addition, the two year limit does not take into account any time spent:

- Studying below Bachelor's level (before 31 March 2009);
- As a Tier 4 (General) student, when 16 or 17 years old;
- As a Tier 4 (Child) student, when under 17 years old; and
- Any other non-Tier 4 category which permits study (*Guidance for Applicants* para 107)

Other time limitations which apply to entry clearance include where a migrant would spend five years in the UK (r245ZV(ga)). This provision was designed to make it more difficult for a student to meet the requirements of the 10-year long lawful residence rule. However, exceptions to the five-year rule include:

- Migrants studying for a Master's degree after completing an undergraduate degree (where the course duration was four or five years). For these students the limit will be set at six years (r245ZV(ga)(i));
- Those studying for a PhD. However if on completion of the PhD the time spent in Tier 4 (General) exceeds eight years, no further leave will be granted in Tier 4 (r245ZV(ga)(ii) and r245ZV(gb));

- Those following courses in architecture, medicine, dentistry or law (where the applicant has completed a law degree in the UK and is progressing to study higher level law qualifications, e.g. a law conversion course);

- Those studying veterinary medicine and science, and music at a music college that is a member of Conservatoires UK (CUK) (r245ZV(ga)(iii))

As above, calculations as to whether the applicant has exceeded the time limit are based on the grant of leave rather than the time studied (r245ZV(ga)(8)).

UKVI will only adjust the period taken into account where there are exceptional compelling and compassionate circumstances justifying this (*Guidance for Applicants* para 118).

Example

Huang is present as a Tier 4 student. He wants to apply for leave to remain for a further course. He has so far studied for four and a half years at undergraduate and masters level in law, and now wishes to study for the Legal Practice course.

Although in general a student may not spend more than five years in the UK as a student, Huang is permitted to do so in the subject of Law where he will be moving onto the LPC.

Appendix A: substantive criteria

The Certificate of Acceptance for Studies (CAS)

The requirements for a CAS are stipulated at A116-A117:

- Being issued no more than six months before the application is made (A116(a))

- No more than three months before study is to commence (A116(b))

- The offer from the Sponsor remains extant and the Sponsor had (and has retained) their Tier 4 licence (A116(c), (e))

- Studies with legacy Sponsors are permissible only for retaking exams or repeating course modules (A116(da)-(db))

- The CAS may only be used once, where the application was approved or refused (though it may be reused where the application was merely rejected as invalid) (A116(ea))

- Details are provided by way of the applicant's name, birth date, gender, nationality and passport number, and course title and level, full/part-time status, and start and end dates, the main place of study, details of how English language was assessed and test scores where required, details of any work placements, accommodation fees and boarding costs, details of any partner institution where the course is provided by another education provider, whether an ATAS certificate is required, whether a certificate is required from the Postgraduate Dean because it is a Foundation Programme for doctors or dentists, and any overseas higher education institution backing a "study abroad programme" (A116(f)) (those studying music, drama or dance can undertake work placements which involve a professional performance under a concession in the Guidance where studying at RQF level 6/SCQF level 9 plus, and this is assessed as integral to the course by the Sponsor)

- Although obviously usually a CAS will relate to a course of studies, it may also be issued for work as a Student Union Sabbatical Officer or for the doctorate extension scheme (so long as issued within 60 days of the expected end date of a PhD course) (A116(g)-(h))

- The reference number must link to a CASCS entry naming the applicant as the relevant migrant, which has not been withdrawn or cancelled by the Sponsor or Home Office since being assigned (A117)

A student can apply for further leave to resit exams: the CAS should make this purpose clear. They apply on the basis of exam resits no more than once (unless the Sponsor has Tier 4 Sponsor status) (A119).

Examples

Christopher plans to seek entry clearance for a course in Biology as a Tier 4 student which starts in nine months' time. He wants to apply in good time to be confident of getting a place on the relevant course.

The CAS must not be issued more than six months before the application is made, and the entry clearance application must be made no more than three months before the course starts.

Christopher's application is made and succeeds. He arrives in the UK with his CAS. However, when the immigration officer checks the register of CASs online, he discovers that the CAS was cancelled because the offer has been withdrawn.

Christopher can be refused leave to enter because of a change of circumstances. Where the offer has been withdrawn, a key Appendix A requirement will no longer be satisfied. The situation would be the same if the institution's licence had been revoked.

Ashfar plans to make an extension application within Tier 4 and has a Sponsor lined up; they have confirmed they will make him an offer as soon as he has the paperwork in order. He does not have a suitable English language test result yet, and is planning to sit a test soon.

Ashfar should get on with getting the test result. The CAS will not be issued until he has satisfied the college of his English language proficiency. A delayed test result could prevent the CAS being issued, which could mean that he has to make an application for further leave to remain without a CAS in the hope that one reaches him to forward to the Home Office before his application is decided. There is no legal obligation on UKVI to await the document, however: Mudiyanselage [2018] EWCA Civ 65.

Orinoco is studying at Womble College. He has applied for further leave under Tier 4. However, the College has its licence revoked before his application is decided. When the UKVI decision maker looks up the CAS, they will see that the College is no longer entitled to issue valid CASs. So the application is liable to be refused.

However, there is a policy to limit leave at this point to 60 days, providing the student is not suspected of involvement in the malpractices leading to revocation. So the decision maker should remember this policy and give Orinoco the benefit of it. Orinoco will then be able to use this period to find another Sponsor, or find an alternative immigration application to make; otherwise he must leave the country.

The policy does not apply where the CAS if withdrawn or invalidated by the Sponsor, even if the migrant is not at fault. In Patel [2018] EWCA Civ 229 it was held this was not unfair – the student's only remedy lay against the Sponsor. However, if UKVI is responsible for the problem arising having revoked the Sponsor's licence, then they should given the student the benefit of the policy: EK (Ivory Coast) [2014] EWCA Civ 1517.

The CAS and English language requirements

Sponsors are responsible for ensuring that applicants meet the required English language proficiency for their course of study. A118 basically provides that a CAS will not be valid unless an applicant is proven to be proficient in English. There are several ways to demonstrate this, and at least one requirement must be satisfied. The various means of doing so will be familiar to anyone who has used Appendix B in order to assess English language proficiency in other PBS routes. However, Tier 4 contains its own indigenous language assessment system within Appendix A, rather than situating its requirements in Appendix B like most other routes.

A118 divides up applicants into three classes at A118(i), (ii) and (iii). These are

- Degree level studies with a UK recognised or publicly funded body
- Degree level studies with a body that is not a UK recognised or publicly funded one (they may rely on positive results from an approved English language test provider if they do not satisfy one of the other possibilities)
- Studies below degree level

The ways in which proficiency may be shown are by satisfying one of these routes:

- Being from or having previously completed an academic qualification equivalent to UK degree level in a majority English speaking country. Nationality must be confirmed through specified documents set out in A120-SD(b). The equivalence of the qualification abroad with a relevant level of award in the UK must be confirmed by UK NARIC (A118(b)(i)(1) and (2))
- Having previously completed a degree in the UK (A118(b)(i)(3))
- Short-term study for up to six months if the applicant's course of study is the overseas element of a course with a higher education institution in the USA, and leads to an academic qualification that UK NARIC deems to be equivalent to UK degree level (A118(b)(i)(4))
- Having completed a course of six months or more as a Tier 4 (Child) in the UK which ended within two years of the date the CAS is assigned (A118(b)(i)(5)); or
- Having a CASCS entry which confirms knowledge of English equivalent to level B2 – this assessment can be conducted by the Sponsor institution for degree level students with publicly funded/recognised bodies (A118(b)(i)(6)), but otherwise must be assessed via an English language test result in reading, writing, speaking and listening (subject to a disability exemption from one

component) from an approved provider for study at lesser institutions (A118(b)(ii)(6)) or for non-degree level studies (A118(b)(iii)(5))

It should also be noted that the required English language proficiency varies with the level of study that the applicant is proposing to undertake:

- For degree level courses and above, English language must be at level B2 CEFR (reading, writing, speaking and listening) (A118(i)(6));
- However, if studying below degree level (RQF level 3, 4 or 5 Scottish Credit and Qualifications Framework (SCQF) level 6, 7 or 8 in Scotland), an applicant will need to show English language proficiency at level B1(A118(iii)(9))

Evidential requirements for English language proficiency differ depending on the level of the course and type of provider. In particular, where the course is at degree level, and provided by a publicly funded Sponsor, there is no requirement for the student to provide a test certificate.

There are exceptions to the English language requirements, for example, disability (the *Guidance for Applicants*, paras 142ff). There is significantly more detail about English language processes in Chapter 1: *General themes in PBS cases.*

Example

Darshan wants to apply for entry clearance as a Tier 4 student. He has evidence of English language proficiency as he has passed the relevant test with a provider listed in Appendix O to the Rules at level B1 across the board. He is nervous about speaking English under pressure, though, and seeks reassurance.

Darshan can be invited for interview and asked to demonstrate his English language proficiency. He will not be expected to sit a formal English language test – the test is whether his English skills are at the level indicated in the CAS. Indeed, it is even possible to be interviewed at the port of entry after entry clearance has been issued.

Minimum academic requirements

Points will only be awarded under a CAS if it meets the standards laid down in A120. This states that the CAS must be issued for a course which meets one of these requirements:

- Leads to an "approved qualification" (see below);
- Is at Regulated Qualifications Framework (RQF) level 3, or level 6 of the SCQF (or RQF level 7 or SCQF 11 if part-time in England/Scotland) or above if the Sponsor is an Highly Trusted Sponsor (HTS), or RQF4/SCQF7 or above they are a Probationary Sponsor (A120(a)(i)-(iv))
- If for a person studying at an overseas Higher Education Institution (HEI), is a short-term Study Abroad Programme at degree level (A120(a)(v))

- At minimum level B2 CEFR if for an English language course (A120(a)(vi)) or
- Is a recognised Foundation Programme for postgraduate doctors or dentists (A120(a)(vii))
- A course delivered under a partnership between a higher education institution and a research institute must be accredited at RQF level 7 or above (Level 11 or above under the Scottish SCQF)

Furthermore, the CAS must be for a single course of study unless

- It relates to a pre-sessional course of no more than three months plus a course of degree level study or
- There is a pre-sessional course of no more than three months in order to ensure the applicant reaches B2 English language proficiency before starting the degree level study
- So long as in either case the degree-level study begins no later than one month after the end date of the pre-sessional course (A120(b)).

If the student is studying towards an ACCA accountancy qualification or foundation qualification, the Sponsor must be an ACCA-approved learning partner at Gold or Platinum level (A120(ca)).

Approved qualifications
Per A120(cb), an approved qualification is one that is either:

- Validated by Royal Charter (A120(cb)(1))
- Awarded by a recognised body (the list is produced by the Department for Business, Innovation and Skills) (A120(cb)(2)) or recognised by a formal awarding body (A120(cb)(3))
- RQF level 3 or above, or level 6 of the SCQF in Scotland (A120(cb)(4) and (5))
- An overseas qualification which is deemed equivalent to RQF level 3 (A120(cb)(6))
- A qualification covered by a formal legal agreement between a UK-recognised body and another education provider (A120(cb)(7))

The course must also be (A120(e)):

- A full time course at degree level, or overseas equivalent offered by a UK Higher Education Institution, or
- A full time course of study involving a minimum of 15 hours per week organised daytime study
- A part time course sponsored by a UK recognised body or a body in receipt of public funding as a higher education institution

Restrictions also apply to courses where there is a work placement involved. The general rule is that this cannot exceed a third of the total length of the course (A120(f)). The exceptions however include where:

- There are statutory requirements of that state the placement should exceed one third of the total length of the course or

- Where the placement does not exceed one half of the total length of the course and the student is following a course of degree level study

Specified documents
There are requirements for the specified documents which are provided to satisfy the Appendix A criteria:

- For qualifications, the dated award certificate (or transcript, or a printout from the awarding body's online checking service), showing the applicant's name, the award title, and the name of the awarding institution

- Alternatively the Sponsor may have assessed the applicant using one or more references, in which case the CASCS entry must include details: the reference or a copy backed up by a dated letter from the Sponsor confirming they saw the original, giving the applicant's name, confirmation of the type and level of course or previous experience, and dates thereof, and the referee's contact details, and confirmation that the qualification is at degree level or above from UK NARIC if the qualification comes from a listed country (A120-SD(a))

- For nationality, valid passport or travel document, or where these are not available, a current national identity document or letter from the home government or embassy confirming their full name, birth date and nationality (A120-SD(b))

Where the applicant has provided print outs as evidence of previous qualifications, the Home Office reserves the right to request the certificate of qualification or the transcript of results, and to refuse the application if these are not forthcoming (A120-SD(c))

Applications for leave to remain

Switching into Tier 4 (General)
The ability to apply for leave to remain has been curtailed in recent years, so that the ability to "switch" into Tier 4 is now fairly limited. There are now only a handful of classes of applicant who are able to switch into Tier 4 (or extend leave within the route), as follows:

- Tier 2 (General)

- Tier 2 (Intra-company transfer)

- Tier 2 (Minister of religion) and

- Tier 4 (Child)

- Tier 4 (General) – however, not every student can do so, it depends on the quality of their Sponsor. They must have last been sponsored by a UK recognised body, body in receipt of public funding as a higher education institution, an Embedded College offering Pathway Courses, or an independent school

In-country applications for Tier 4 (General) visas can also be made when a student is nearing the end of their course.

The new course will need to begin within 28 days of the applicant's current leave to remain expiring (r245ZX(l)). Where the gap between the leave running out and the new course is more than 28 days, the student is expected to return home and apply for entry clearance. In practice UKVI recognises that, given the extension of leave given by section 3C of the Immigration Act 1971 following an in-time application, the new course must start within 28 days of the date of that decision.

This would help somebody whose CAS expires on 31st July where their new course is to begin on 1st September. They could submit a Tier 4 application by post on 30th or 31st July, and could then submit their biometric information towards the end of the 15 working day time limit. This would bring them closer to bridging the potential 28-day gap between the caseworker making a decision on the application and the course's actual start date.

Academic progression

For leave to remain to be granted, it will have to be shown that the proposed studies represent academic progression. The provisions are found in A120A. For example, if the course is at the same level as the last one, as where the applicant wants to study for a second Bachelor's degree, they run a risk that the new course is not accepted as representing sufficient progress. There are a series of exceptions:

- Resitting examinations or repeating modules (A120A(a)(i))
- Completing a PhD or doctoral qualification for which the CAS for the previous period of leave was assigned (A120A(a)(ii))
- Making a first application to move to a new institution following revocation of the original Sponsor's licence (A120A(a)(iii))
- Undertaking a Student Union Sabbatical Officer role or resuming studies after completing that role (A120A(a)(iv))
- Applying under the doctorate extension scheme or as a postgraduate doctor/dentist on a recognised Foundation Programme (A120A(a)(v))
- Applying for leave to undertake an intercalated Bachelor's or Master's degree or PhD where studying medicine, veterinary medicine and science, or dentistry (A120A(a)(vi)) (*intercalated* studies allow the student to pursue a separate but related research degree) (the Guidance states that it is only when the intercalated course can be completed within the student's extant period of leave that they are not required to submit a new application to the Home Office)
- Applying for leave to undertake a study abroad programme or work placement which is both integral to, and assessed as part of the course; or to complete their course, having completed a study abroad programme or work placement (A120A(a)(vi))

For academic progress to be established, it is necessary that the applicant *either*:

- Has successfully completed the course for which the last CAS was allocated (or the course into which they permissibly switched) (A120A(b)(i))
- Is applying for leave to allow them to progress from Bachelors to Masters as part of an integrated Masters course, or Masters to PhD as part of an integrated Masters to PhD programme, having been offered a place on a higher level course by the Sponsor after assessment of their academic ability (A120A(b)(ii))
- *And* the course is above the level of that under the previous CAS (A120A(b)(iii)) *unless*

- The course is taught by a UK recognised or publicly funded body which is also the (Tier 4) Sponsor, and is at degree level or above, and not at a lower level than the previous course for which leave was granted, and the Sponsor confirms that the course is related to the previous course in the sense it is connected to it, part of the same subject group, or involves deeper specialisation, or this course of studies supports the applicant's genuine career aspirations

Generally speaking, the Sponsor's assessment in the CAS must be accepted as the last word on the subject, unless there is concrete evidence that the college made an assessment which was plainly inappropriate on the face of the documents (as explained in Pokhriyal [2013] EWCA Civ 1568).

Where UKVI does investigate the matter for itself, as where the courses are at the same level, then it will look at

- The level and subject matter of the courses
- The applicant's education history, and
- The credibility of the rationale for the educational decision and whether it is sufficiently explained by the Sponsor.

In these circumstances, applying for a course at the "same level" may nonetheless represent progression. There are further exemptions from this rule which include:

- Switching to Tier 4 (General) from a Tier 4 (Child) student visa;
- Making a Tier 4 (General) application from overseas; or
- Making a first application to complete an existing course commenced at a Tier 4 Sponsor that had its licence revoked (para 57)

Example

Harpreet was granted entry clearance as a student to study tourism and hospitality at QCF/RQF level 4. He now wishes to extend his leave to remain to study Hospitality Management. When you look up the courses, you see that the new course is also at QCF/RQF level 4.

As he was previously granted leave as a student, he must show academic progression. Consecutive courses at the same level clearly do not necessarily demonstrate this. He does not benefit from one of the exceptions, e.g. resitting, PhD studies, loss of the Sponsor's licence, student sabbatical officer, etc. As no exception applies, the requirements of A120(b) must be satisfied: so as this does not represent degree level studies, the course must be above the level of the previous course for which a CAS was issued. Harpreet must rethink.

Extensions

Those completing a PhD in the UK can apply for an additional 12 months leave under the Doctorate Extension Scheme. This can be done up to 60 days before the course end date (r245ZX(n)(4)) (see also *Guidance for Applicants*, para 120ff). Under this scheme, applicants will also need to demonstrate that they have sufficient funds to cover living expenses for two months (*Guidance for Applicants*, para 194).

Examples

Ronaldo applies to study a course below degree level under the Tier 4 (General) route. When making the application, Ronaldo is 17 years and 4 months old. He is granted entry clearance, and granted a visa for the duration of the course (two years). It is now approaching the end of Ronaldo's course, and he would now like to apply to university to study marine biology.

Can Ronaldo apply for leave to remain? Yes. The time spent in the UK before Ronaldo was 18 will be discounted, meaning that he has not spent more than two years in the UK studying below degree level. Therefore, so long as Ronaldo has a valid CAS and meets the minimum maintenance funds, he will be able to apply for leave to remain under a Tier 4 (General) visa.

Aiman is a citizen of Malaysia present as a Tier 4 student. He wants to apply for further leave to remain for 12 months in order to study for a NCC Education Level 4 Diploma in Business. You look at his immigration history and see that he has spent 18 months in the UK achieving a Level 4 Certificate in Professional Marketing; he tells you he passed that course in 11 months of study.

As he has already been studying courses that are below degree level (you can use the Ofqual Register of Regulated Qualifications to assist with assessing qualification levels), he must watch out for the rule on "below degree level" studies: he must not have spent more than two years in this immigration route studying courses at that level. The Rules make it very clear that it is the length of leave and not the length of study which matters. Accordingly it is clear that the new course would take him over the maximum permitted.

Appendix C: The required funds for maintenance

Students will be expected to show that they hold sufficient funds to cover either

- The full costs of their course fees or
- Fees for the first academic year where the course will last for a year or more

They must also show available funds of £1265 for maintenance if studying in London (£1015 for those studying outside London)

- For each month of the course
- Up to a maximum of nine months

The money must be held in the relevant account at the date of the application and for a consecutive 28 day period beforehand, evidenced by bank statements dated no earlier than 31 days before the date of application (C1A(c) and C1A(h)).

"London" for these purposes has a very distinct (and somewhat medieval!) definition (C12AA).

For further information on supplying documentary evidence in relation to maintenance funds, see Chapter 1: *General Themes in PBS cases* (see also the Guidance, paras 177ff)

Period and conditions of grant across Tier 4

In general, Tier 4 visas are granted for the duration of the course of study, plus a little extra either side (r245ZW(a)).

The period of leave granted is linked to the length of course, permitting a certain amount of time to get established in the UK and a period at the end of one's leave, which may be used to identify a further route under Tier 4 or otherwise to extend one's stay or to plan one's return abroad (r245ZW(b)):

- A course for 12 months or more: one month before the course starts and four months after completion;

- A course for six months or more but less than 12 months: one month before the course starts and two months after completion;

- Pre-sessional course of less than six months: one month before the course starts and one month after completion;

- Course of less than six months which is not a pre-sessional course: seven days before the course starts and seven days after completion; and

- Postgraduate doctor or dentist: one month before the course starts and one month after completion

Note: applications have to meet routine conditions, for example, no recourse to public funds and, if required by paragraph 326 of the Rules, registration with the police (r245ZW(c)).

If a course finishes early because of an earlier than expected completion, leave will be curtailed with a view to giving the same "wrap-up" period of leave as was originally allotted under the provisions above – so a person studying for a course exceeding a year's length would have enjoyed four month's "wrap-up" leave, and now will continue to do so (Guidance para 365ff).

How many hours per week can Tier 4 (General) students work?

Employment is permitted only in the following circumstances (and generally only where the course is one of full-time studies):

- Employment during term time of no more than 20 hours per week for those studying at degree level and above (r245ZW(c)(1));

  Employment during term time of no more than 10 hours per week for those studying below degree level (including Foundation degrees), but only at certain colleges, and Employment of any duration during vacations (for those permitted to work)(r245ZW(c)(2));

- Employment as part of a course-related work placement which forms an assessed part of the applicant's course and provided that any period that the applicant spends on that placement does not exceed half of the total length of the course undertaken in the UK (r245ZW(c)(4));

- Employment as a Student Union Sabbatical Officer, for up to two years, provided the post is elective and is at the institution which is the applicant's Sponsor (r245ZW(c)(5));

- Employment as a postgraduate doctor or dentist on a recognised Foundation Programme (r245ZW(c)(6)); and

- Self-employment, if the applicant has applied for leave to remain as a Tier 1 (Graduate Entrepreneur) Migrant (r245ZW(c)(8))

In addition, a Tier 4 (General) student may not be self-employed, or employed as a Doctor in Training other than a vacancy on a recognised Foundation Programme, professional sportsperson (including a sports coach) or an entertainer, and must not fill a full time vacancy other than a vacancy on a recognised Foundation Programme (r245ZW(c)(8)(c)).

Lastly, applicants may undertake a "supplementary course" whilst in the UK, e.g. an evening class, so long as it does not hinder their academic progress on their main course of study (r245ZW(c)(8)(iv)(c)).

A student can only study on the course identified in the CAS, save for the exceptions mentioned in the introduction.

Neither UKVI nor the Sponsor have to be told about supplementary studies. (Guidance for Applicants, para 333).

Those given leave to enter or remain to study at publicly-funded further education colleges are prohibited from working.

Example

Edna and Josephine have been granted leave as Tier 4 students. Edna will be studying for a law degree at Bristol University. Josephine will be studying for a Level 5 foundation degree at Bolton University. Each wishes to know whether they can work in the UK and on what terms.

Edna is studying a degree level course at a UK recognised body (Bristol University is on the list at the *Check if a university or college is officially recognised* website here) and so can work for up to 20 hours weekly in term-time (and longer outside term-time).

Josephine is pursuing a course that is below degree level (see the GOV.UK website What qualification levels mean) and so can work for no more than 10 hours per week (and longer outside term-time).

The Tier 4 (Child) route

Overview

Beginning at r245ZZ, this route is for children at least four years old and under the age of 18 who wish to be educated in the UK in private independent schools. Applications to study at level 2 RQF or below must apply through this route.

The types of courses which can be studied on a Tier 4 (Child) student visa are set out at paragraph 243 of the *Guidance for Applicants.*

Lastly, unlike Tier 4 (General) applications, there are no English language requirements for this route.

Requirements for entry clearance
As with Tier 4 (General) visas, Tier 4 (Child) applicants will need to obtain a minimum of 40 points through both a CAS and maintenance funds (r245ZZA(b)-(c) and C15-22). This is also set out at Appendix A Table 17.

Note: the genuine student provision (as above for Tier 4 (General) applications) applies to child applicants over the age of 16 (r245ZZA(j)).

Finally, if a foster carer or relative will be responsible for the child then additional documentary evidence must be provided (r245ZZA(f)). The specified documents, details and requirements pertaining to care arrangements are listed at r245ZZE. This provision outlines that applicants must provide a letter from their intended carer with the following information:

- Name, address and contact details of the intended carer;
- The nature of the relationship;
- That the intended carer has at least £570 per month (up to a maximum of nine months) available to look after and accommodate the Tier 4 (Child) student; and
- A letter must also be provided by the child's parent or legal guardian setting out: (a) the nature of their relationship with the intended carer, (b) the address where their child will be living with the intended carer, and (c) evidence that the intended carer is settled in the UK, e.g. a current passport, travel document or certificate of naturalisation (copies will be accepted) (r245ZZE(4))

Appendix A: The key requirements
The same rules apply as under the Tier 4 (General) route in relation to a CAS, which include:

- Being issued by an independent school no more than six months before the application is made;
- No more than three months before study is to commence; and
- The offer from the Sponsor remaining valid (A124)

A125A also states that a CAS will only be valid if the applicant supplies evidence of previous qualifications (the specified documents are set out in paragraph 125-SD).

Appendix C: adequate funds for maintenance
In terms of demonstrating the requisite funds, Tier 4 (Child) applications differ slightly from Tier 4 (General) visas. The following variations apply:

- **Residential independent schools**
  For a child studying and boarding at a residential independent school the Home Office will require evidence of sufficient funds to pay school fees for a year plus any additional accommodation fees required by the school. Access to funds will need to be demonstrated through either money in the child's own name or money in accounts held by a parent or legal guardian

- **Non-residential independent school (private foster care arrangement)**
  For a child studying at a non-residential independent school in a private foster care arrangement, the Home Office will require evidence of sufficient funds to pay school fees for one year plus an undertaking from a UK resident or citizen to provide maintenance and accommodation for the duration of the course. The undertaking must set out the nature of the relationship with the child and the child's parent(s). In addition, the individual providing maintenance and accommodation will need to be able to demonstrate that they have accommodation and the funds to support a child in addition to their own existing commitments (available income of at least £570 per month will be required up to a maximum of nine months) (r245ZZE(6))

- **Independent school (parent accompanying a child under 12)**
  The Home Office will continue to allow children studying at independent schools under the age of 12 to be accompanied to the UK by a parent who will be responsible for their care. In this case, the Home Office will require evidence of funds required to pay school fees for one year plus £1560 per month for each month up to a maximum of nine months. If more than one child is studying then as well as evidence of ability to pay annual fees for each additional child, evidence of a further £625 per month will need to be shown to be available for each additional child

If the applicant is 16 or 17 years old and living independently, they will need to show that they have:

- £1,265 per month for living costs if studying in London; and

- £1,015 per month for living costs if studying outside London or anywhere else in the UK

These criteria must be proved by specified documents:

- Personal bank or building society statements covering a consecutive 28 day period ending no more than 31 days before the date of application

Bank statements which merely show an applicant's balance on a particular day will not be accepted.

Private foster care arrangements
If the applicant will be staying in a private foster care arrangement, they must also receive permission from the private foster carer's UK local authority. This is explained in the "Children (Private Arrangements for Fostering) Regulations 2005". Details of the Act can be viewed at: www.opsi.gov.uk/si/si2005/20051533.htm (*Guidance for Applicants*, para 293ff).

The following documentary evidence must also be provided if the applicant is under 16 years old and intending to stay in a private foster care arrangement:

- A copy of the letter of notification from the applicant's parent(s), legal guardian or intended carer to the UK local authority. This must confirm that they will be in the care of a private foster carer while in the UK; and

- The UK local authority's confirmation that it has been notified of the foster care arrangements (r245ZZE(4)(iv))

Applications for leave to remain
Applications for leave to remain are substantially similar to applications for entry clearance. However, as with Tier 4 (General) applications, the new course will need to begin within 28 days of the applicant's current leave to remain expiring (r245ZZC(j)).

Where the gap between the leave running out and the new course is more than 28 days, the child is expected to return home and apply for entry clearance.

The general grounds of refusal
Child-specific grounds for refusal or curtailment in Part 9 of the Rules are sparse; however they do include:

- Failing to show an immigration officer written consent from an applicant's parent(s) or legal guardians (r320(16))

This will "normally" lead to the applicant being refused entry clearance. In addition, the same considerations as mentioned before in relation to Tier 4 (General) visas apply (though of course, excluding the English language requirements).

Period and conditions of grant for Tier 4 child students
If the application is made when the child is under 16 leave will be granted for:

- The length of stay that is asked for;
- The length of the course; or
- Six years (245ZZB(ii))

The shortest leave will be granted, e.g. if the applicant's course is five years long, this will be the total grant of leave rather than six (plus four months after the end of the course (r245ZZB)(iii)). In addition, leave will be granted for a maximum of one month before the course commences.

Note: for applicants over 16 a maximum of three years will be granted rather than six (r245ZZB)(b)(ii)).

How many hours per week can Tier 4 (Child) students work?
Firstly, applicants under 16 years old cannot work *at all* (r245ZZB(c)(iii)).

However, for those aged over 16, employment is permitted:

- During term time for no more than 10 hours per week (r245ZZB(c)(iv)(1);
- Without limit during vacations (r245ZZB(c)(iv)(2));
- Where there is a work placement involved, the general rule is that this cannot exceed a half of the total length of the course (except where there is a UK statutory requirement that the placement should exceed half) (r245ZZB(c)(iv)(3))

Chapter 7: Representing Tier 2 and Tier 5 Sponsors

Introduction

This Chapter explains the system for sponsoring workers from the Sponsor's perspective, with a general overview of the process. Chapter 8: Tier 2 and 5 Sponsors - Compliance Issues concentrates on issues surrounding compliance including the consequences and possible remedies when things go wrong.

In recent years the use of non-EEA migrant labour in the UK has been regulated ever more intensely. There are two major routes to joining the UK labour market, found in Tier 2 and Tier 5 of the Points Based System. Tier 2 is for workers coming on a long-term basis, and indeed some branches of the route can lead to settlement. Tier 5 offers opportunities for temporary work and exchange schemes, and for work experience and training. See Chapter 5: Tier 2 Sponsored Workers and Chapter 9: Tier 5 Temporary Workers and Youth Mobility Scheme Temporary Migrants for information about both these routes from the perspective of the migrant and their situation within the immigration system.

Sponsorship is a major area of immigration advisory work. In late 2017, the Sponsor register included 29,240 organisations currently licensed to sponsor migrants under Tiers 2 & 5 of the Points-Based System. It is understood there were some 150 new applications for Sponsor licences a week by late 2017, with a 20% refusal rate.

Of course, EEA nationals, and individuals who are settled here and some migrants otherwise resident in the UK may have the right to work, and students from outside the EEA have a limited ability to work within the constraints of the particular visa they hold. Their employers must ensure they follow the required right to work checks when employing these individuals and retain evidence of their entitlement to work. Sometimes a potential employee who will struggle to meet the Tier 2 requirements might nevertheless be able to come to the UK as the dependent of their partner, which may offer an alternative possibility where the relevant immigration category permits them to do so and to work following their arrival. These are issues which we deal with elsewhere: this Chapter concentrates firmly on sponsored workers.

The idea of the Sponsorship system is that the Sponsor steps into the shoes of the immigration service, to the extent that they guarantee that they employ only those workers who represent a safe level of risk to immigration control, and that they will maintain record-keeping and reporting systems that are appropriate to this level of responsibility. But beyond this, the employer is also the guardian of the domestic labour market, and they also have to undertake and honour obligations to ensure that they only recruit to jobs for which there is no settled worker available.

There is a detailed procedure for applying for a Sponsor licence. There are various tier-specific criteria, for information technology and digital technology jobs, and for intra-company transfers, for sportspersons, nurses and midwives, and for the various sub-routes under Tier 5. The applicant organisation has to show a good case for needing migrant workers, and has to provide a hierarchy chart or equivalent information setting out its structure, showing where sponsored workers would be located.

The firm must show its *eligibility* to be a Sponsor by providing numerous documents of various classes as set out in Appendix A to the Guidance: these demonstrate that the entity is appropriately registered and regulated in whichever sector it operates, and that it is registered with HMRC and makes the appropriate tax returns. It must also demonstrate its *Suitability*: i.e. that its human resource and recruitment systems are sufficiently robust to meet the heavy record-keeping and reporting requirements. A Sponsor must keep copies of immigration status documents showing the length of leave to remain and entitlement to work, a history of contact details of its migrants and all relevant details of their recruitment, a formal document recording their national insurance number, and records of absences.

When awarded, licences are given for four years, subject to earlier surrender or revocation. A refusal may be challenged via the *Error Correction Request Form* process, which looks at whether relevant evidence was overlooked (it does not permit further evidence to be supplied).

The Sponsor reports to the Home Office via the Sponsor Management System (the SMS). The entity's key personnel are responsible for the SMS. They have to report changes to their own details, to the organisation's structure and regulation/registration including entering into compulsory financial arrangements and mergers and takeovers, and convictions. They must also record significant changes in the sponsored migrant's circumstances and unauthorised absences.

The roles of key personnel have to be filled: the authorising officer with overall management responsibility, the key contact, and level 1 and level 2 users, who carry out the more mundane filing of information. These roles must all be filled, though they may be the same person; some large Sponsors might appoint a legal representative to one of the lesser roles. They must be persons of good character, free from relevant criminal or financial misdemeanours. Indeed, UKVI reserves the right to check other responsible figures in an organisation, beyond the SMS users. SMS users have the ability to assign CoSs to migrant workers, and they must do so responsibly: for example, they must not assign a CoS to themselves of a close relative or partner.

The holder of a licence is allocated a distinct number of Certificates of Sponsorship (CoS). The Sponsor may then assign a CoS to a worker they wish to employ. There are restricted CoSs, subject to an annual limit; these are released in 12 monthly instalments. Sometimes they run out (in which case they are allocated according to a points system that privileges factors such PhD-level and skill shortage occupations, public service work, and salary rates) so employers need to plan ahead. The period of employment is closely linked to the CoS to which it relates; so a restricted CoS will only be valid within three months of its assignment to a worker.

There are also unrestricted CoSs, not subject to such a limit. These can be assigned to workers who for one reason or another are not seen as a threat to the domestic labour supply, because they are already present and established in work, or are a high earner or similar:

- Those extending their stay in the same or a new job with the same or a different Sponsor
- High earners and posts associated with what is called "high value inwards investment"
- Those entitled to switch into the category, although not the dependents of students who require restricted CoSs
- Doctors and nurses
- Before 1 July 2018, Croatians applying for worker authorisation: Croatia's accession to the EEA required arrangements to be put in place giving limited access to the domestic labour market. However those arrangements have now ended, and Croatian nationals are in the same situation as any other EU national

When assigning unrestricted CoSs, it is important to check that the job is at the right skill level, that the Resident Labour Market Test advertising requirements have been met, and that the salary package is at the appropriate rate. Each of these requirements is the subject of extensive provisions.

Generally speaking the job must involve activities which are measured by the UK's national qualifications framework at RQF level 6 or higher. The codes of practice for skilled work are listed at Appendix J of the Immigration Rules, so the job in question can be measured against the occupations and descriptions of skill levels listed there via the Standard Occupation System of codes (SOC Codes). There is some provision for less highly skilled workers, for some specialist roles in the creative sector, and for those were previously under the ICT route within certain dates.

The appropriate pay rates are set out in Tables in the Immigration Rules: there are two specified rates for the Intra-Company Transfer category in Tier 2, and a multitude of different salary rates for Tier 2 (General), linked to the salary figures given in Appendix J for each SOC Code, which differentiate between established workers and new entrants.

The Resident Labour Market Test (RLMT) is a trap for the unwary. The central requirement is the need to advertise vacancies to ensure that no settled worker is available for the role. There are some exemptions, including for those extending leave with the same employer in the same role, for shortage occupations (listed in Appendix K), some students who previously studied at degree level or above, for high earners, and some speciality training and non-essential research positions. Where the RLMT is required, all the critical requirements of the role, from salary to skills and experience, have to be advertised via closely-defined media for specified time periods. Most importantly from the Sponsors perspective, exhaustive records must be kept, which show that the RLMT was satisfied, particularly with regard to the dates over which advertisements were publicised (which may well require screen-shots of web-based recruitment media).

These requirements may be audited by the Home Office in compliance visits: RLMT records can be scrutinised, pay rates checked, and they may interview migrants, their colleagues and management about the *reality* of their role, and then assess whether the function truly meets the requirement of the job as described on the CoS and as required via the SOC Code in Appendix J.

Where a compliance visit raises questions about a Sponsor's ability to meet its obligations, then the A-rating that all new Sponsors initially receive may be downgraded to a B-rating, with a time-limited action plan as to the steps they will have to take to win back the full trust of the Home Office. If they fail to implement the plan adequately, then their licence may be revoked. A Sponsor may have no more than two action plans within the currency of a licence period.

We deal with questions of revocation, suspension and downgrading in detail in Chapter 8: Tier 2 and 5 Sponsors – Compliance Issues.

Structure of the regulatory system

The rules and procedures for Sponsors (rather than migrants) which are the core of the sponsorship system itself are found entirely within the Guidance regularly published and updated by the Home Office. Presently this is *Tiers 2 and 5: Guidance for Sponsors* (Version 01/18; effective from 11 January 2018).

There is no separate more formal underpinning of Rules that are overseen by Parliament. The decision of the Supreme Court in New London College [2013] UKSC 51 explains that this relatively informal way of running things is lawful. Lord Sumption also made clear in that case that the Guidance might be burdensome, but it was a voluntary scheme: so Sponsors had to like it or lump it! As he put it:

> There are substantial advantages for sponsors in participating [in the Tier 4 scheme], but they are not obliged to do so. The rules contained in the Tier 4 Guidance for determining whether applicants are suitable to be sponsoring institutions, are in reality conditions of participation, and sponsors seeking the advantages of a licence cannot complain if they are required to adhere to them.

The main Guidance has a series of Annexes at the end of the document, addressing the mandatory and discretionary refusal of original applications to become a Sponsor (Annexes 1-2), the circumstances in which downgrading (Annexes 3-4) and revocation (Annexes 5-6) will take place, and listing the relevant kinds of unspent conviction that will be taken into account (Annex 7) and further details on the approach taken to mergers and takeovers (Annex 8).

There are also a series of associated Appendices: for example, Appendix D gives the documentary requirements for Sponsors.

A large part of the Guidance summarises the content of the Immigration Rules addressing various categories of sponsored migrant. When reading those sections of the Guidance one should bear in mind that it is the original underlying Rules that are the primary source of law – the Guidance may be out-of-date, or fail to take account of a particular nuance of a Rule change, so it is unwise to rely on it without casting an eye at the underlying Rule.

Casework Tip

It is a very good idea to store each generation of Home Office Guidance. Although it is the current Guidance which will apply when advising Sponsors of their present obligations, when things go wrong the relevant Guidance will crystallise as that in force at the date of compliance action being taken. You may be able to find older generations of Guidance at the UK Government Web Archive.

Recurring concepts

The cap: the Tier 2 (General) limit

There are only a limited number of CoSs actually available for those jobs which falls into the category of "restricted" – essentially sponsored workers entering the UK from overseas as a "new hire" and family members (dependants) of Tier 4 migrants who are switching to a Tier 2 visa.

The Certificate of Sponsorship

The CoS is central to the system and it is a virtual document rather than a paper one. Copies may be printed off, but it is the one held on the central database that is the true record. Sponsors are allocated a set number of unrestricted CoSs (based on their evidence-backed estimate of how many Tier 2 and Tier 5 certificates they'll require) which they may then assign to migrant workers. Restricted certificates may only be assigned through the sponsorship management system (SMS).

RQF levels

The UK measures skill levels via the national qualifications framework: generally speaking, Tier 2 workers must be functioning at RQF level 6 or higher, though there are a few exceptions addressed below. A job's skill level can be measured via the Standard Occupation System of codes (SOC codes) which are set out in Appendix J to the Immigration Rules.

Appropriate pay rates

Workers under Tier 2 must earn certain minimum levels of income. These are identified in Appendix A to the Immigration Rules, although the UKVI Guidance repeats them. They are also found alongside the SOC Code and occupation descriptions found in Appendix J.

The Resident Labour Market Test
The link between immigration and employment is a famously controversial issue. The UK's settled workforce is protected via the RLMT, which specifies procedures and periods over which a vacancy must be advertised to make sure that those already entitled to be in the country loses out. Some jobs are exempt, though.

The Sponsorship Management System (SMS)
This is the system by which Sponsors communicate with the Home Office to report changes in their own circumstances and those of their employees.

Genuine vacancies
UKVI are very concerned about the possibility that CoSs are assigned at a level which does not generally reflect the underlying job, and they may audit this by interviews and assessments of a sponsored migrant's work during and following compliance visits.

The skills charge
The skills charge is levied on employers of migrant workers and its proceeds are to be invested in improving the skills of the UK workforce: £1,000 per person, per year; charities and small companies only pay £364 per person annually.

Government agencies
Government agencies which support inward investors or exporters play a role in the system, in that they may support certain applications; for example, for a small company to employ sponsored digital technology workers. There are equivalent agencies to the English-based regulatory and government agencies in the devolved governments of Scotland, Wales or Northern Ireland. To save space we just refer to the central government entity, e.g. the Department for Information Trade (DIT), though the economic devolved government departments in Scotland, Wales or Northern Ireland offer the same functions.

Children
Employers must make suitable care arrangements for children working in the UK by way of their travel, reception and living arrangements, including ensuring appropriate parental consent.

Enquiries made to the Home Office
The contact points given are the Business Helpdesk and the telephone number 0300 123 4699. Where the Guidance leaves the Sponsor unsure as to the position, then they raise an individual query rather than follow their instinct.

Overview of Sponsorship

The guidance explains the two overriding features of the Sponsorship system:

- It provides evidence they are filling a genuine vacancy for which no settled worker is available
- The Sponsor pledges to uphold the expected duties

Broadly speaking there are two kinds of Sponsors:

- Educational establishments
- Employers

Employers need to be aware that the migrants they sponsor will be under various limitations as to how long they can spend in the UK.

There are four primary aspects to a Sponsorship application:

- Being a genuine organisation operating lawfully in the UK

- Being honest, dependable and reliable, having regard to the applicant's history and background, and the key personnel involved in the business

- Showing an ability to meet the Sponsor licence requirements

- For those applying to sponsor Tier 2 (General) migrants, showing that the employment proposed genuinely meet the skill level and pay rates which are required

Once an application is made, the information provided may be used in line with the Home Office Personal Information Charter. Details may be passed on to other government departments and agencies, local authorities and fraud prevention agencies such as HM Revenue and Customs (HMRC), Department of Work and Pensions (DWP) and Credit Industry Fraud, Avoidance System (CIFAS)) for immigration purposes, the prevention of fraud and criminality and/or to help them carry out their functions.

There are two relevant routes:

- Tier 2 for skilled work

- Tier 5 for temporary work and exchange schemes

Like everyone else, Sponsors must ensure their employees are entitled to work in the UK. There are civil and criminal penalties for employing workers without such permission. Compliance officers will refer cases of illegal working for prosecution or the issue of a civil penalty. Sponsors caught in this situation will face suspension of their licence, and their future licence applications may be refused.

Representatives may assist with preparing an application, but the Sponsor has to send it themselves, otherwise the application will be invalid and the fee retained. If a representative is desired once the licence is issued, then they must be appointed using the Sponsor Management System. They may be appointed at the application stage only if they are to be the Key Contact. A Sponsor must nevertheless have a level 1 user who is their own employee.

There are fees for initial applications, extensions, scope changes, and for each Certificate of Sponsorship (CoS) that is assigned under the licence.

Although Sponsors tend to be private firms, sometimes government bodies may be a Sponsor: as where a local authority sponsors teachers in self-governing schools, or where the Deanery, Local Education and Training Board, or provider/commissioning organisation, a Strategic Health Authority has funding control over training posts for doctors and dentists.

Applying for a licence
Sponsor licences are valid for four years, subject to their earlier surrender or revocation. The key aspects of an application are

- Completing the online application process

- Paying the fee

- Providing proof of certain documents to confirm genuine operation and lawful trading in UK – including proof of holding appropriate planning permission or Local Planning Authority consent where require, and if a food business, evidence of registration with a relevant food authority

- Meeting the eligibility and suitability criteria

- An audit of the application by the Home Office, which may include requests for further information or a site visit, looking for evidence suggesting a threat to immigration control or of a failure to comply with a public body's rules

- Applications may be refused, rejected or granted; grants receive an A-Rating

Once the application is granted, then CoSs may be granted. From this time, the reporting and record keeping duties kick in. Once the application is granted, key features of the scheme are:

- A limitation on the number of CoSs to be assigned

- Visits to check compliance

- Referring incidents of non-compliance to the appropriate authorities, for civil penalties or possible prosecution

- General duty to act honesty in all dealings with the Home Office, avoiding making false statements and ensuring all relevant information is disclosed in the application process and thereafter

Sponsorship failings may lead to downgrading to a B-Rating, in which case a Sponsor will receive a time-limited Sponsorship action plan showing the necessary steps to retain the licence. Sponsor ratings are published on www.gov.uk.

Example

Oasis Enterprises are a firm contemplating becoming a Sponsor. Before they apply, they need to look at every aspect of the Guidance, particularly the record-keeping and reporting duties, to ensure that they have the relevant processes in place – and they have to be able to operate those procedures with the mindset of the immigration service, not simply as a benevolent human resources department. And there might not be much chance to get one's house in order: compliance visits may take place as part of the application process, or when an extension application is made, or may simply be unannounced.

Good ideas are to:

- **Ensure the supporting documents are ready: a failure to do so once the online application process is activated can lead to delay and cost, as the documents must be supplied within five working days of the initial application**
- **Identity the necessary arguments and evidence to support the request for a particular number of Certificates of Sponsorship**
- **Check that the authorised users are all able and willing to take up their roles, and they have no blemishes on their character that may derail the application**

The Certificate of Sponsorship

The CoS is central to the system and it is a virtual document rather than a paper one. Copies may be printed off, but it is the one held on the central database that is the true record. Sponsors are allocated a set number of CoSs, which they may then assign to migrant workers. The operation of the CoS is explained in detail in section 23 of the Guidance.

When created, the CoS receives a Unique Reference Number which the migrant can cite in order to support their immigration application which is based upon it. Once assigned, a CoS can be used by a sponsored migrant to support their immigration application. The CoS will then show as "used" in the Sponsor's SMS account, and cannot be used again; if their application is refused and they wish to re-apply a new CoS must be assigned. If their application is rejected (i.e. declined as invalid rather than refused in substance) or withdrawn, then the CoS should show up as "assigned", and can be re-used for a further application (23.4). They must use the CoS within three months of its issue (and a migrant may not rely on it more than three months before the job's stated start date).

Migrants who are abroad can be granted entry clearance no more than 14 days before the CoS start date; the start date may be delayed following the grant of entry clearance, but they may not begin work more than 28 days from the CoS's start date (including appropriately reported changes to that date) or the date of entry clearance being granted. The start date given on the CoS must be the date that the migrant is expected to start working at the time the CoS is assigned. A migrant cannot apply for leave more than three months before their CoS's start date.

Assigning a CoS does not guarantee that the beneficiary's immigration application will succeed; they must still satisfy all the requirements of the Immigration Rules.

A group CoS may be assigned to all members of a group entering under the Tier 5 Temporary Worker Creative and Sporting category.

In general access to the UK labour market is tightly controlled. There is a maximum annual allocation of Tier 2 (General) CoSs.

There are also unrestricted CoSs which escape that regime, essentially because some classes of applicant are not seen as competing with domestic workers or are established in sponsored work already. These are those

- Extending their stay with the same Sponsor, in the same job or changing job into a different SOC code

- Tier 2 (General) workers who are already working here and are changing Sponsor

- High earners applying from overseas with a salary package exceeding the maximum (presently £159,600)

- Already present with leave in the UK and permitted to switch into Tier 2 (General) (however, where they are present in the UK with leave as *dependent family members of Tier* 4 (i.e. student) migrants, they will count towards the annual limit, and thus require restricted CoSs)

- High value inwards investment posts (see Chapter 5: Tier 2 Sponsored Workers under the section *Relocation of high value business/significant new inward investment project*)

When assigning an unrestricted CoS, it is important to identify that

- The right kind of CoS is assigned (i.e. one of those above)

- The job is at the right skill level
- RLMT requirements have been complied with
- The salary package is at the appropriate rate

When a licence application is made, the Sponsor is asked for a number of CoSs that are to be assigned in the first year. They will not necessarily receive the full allocation requested. They will receive a zero allocation if they are unsure as to their migrant recruitment intentions, and the allocation is particularly likely to be lower if they are B-rated and on an action plan, or are a start-up organisation or have no history of complying with the Immigration Rules. Other factors are the business's sector and size, and the time the firm has been trading, whether it intends to use agents for recruitment who have previously been linked to immigration abuse, and whether the number of CoSs sought is credible in all the circumstances.

Example

Oasis Enterprises wants the option of employing up to 10 sponsored migrants once it receives its licence.

The firm must make a strong argued evidence-backed case for this number of CoSs, having regard to its past employment record and the challenges it has faced when recruiting for skilled roles. The firm should factor in any business aims and projections which may have a material impact on staff recruitment needs over the next 12 months. The greater the detail given, the better are the chances of getting the number of CoSs requested.

Moving forwards, Oasis should also plan ahead for the next year, and ensure that it files a request for a new allocation ahead of the annual April deadline. Failure to sort this out in good time could leave the firm with a zero CoS allocation. They would then not be able to sponsor migrant workers without making an in-year renewal request, which will take time to prepare and receive a decision from UKVI.

CoSs must be allocated within the year running from the licence start date. Unused CoSs are removed from the SMS account at the year's end and cannot be carried over. Where possible UKVI will write giving the next year's allocation in advance, based on the number assigned in the previous year.

A Sponsor may apply for further unrestricted CoSs via their SMS account, though restricted CoSs can be applied for only under the *application cycle* process. The allocation may be reduced due to compliance action or if the firm downsizes.

A CoS may be cancelled by UKVI if they suspect it was assigned through misrepresentation or fraud, or if it was improperly assigned, and the Sponsor can also withdraw a CoS that has not yet been used to support an immigration application. In the former case, their leave will be curtailed to 60 calendar days, to give them a chance to find a new Sponsor (and provided it is accepted that they were not involved in the reasons leading to the improper assignment).

A migrant can only have one CoS assigned to them at a time, so if they do not take up a job offer with the potential employer who first issued them a CoS, they cannot obtain a new CoS with the successful employer until the first CoS is withdrawn. Failing to action a migrant's request for cancellation of a CoS may be relied on by UKVI to justify compliance action being taken.

A restricted CoS must be assigned within three months of the allocation date appropriate to the application: that date is calculated by reference to monthly application cycle, discussed further below. If UKVI seek further information which is not supplied within time, or subsequent checks related to that material cannot be completed within time, the application will be rejected. After three months the CoS will be removed from the Sponsor's SMS account.

Section 24 of the Guidance explains that when an employer issues a CoS, they are essentially confirming to the Home Office that they have met all the requirements of the Guidance and that the migrant will be able to make a successful immigration application.

There is detailed Guidance on the practicalities surrounding the issue of a CoS in the guidance *Creating a CoS: guide for Tiers 2 and 5 sponsors* (SMS guide 8A).

The cap: the Tier 2 (General) limit
As we touched on above, even satisfying all the requirements of the Immigration Rules does not guarantee that a potential sponsored migrant can work in the UK, because there are only a limited number of CoSs actually available for those jobs which fall into the category of "restricted" – essentially sponsored workers entering the UK from overseas as a "new hire". The Home Office *Guidance on Allocations of restricted certificates of sponsorship* shows the number available each month: usually some are carried over as not every restricted CoS is taken up.

The Guidance addresses restricted CoSs in detail in section 29 of the Guidance.

- The limit is specified in Appendix A (A80 onwards): 20,700 presently
- A Sponsor must apply for a CoS to the Secretary of State
- To obtain a CoS, they must score points under Table D: at least 20 points for the nature of the job and at least 1 point for salary – the idea is that the more valuable the job, the more points are scored; and the higher the salary, the more points are awarded
- Table 11D of Appendix A sets out various jobs and salaries:
    - **Jobs and recruitment**: Shortage occupations receive 130 points, PhD occupations that pass or are exempt from the RLMT receive 75, new graduate jobs that pass the RLMT and the student switching control receive 30, certain public service occupations in health and science/language teaching receive 30, and jobs that pass the RLMT or benefit from an exemption receive 20
    - The job in the CoS must (A81A)
        - Appear on the list of occupations in Table 2 of Appendix J, or
        - Be one of the creative sector occupations at RQF level 4+
        - Appear on the SOL in Appendix K (at the time the application is decided; contracted working hours being for 30 hours weekly, and the special nurse and Scotland provisos must be met: A81B)

- PhD level jobs must be must be listed in Table 1 of Appendix J (A81C)

- For the RLMT to be satisfied or an exemption established, the Sponsor must certify that the RLMT advertising requirements are met, or that the Post-Study Work exemption or one of the other exemptions is satisfied (A81D)

- **Salaries** (to be calculated via the usual constraints as to guaranteed income shorn of all extras: A81E, and only via hours up to 48 weekly A81G) from £100,000 receive 60 points; then there are bands by which salaries that are relatively high receive between 45 and 55 points, and finally salaries under £65,000 are grouped in decreasing bands receiving from 1 to 40 points

    - The salary must exceed the Appendix J code of practice level (A81F)

    - Points are only awarded if the vacancy is considered genuine and not tailored to exclude resident workers, as set out above (81H-81I) – which may include reasonable grounds for not believing that the regulatory requirements for nurses will be met (81H(c))

Once the Sponsor has scored sufficient points, they are eligible for inclusion in the allocation of CoSs via the process set out in the Monthly allocations provisions of Appendix A (paras 82 onwards). The monthly allocation runs in line with the financial year from 6 April to 5 April, with more (2,200) at the start of that year than at the end (1,000) (the allocation pattern is set out in Table 11E). The approvable applications are determined on the 11th of each month.

Historically it has been relatively rare for the threshold to be exceeded, so that Sponsors seldom lose out. However demand can exceeded supply, as happened in the summer of 2015, and in December 2017 and January 2018. Where there is a shortage of CoSs available for allocation, they will be allocated to the jobs with the greater number of points, having regard to factors such as being on the shortage occupation list, requiring PhD level employees, "new graduate" jobs, key "public service occupations", and then via salary level. Given that unsuccessful applicants in a month that the cap bites may well apply the following month, there is scope for a logjam, so Sponsors have to plan carefully when this happens.

Very exceptionally, UKVI may authorise issue of a CoS outside the allocation process: the examples they give are where their own delay has prevented a migrant starting work earlier, or where a doctor's application must be expedited because patients need life-saving surgery (of course, doctors now get an easier ride generally as they can access unrestricted CoSs).

Casework tip

In most cases, the best way of beating the cap will be to offer a higher salary (the corollary being that the cap bites more sharply on lower-paid areas, e.g. teaching): it is worth checking the salary bands, as sometimes a small raise may move the applicant into a category that scores more points.

However, if the last job advert did not promise a salary in this range, then the RLMT would have to be repeated. When re-applying, it is important to check that the last RLMT is still valid, which requires that it was run in the last six months.

Sponsoring migrants

Section 24 of the Guidance addresses various aspects of the actual sponsorship process for migrant workers. Chapter 5: *Tier 2 Sponsored Workers* examines this process from the perspective of the migrant's immigration application, and gives examples of how the various facets of the scheme works.

A couple of points to look out for are that:

- Before applying for entry clearance, from 6 April 2017, Tier 2 General applicants have had to provide a criminal record certificate from each country in which they have lived for 12 months in total, cumulatively or consecutively, in the decade running up to the application date

- Once employed, all payments must be made directly to their bank accounts, in the UK or abroad; they must not be paid in cash (24.4)

Skill levels under Tier 2 (General) and ICT

There is a general requirement that employees must be *working* at a level equivalent to **RQF level 6**: to emphasise, *working* at that level, not simply having been *educated* to that level. This requirement emanates from the Immigration Rules themselves (Appendix A at A74). There are some exceptions: where

- The migrant will be sponsored under Tier 2 (General) for a shortage occupation listed in Appendix K

- They will be sponsored in some identified codes within the creative sector, such as artists, dancers, product and clothing designers

Whenever one of these scenarios applies, the Sponsor should add a Sponsor note when assigning the CoS explaining which exception applies and recording the evidence that justifies this conclusion.

The SOC code system

It is very important to ensure that the right SOC code is identified; these are listed in Appendix J. Section 25 of the Guidance gives some detail about the system.

- Simply believing that the role in question is highly skilled is not the issue: the employer must identify the precise SOC code for the job for which they are recruiting and ensure that the role is RQF level 6 or above

- If the planned job title dovetails neatly with an existing SOC code, this should be easy enough; but if it does not, then it may be necessary to search for aspects of the job title within Appendix J until a SOC code that more or less matches the function in question is found

- Remember: the Home Office do not have to accept a bare assertion that a particular job truly reflects the SOC code attributed to it by the employer: they could refuse an application if they feel that the job's content is being exaggerated

- If you can't find a close enough match, then you can email the Office for National Statistics on occupation.information@ons.gov.uk giving the job title, description, and the necessary qualifications

- Occasionally the SOC code system is revised, which means that a role may fall out of the level at which it was originally identified. Migrants whose CoS was assigned before 6 April 2013 can still extend their leave notwithstanding a diminution of their job's SOC code

Casework Tip

Always ensure that Sponsors understand the importance of using the appropriate job title during the course of an employee's sponsored work. Some firms use different job titles for dealing with colleagues and clients (e.g. the word "sales" may be avoided in client communications): this is a recipe for problems though in the event of a compliance audit.

Digital technology jobs

There are some particular conditions to be satisfied before a migrant can be sponsored for digital technology role, set out at Table 5 of Appendix A to the Guidance:

- That the company has between 20 and 250 employees (a smaller company must get a letter from the Dept for International Trade) confirming they have been working with the company vis-á-vis trade of investment activity

- The company must be independent in the UK (i.e. not more than 25% owned by a company with other establishments in the UK where one of those establishments has more than 250 employees; though a firm may be owned partly or wholly by an overseas company with no other branch, subsidiary or other representative in the UK)

- The company must not have been established in the UK for the purpose of supplying services exclusively to another company here

No more than 10 such employees can be sponsored via any kind of CoS, restricted or unrestricted. If a firm expands so it has more than 250 employees, the Home Office must be notified, and no further workers can be recruited under these shortage occupation provisions. However, more migrants may be recruited into the roles so long as the Resident Labour Market Test is carried out.

Rates of pay

Section 26 of the Guidance addresses pay rates. From 6 April 2011, migrants sponsored under Tier 2 (General) and ICT must be paid in line with the relevant minimum. These are set out at Appendix A of the Immigration Rules at Table 11AA for ICTs. Their requirements are:

- £41,500 for long term staff

- £23,000 for graduate trainees

Before 6 April 2017, there was a further sub-category within ICT, for Short-term Staff: there the threshold was £30,000, or £24,800 if the migrant was first sponsored before 24 November 2016.

For Tier 2 (General) (the Immigration Rules at Table 11CA), minimum salary is the *higher* of

- £30,000 or

- The appropriate pay rate in the Appendix J codes of practice

There Appendix J pay rates cater for new entrants to the sector who will inevitably start off with lower earnings. This includes certain public service occupations, medical radiographers, nurses and paramedics, and maths, physics, chemistry, computer science and Mandarin schoolteachers.

If a salary package is subsequently reduced to a level below that stated in the CoS, then the new pay must still meet the minimum level; the SMS must be used to report such a reduction. However, there are some exceptions, such as where the pay cut is down due to taking professional exams, various forms of parental and adoption leave, or a doctor goes abroad to help with the Ebola crisis.

Any changes to salary must be recorded via the SMS; UKVI acknowledge that sometimes circumstances may legitimately change in between the application for a restricted CoS and its allocation; this should be recorded via a Sponsor note. Salary increases are permitted only where this does not take the role into a salary range above that which was advertised.

We discuss pay rates in more detail in Chapter 5: Tier 2 Sponsored Workers under the section *Appropriate salary*.

When a CoS is assigned, these three pieces of information must be given:

- The gross salary figure
- A separate figure for all allowances and guaranteed bonuses
- A breakdown of those allowances and guaranteed bonuses

These figures must not be inflated to take account of any expected tax relief that would be received for a settled worker but not incurred for a migrant. For example, a resident worker might receive £25,000 before tax, whereas a migrant worker would receive £21,000 after tax: the CoS must show the lower amount.

Section 29 of the Guidance sets out other information to be provided in the CoS, which must show full details of when and where the job was advertised, any advertisement reference numbers, and the appropriate Find a job/Jobcentre reference number.

The Resident Labour Market Test

One key feature of the sponsored worker system is the protection of the settled workforce via the Resident Labour Market Test (RLMT). It is generally essential to advertise vacancies in line with the RLMT requirements in order to demonstrate that no settled worker is suitable for the role; and if there are applicants of both kinds, preference must always be given to a settled worker who meets the requirements of the vacancy's skills and experience requirements (even where a migrant worker may be *more* skilled and experienced).

The only exceptions to the RLMT requirement are where the job is exempt from the requirement, because

- The migrant is already working for the employer and are remaining in the same occupation, and needs to extend their leave
- The job is on the shortage occupation list (unless it is a nurse under SOC code 2231, where the RLMT is nevertheless required) and involves at least 30 hours of work a week
- The migrant is applying following studying in the UK in various circumstances, including as a Tier 4 student at degree level or above
- The salary exceeds £159,600

- The post-holder is returning from academic leave having previously held the role as a Tier 2 (General) migrant

- Supernumerary research positions over and above normal staffing requirements

- Postgraduate doctors and dentists in speciality training

- Where the work is for a high value inwards investment post

A CoS must be assigned within six months of the job vacancy first being advertised subject to certain exceptions:

- For university milkround recruitment (within 48 months of the milkround so long as the job was offered to the migrant within 12 months of the recruitment campaign)

- PhD level SOC codes (within 12 months of the recruitment campaign)

- Trainee barristers SOC codes (within 12 months of the pupillage position first being advertised) and

- Orchestral musicians (within 12 months of the date the job was first advertised) (see generally Chapter 29 of the Guidance).

We deal with the RLMT in more detail in Chapter 5: Tier 2 Sponsored Workers.

Applying for a Sponsor licence

Section 3 of the Guidance addresses general considerations arising from the application process, and section 4 sets out the main sector-specific categories and their individual features. The short general guidance *UK Visa Sponsorship for employers* is also helpful.

A would-be Sponsor must register online via the *Online Sponsor application registration* after which they can log into the *Sponsor application log in*. The process is expected to take some 30 minutes. Once the online application has been sent, the original submission sheet must be sent too, signed and dated by the authorising officer, with original or certified copies of all the mandatory documents listed in Appendix A.

If essential items are missing, the application will be treated as invalid, and rejected, with the application fee refunded (though not if consideration was underway when an application is withdrawn: Guidance 1.15). If non-mandatory documents are missing from the application then the Home Office will contact the Applicant by email giving five working days to supply the missing information; an applicant so doing should reply to the email at once to confirm the documents are en route. The authorising officer and key contact should be available over the consideration period, to deal with any forthcoming requests. It is the key contact who will be emailed for further documents and information.

Tier-specific provisions

Information technology jobs

Appendix K lists information technology jobs for Sponsors where the work requires certain experience (e.g. five years of cyber security work) and where the Sponsor meets the appropriate requirements, which are tested via a pre-clearance process.

Religious organisations

Only a bona fide religious organisation may apply for a licence for Tier 2 Ministers of Religion and Tier 5 Temporary Religious Workers. Other requirements are

- Being a registered, excepted or exempt UK charity, or ecclesiastical corporation set up for charitable purposes

- Having the structure for a faith-based community with a common system of beliefs and spiritual goals existing to support and/or propagate common beliefs and practices; the beliefs must include religious or philosophical belief in something transcendental, metaphysical or ultimate, and leave out any political or philosophical belief concerned with man, unless said belief is similar to a religious one

- The organisation does not exclude community membership on gender, nationality or ethnicity grounds; nor breach or encourage others to breach any UK legislation; nor works against the public interest or have a detrimental effect on personal or family life as commonly understood in the UK

- Receives financial and material support from the congregation/community on a voluntary basis, without promise or coercion

Intra-Company Transfer

The Intra-Company Transfer route permits the transfer of staff between two linked companies, which the Guidance styles "entities". A Tier 2 ICT Sponsor must show a direct link by common ownership or control with the overseas entities from which migrants will be brought, shown by one of the following:

- One entity controlling the other's board's composition or half the maximum number of votes at the other's General Meeting

- Holding more than half the issue share capital of the other

- A common parent that itself or through other entities meets the above requirements vis-á-vis the two entities comprising the ICT arrangements

- One entity being related to the other as both are party to a joint venture agreement, or one is formed by the joint venture agreement to which the other is party, or they would be so party were their country of operation to permit such ventures

- Both entities are accountancy or law firms, and one is related to the other by agreement allowing both to use a trademark registered or established under UK law and the jurisdiction of the other entity's country of operation – or where the relationship by agreement allows both to run under the same name in the UK and in the jurisdiction of the other entity's country of operation

- If the entities are unincorporated associations, the receiving one may be considered to be a linked company if it is a registered company and its Articles of Association with the sending entity show a relationship of control, e.g. one member has the power to appoint the other's trustees

- If the link between the two transferring entities arises from the ownership of shares in both by an individual, then that individual must own a majority of shares in both

Where the firms are involved in a joint venture, the Home Office must be assured there is a genuine migrant vacancy: several pieces of evidence will be required. Informal agreements are not enough – the venture must be operating and the vacancy must already exist. Additionally, some or all of the following may be required:

- References from Companies House and confirmation of the entities involved and of the owners of the new company

- Public announcements of the joint venture

- A copy of an official letter from the overseas company/investor to Ministers confirming their intention to invest, naming the entities

- A copy of the binding contract or partnership agreement, signed appropriately, between the entities, including the names and positions of the signatories, the investment or ownership agreement, and timescales and phases of the projects

- Where the joint venture has a previous history of working with the DIT, or economic devolved government departments, evidence of the DIT listing may be accepted

When a CoS is assigned under the ICT route, the Sponsor guarantees that the job is an Intra-Company Transfer, that the migrant has previously been employed for the specified period before the move, that if they are being paid other than in sterling then the salary rate on the CoS has been appropriately converted via the www.oanda.com website, and that they will be paid at least the appropriate rate, including relevant allowances.

Sportspersons (Tier 2) and Creative and Sporting (Tier 5)
Here the Sponsor must be an events or other kind of organiser aiming to work in the sporting sector, a sporting body or sports club, and must have an endorsement from the Home Office approved sports governing body. This endorsement provides confirmation of the genuineness of the Sponsor and their requirement to bring sportspeople to the UK. Where there is no such governing body, then the Economic Migration Policy team should be emailed, who will contact relevant sports councils and the Department for Culture, Media and Sport, and the Central Council of Physical Recreation, to identify a suitable body.

When a new appropriate governing body is identified, then they will be added to Appendix M – as there are two annual updates typically to the Rules, in April and October, there may be some time to wait. Applications made before that date will fail, and a CoS is only valid for three months once assigned, so timing is crucial.

Once the governing body is identified and their endorsement is agreed, an application may be made for the Sponsor licence, providing all relevant documents under Appendix A, including the sporting body endorsement. The online application only provides for one sport to be identified in the Sporting body endorsement section: other sports can be identified together with the reasons for the number of CoSs sought.

Those migrants using the Creative and Sporting Concession should apply for leave before entering the UK from Ireland (Guidance at 34.22).

Non-EEA trained nurses and midwives
There is a specific regime in place for this class of health professionals (within section 15 of Guidance): they have to register with the Nursing and Midwifery Council (NMC), passing appropriate tests of competence, via a two part exam, Part 1 being a computer-based test taken at Pearson VUE test centres and Part 2 comprising an objective structured clinical examination, available only at NMC-approved test centres.

Where workers are sponsored at SOC Code 2231 for Nurses or Midwives at pre-registration level, they must satisfy the language requirements by reaching 7.0 at the IELTS (or passing the Occupational English test) within the last two years, practised for at least 12 months full time (or an equivalent period part-time), been registered with the licencing authority or registration body and confirm this via the appropriate documents in any country they have worked, achieved a decade of school education before starting post-secondary education in nursing or midwifery training and then registering in their home country at entry level, having passed the NMC eligibility assessment, passed the test of competence and met the registration requirements.

There are detailed provisions for their taking and resitting of exams. The Guidance warns that there are some non-EEA nationals sponsored under Tier 2 (General) on the basis they were to complete the Overseas Nursing Programme and obtain registration with the NMC; if they failed to apply for permission before the scheme closed on 31 March 2015, it is too late to apply now.

Tier 5 Temporary Worker Charity Workers
The Sponsor charity must be a registered, excepted or exempt UK charity in line with the relevant charity legislation in the charity's part of the UK; or an ecclesiastical corporation, established for charitable purposes.

Creative Sector (Tier 5)
The Sponsor must be operating, or intending to operate, in the creative sector: e.g. as a national body, event organiser, producer, venue or agent, or other similar organisation.

Tier 5 Government Authorised Exchange
This route is for migrants coming via approved schemes aiming to share knowledge, experience and best practice. Establishing a new scheme is time consuming, the process taking three to four months for approval, and even then there may be a further wait before migrants can actually be sponsored, because of the need to await formal addition of the scheme to Appendix N, which lists the existing schemes. The January 2018 Guidance was rewritten to emphasise that the central elements of the scheme are endorsement by a government department, and administration by a single overarching Sponsor. The need to avoid proliferation of such schemes means that the fact a government department endorses a scheme does not guarantee UKVI acceptance. The ability of a government department to rigorously police such a scheme will be given particular attention.

There are four steps:

➢ **Step 1: Agree overarching body** – there may be an organisation in the same overall sector which is appropriate, and an applicant should read Appendix N to identify one

➢ **Step 2: Government department/executive agency endorsement** – the prospective overarching body must approach a government authority to ask if they will endorse the scheme. Absent any contact point of their own, they should email the Tier 5 (GAE) team for help in finding one.

  It is necessary to explain to the relevant government authority why the scheme is necessary, its benefits to the sector and the UK, the roles and skill levels of participating migrants and the salaries/payments made to them. If they agree, then their Accounting Officer must write to the UKVI Director for Immigration Operations giving details of the overarching body and confirming that the scheme satisfies all relevant requirements for such schemes and meets their aims or objectives, and that they are satisfied with the Sponsor's ability to meet their duties, and recognising that if large numbers of migrants under the scheme breach the Immigration Rules it may be appropriate to end it.

  Relevant considerations will be that the scheme

  - Must help the government authority meet its published aims or wider objectives

  - Not harm the resident labour market (i.e. roles must be supernumerary, over and above normal staffing requirements and not filling existing vacancies)

- Work must be at RQF level 3 or above, unless part of the EU Lifelong Learning Programme when a lower skill level may be employed

- Meets all relevant UK and EU employment legislation including the National Minimum Wage Act and EU Working Time Directive

- Includes anti-abuse measures

➢ **Step 3: Approval** – the full proposal and relevant government endorsement must be emailed to the UKVI Tier 5 (GAE) Team, who retain the last word on approval, which they will communicate to the endorsing department who will send a copy of the letter so doing to the applicant

➢ **Step 4: Licensing** – once the scheme has been approved, the Sponsor licence may be sought, the applicant sending all relevant documents identified in Appendix A for the application to be validated. As with sportspersons, the need to wait for the scheme's addition to the published bi-annual update of the Immigration Rules, combined with the fact that CoSs are valid only for three months from issue, combines to mean that the timing of the issue of CoSs must be addressed with care.

Tier 5 Temporary Worker International Agreement
This route is for those wishing to sponsor employees of overseas governments or international organisations, or private servants in diplomatic households or for the staff of those working for international organisations. An applicant for the international organisation route must be named on the published *List of international organisations whose employees qualify for exempt entry clearance*.

The Home Office is entitled to seek a limited waiver of diplomatic immunity and inviolability for the purpose of compliance visits to the Sponsor's premises; to be given by the Head of Mission or Head of Organisation. Applications are to be supported by a signed letter from the relevant Head confirming they agree to the application, wish to sponsor migrants under this route and accept the sponsorship requirements.

Contractual Service Suppliers and Independent Professionals
Where the applicant has contracted with an overseas supplier for delivering services under an international trade agreement listed in Appendix F then those coming to deliver such services must be sponsored under the International Agreement sub-category. CoSs may only be assigned for this purpose by a Sponsor holding only this kind of licence.

The skills charge
The Immigration Skills Charge Regulations 2017 provide the legal basis for this regime, the proceeds of which are to be invested in improving the skills of the UK workforce. The skills charge is £1,000 per person, per year. Organisations with charitable status or subject to the small companies regime as set out in the Companies Act 2006 are eligible to pay the "small" charge of £364 per person per year.

The skills charge applies for nationals of non-EEA countries and Switzerland applying for visas exceeding six months (if applying from abroad); and for all visas (if applying to switch/extend leave in the UK). Some classes of worker are exempt:

➢ Those applying for a visa from abroad of less than six months;

➢ A worker sponsored in Tier 2 before 6 April 2017 and is now extending their leave;

➢ A Tier 2 ICT Graduate Trainee

- Tier 4 students switching to Tier 2 (General)
- Tier 2 (General) applicants performing a PhD — level occupation under Appendix J

Family members who are a worker's dependents only have to pay the skills charge if themselves entering the UK in the Tier 2 General/ICT categories.

CoSs are only valid once the full charge has been paid. There will be a reminder from the Home Office, but if payment is not then made within 10 working days, the migrant's immigration application will be refused.

There is provision for refunds:

- Of the whole charge, if the visa application is refused, the application is withdrawn, or the application is granted but the worker never travels or commences work for the Sponsor (refund decisions should be made within 90 days of the Sponsor notifying UKVI via the SMS that the worker did not come to the UK, or within 90 days of the CoS expiry date if no valid immigration application was made, or, where the application is refused, within 90 days of the administrative review deadline or of any such review failing
- Partially, for each *whole* unused six-month period of leave, except where a worker leaves their post during the first year of employment
    - E.g. where a shorter visa is granted than sought
    - A voluntary change of Sponsor, when the first Sponsor will receive the difference between the charge paid and that actually due on the basis of the period worked
    - The worker leaves their post early due to illness, redundancy/dismissal, probation failure, or not obtaining a relevant qualification
- No refund will follow where a worker changes job but stays with the same employer, switches from Tier 2 General/ICT but remains in the same job, or where their leave is curtailed for breach of their leave's conditions, due to their own or their Sponsor's actions

Structure of the Sponsor's organisation

Section 5 of the Guidance discusses business structures. Those organisations which have multiple offices or other business places across the UK, styled as "branches" by the Guidance, have options as to how to apply for Sponsor licences. Thus they may apply for

- A national licence for head office and all branches
- Separate licences for each branch
- A licence covering a particular region with several branches

The Home Office may request evidence of the common ownership or control said to unite the branches – they require the same kinds of evidence as identified above in the context of assessing the relationship between parties to Intra-Company Transfer.

Where licences are the subject of action by the Home Office:

- A branch may not be added to a Sponsor licence where the licence-holding branch has had its licence suspended for the time being, or revoked within the last 12 months (a B-rated Sponsor can no longer add branches to its licence (5.2); this change was introduced in January 2018).

- Where one branch has its licence revoked or downgraded, the others will face investigation, although no automatic sanction will be imposed against them.

- Where a licence for head office and branches is revoked, this will apply to all branches nationally

- Evidence of previous abuse or non-compliance will be considered, and its background, when future applications from individual branches within an organisation are considered

There are some limitations on the form of work which is carried out.

- **Employment agencies/intermediaries**: these may only sponsor workers who are directly employed by the agency itself, not for those who are then supplied as labour onwards to another organisation, under any kind of contractual arrangement. A Sponsor wishing to employ a migrant worker provided to them by such a business can do so only where they themselves have genuine responsibility for deciding all the duties, functions and outcomes, or outputs of the job done by the migrant, and for agreeing and paying their salary

- **Franchises**: where one business controls franchises, then they may be licensed in the same way as a head office and branches; however where the franchises are not under the common control of a parent business, then separate licences are required

Example

Rashid is a Tier 2 worker in the IT sector. His Sponsor plans to subcontract him to another firm to carry out particular duties there.

His Sponsor needs to tread carefully. It is possible to have time-limited subcontracting of sponsored workers, but the Guidance repeatedly rules out the mere provision of "labour" or a Sponsor working as a disguised employment agency. So the less control that the Sponsor has over a subcontracted worker, then the more chance they have of a compliance visit taking a dim view of their arrangements.

Key personnel

Section 6 of the Guidance sets out the system of key personnel. There are four key roles:

- Authorising officer
- Key contact
- Level 1 user
- Level 2 user

Only the level 1 and 2 users have access to the SMS once the licence is granted; persons given the other roles will have to be set up as such if they seek access.

Key personnel must

- ➢ Be based permanently in the UK for the duration of the role
- ➢ Meet criminal conviction requirements
- ➢ Be a paid member of the Sponsor's staff, or an office holder (e.g. holding their role under a statutory appointment, such as company directors/secretaries, board members, appointments under the organisation's constitution such as treasurers and secretaries, or a trustee under a trust deed) with the Sponsor, subject to these exceptions:
    - A level 1 or 2 user may be an employee of a third party organisation to whom human resources functions have been contracted, though as of 6 November 2014 new Sponsors must have at least one level 1 user who is an employee, partner or director, an arrangement which is stated to be best practice for existing sponsors too
    - Level 2 users may be supplied to the Sponsor by an employment agency by whom they are employed
    - An overarching Sponsor licenced via the Government Authorised Exchange in Tier 5 may appoint level 2 users within the organisations taking part
    - An insolvency professional appointed following the Sponsor entering administration
    - A UK based representative may fill the key roles save for that of authorising officer, and the representative's staff may be added to the SMS as level 1 or 2 users in order to help assign CoSs; the acts of the representative will be attributed to the Sponsor

Key personnel may not be

- ➢ A representative not based in the UK
- ➢ A contractor/consultant contracted for a specific project
- ➢ Subject to a Bankruptcy of Debt Relief Restriction Order or Undertaking
- ➢ Legally prohibited from being a company director, except that a person in the "key contact" role may be so prohibited so long as that is solely due to them being an undischarged bankrupt
- ➢ Those who have previously been an owner, director, or authorising officer of a Sponsor that has been ordered to pay legal costs (i.e. have failed to pay the expenses of government lawyers when bringing and presumably losing legal proceedings) against the Home Office which have not yet been paid
- ➢ The Home Office reserves the right to check other individuals associated with the business even though they are not key personnel; this will not be automatic, but their conduct may be taken into account when considering what action to take and as part of the application process

The roles of authorising officer, key contact and level 1 user may be filled by the same person. There may only be one authorising officer and key contact, though further level 1 users can be appointed once the licence is granted.

- Contact details including a secure email address (i.e. accessible by them alone) must be given for key personnel, both on the original application and when new ones are added or changes made; the address must be the main office address, or any branch or head office that is covered by the licence (if a representative is the key contact, then they must provide their main business address)

- If checks made against these key personnel ever reveal unspent criminal convictions for relevant offences (being the offences listed in Annex 7: basically serious ones, such as manslaughter, causing grievous bodily harm, using firearms with criminal intent, holding indecent images of children and sexual offences with children and vulnerable persons, terrorism offences, including attempts to commit such offences), declared on the application or not, or receipt of civil penalties, the present application will be refused (or an existing one revoked), and will not be accepted subsequent nominations for those already granted licences

A SMS user must not assign a CoS to themselves or to a close relative or partner (these are exhaustively defined at 6.12 of the Guidance). At least one SMS user must be a settled worker, unless the Sponsor is a diplomatic mission or international organisation licensed under Tier 5 (Temporary Workers) International Agreement, or the authorising officer has leave as a Representative of an Overseas Business, or under Tier 1 (as a Graduate or full Entrepreneur, or under the Exceptional Talent route).

The **authorising officer** role must be filled for the life of the licence, with the holder always meeting the Guidance's requirements. Despite the role's importance, the holder does not get automatic access to the SMS: they have to be set up as a level 1/2 user, on the application or subsequently, if this is required. They must be

- The most senior person responsible for recruitment of all migrant workers and ensuring that Sponsor duties are met

- A person who full understands the role's importance and has a system in place to check the activities of SMS users

- Responsible for deciding which staff may access the SMS and their level of permission, and for the activities of all SMS users

The **key contact** is usually the main contact between the Sponsor and the Home Office, though the latter may revert to the authorising officer if they require. The key contact needs to be named as a level 1/2 user to get access.

The **level 1** user can be the authorising officer or another person in the organisation. They carry out daily activities under the SMS.

- Only one may be nominated initially, being an employee, director or partner, or office holder, or employee of a third party organisation engaged to deliver human resources services, or a UK-based representative

- Subsequently others can be added, though all will be vetted against the police national computer

- The Guidance advises against having more level 1 users than strictly necessary, taking account of periods of leave or sickness

- They must not be a contractor, consultant contracted for a specific project, a temporary staff member supplied by an employment agency, or an undischarged bankrupt

Level 1 users can perform these SMS actions:

- Request more level 1 users and add/remove level 2 users, and change user details
- Assign CoSs to workers, and withdraw them
- Request an increase in the allocated CoSs
- Report minor changes in details, changes of work addresses
- Report changes of circumstances
- Report worker activity (e.g. not coming to work)
- View licence and key personnel information, and use the bulk data transfer feature
- Access key messages posted by the Home Office
- Apply for a licence renewal and track its progress
- Apply for premium customer service and track that application's progress

Level 2 users have fewer permissions than level 1 users. Their activities are limited to assigning CoSs and reporting worker activities. They may hold the same organisational roles as for level 1 users, and may additionally be temporary staff from an employment agency. However they may not be contractors, project-specific contracted consultants or undischarged bankrupts.

Example

James is the authorising officer for Oasis Enterprises. He is the Director of the Human Resources Department. He is set to take paternity leave.

Because it is essential to have an authorising officer in place at all times, James's departure poses a challenge: whenever the current incumbent takes long-term leave, a Sponsor needs to appoint someone else to fill the role, even though this may only be a temporary arrangement.

Criteria for granting a Sponsor licence

The key overriding requirements are expressed as Eligibility and Suitability, rather like the structure of the more modern immigration routes. Section 7 of the Guidance explains the eligibility and suitability criteria by which an application is assessed, and section 8 explains the supporting evidence that is required, in turn referring to the detailed documentary requirements set out in Appendix A to the Guidance.

Although certified copy documents may be sent with the application, they may only be certified by the issuing authority, a practising barrister, solicitor, notary, or chartered accountant (the latter for financial documents);

they may not be related to the Sponsor, in a personal relationship with them or living with them, or employed by them (this latter change, at 8.3, was introduced in January 2018).

Eligibility criteria

It is necessary to supply the documents listed in Appendix A to the Guidance. The overall objective is to ensure that this is a genuine business with an operating or trading presence in the UK.

There are a series of Tables which list the relevant documents that must be provided. Beyond these, a putative Sponsor must explain:

- Why it is applying for a sponsor licence
- The sector it operates in
- Its opening/operating hours during the week
- Everyone with access to the email address supplied on the application

It must provide an up to date hierarchy chart detailing any owner, director and board members. If the business has 50 employees or fewer, it must list all employees and set out the names and titles of all staff.

It should identify the jobs wished to be filled via CoSs, including the

- Job title and Standard Occupational Classification (SOC) code
- Duties of each job
- Where each job sits on the hierarchy chart referred to above
- The salary guaranteed for each job were it vacant
- Where any migrant has already been identified as a putative sponsored employee (including existing workers), their full name, birth date, nationality, current job title and duties, immigration status, and three monthly pay slips where already working

Supporting documents

There is no substitute for working one's way through the relevant tables. We do not give their full detail here, just an overview.

Table 1 sets out that:

- A public body that appears in the corporate report Public bodies 2013 summary data' on GOV.UK does not have to send any documents
- A public body that does not appear there must send confirmation from its sponsoring government department stating that it is a public body, or a link to the government department website if the public body is listed there
- Government departments, local authorities and companies listed on the London Stock Exchange main market need not send documents

Table 2 explains that, in general, four pieces of evidence are required (an online check by the Home Office will count as one):

- Start-ups (firms operating for less than 18 months on the application date) must provide evidence of having a current, corporate bank account with a FCA-registered bank — plus any mandatory information from Table 3

- Start-ups must also produce a total of four documents listed in Tables 1-4 (that number may include a Table 3 document as just mentioned) — these include, in Table 2, VAT registration certificates, a letter from their corporate banking provider, letters from the Dept of International Trade or similar body confirming the business has a demonstrable business relationship

- Franchises must provide their franchise agreement signed by both parties

- For entities that are registered and inspected by a regulatory body (e.g. nursing care homes, financial insurance businesses, healthcare and medical providers), they may simply identify the body if it is listed in Table 2, or otherwise give verifiable online or documentary evidence of their registration and their last inspection report (the Guidance explains that each branch must provide evidence of inspection records)

- Similarly food businesses registered/approved by a food authority must provide their food hygiene rating via the *Scores on the Doors* scheme

- Charities must explain their registration arrangements under the relevant charity legislation

Table 3 lists the mandatory information required that is relevant to the immigration route in question (e.g. an endorsement from a sport's governing body; for Tier 5 International Agreement cases proof of the contract under an international trade agreement; confirmation of the Government Authorised Exchange arrangements from the endorsing government department; various details of the religion, connection to parent organisation, and the congregation, for a faith body seeking religious workers; and so on).

Table 4 lists various additional documents that can be used to bring the total documents supplied up to the required four: evidence of employer's liability insurance cover for at least £5m from an authorised insurer; FCA or Stock Exchange listing; HMRC registration for the self-employed and partners; current financial report or audited annual report from their accountant; acknowledgment of the Company Tax Return; a HMRC self-assessment return; evidence of local authority planning permission for their class of business at their trading address; proof of ownership of their business premises; an alcohol licence for their premises; and a letter from the bank.

Example

The luxury restaurant Esmerelda is going through the Sponsor application process. It is a registered company. It wishes to employ a business development manager to improve its marketing. The restaurant was established four years ago. It is not a franchise.

As this role will be under Tier 2 (General), the firm must provide the usual justification of why it needs this role. Beyond this, it must identify the relevant documents from the Tables in Appendix A:

- A restaurant does not feature in Table 1, so we can move onwards in Tier 2 (General)

- It is not a start-up or franchise, so none of the criteria relevant to such businesses in Table 2 apply

- However being a food business, it must be approved with a relevant authority: restaurants must **register** with the local council. As the business involves handling meat, fish, egg or dairy products, it must be inspected and approved by its local council. However, the Food Hygiene Ratings given via the *Scores on the Doors* system will suffice to meet this requirement, according to Table 2: so this is the first of the minimum of 4 documents

- Table 3 addresses requirements for categories other than Tier 1 General

- As so far just one document has been identified, three more are required, and these must be identified from the list in Table 4: likely candidates are employer's liability insurance, evidence of registration with HMRC, company tax returns, the accounts produced by an accredited accountant, proof of ownership of the lease, bank statements or an alcohol licence

- Any other essential documents for the firm's legal operation are required, e.g. planning permission for restaurant usage where the local question requires this

- And don't forget, from January 2018 employees of the company may no longer certify copy documents

Make sure the restaurant does not offer a take-away service: this rules it out from being a licensed Sponsor.

Suitability criteria

The Home Office assesses suitability based on the systems in place and the likelihood of the sponsored migrants fulfilling genuine vacancies:

- Demonstrable human resource and recruitment systems

- An ability for the Home Office to make conduct visits and conduct checks to ensure duties are being complied with, which may require access being guaranteed to a third party's premises if sponsored workers will be deployed there

- A genuine vacancy meeting the criteria of the relevant category: this may require inspection of contracts, and if there is minimal office space or a virtual office then the systems in place must provide assurance that the employee's duties can be properly monitored

- Relevant unspent criminal convictions and evidence of any previous non-compliance (applicants must also reveal pending criminal prosecutions, awareness of any involvement with an organisation that has failed to pay VAT or excise duties, or if the proposed Sponsor has been suspended/removed from a Sponsor register in the last five years)

When documents are provided, then the original must be sent or a copy certified "to be a true copy of the original seen to me" by the issuing authority, a solicitor, barrister, notary or a chartered accountant (for financial documents) whose identity is verifiable.

The decision making process

The Home Office will assess the risks based on their experience. They may conduct a site visit to the registered office or any other physical address where migrants might work. Any differences between the situation on the ground and that portrayed in the application are likely to lead to a refusal. If they have concerns about the application, they may make extra checks beyond these (and beyond those associated with the eligibility criteria above; there are also quality assurance measures in place which mean that a percentage of applicants will undergo further checks in any event).

The criteria for refusing applications are set out in Annex 1 and 2, respectively addressing mandatory and discretionary refusal reasons.

These are the Annex 1 mandatory refusal reasons:

- **Dishonesty**, by sending a false document (prosecution may also ensue) (1(a))
- **Sponsorship failings**:
  - Failing to meet a requirement of the relevant tier or category (1(b)) including failing to meet one of the criteria for employing a migrant under the shortage occupation categories (1(r))
  - Failing to have adequate administrative processes in place to meet Sponsorship duties (1(n))
  - Failing to show that resident workers could not satisfy the work requirements (1(o))
  - Having no UK operating or trading presence (1(p))
  - Failing to meet the safeguarding children requirements (1(q))
- **Civil penalties**:
  - For employing one or more illegal workers where the fine was at the maximum (post objections and appeal rights): for 12 months after the penalty was issued (without a fine) or of the fine being imposed (1(c))
  - For giving a residential tenancy to an adult disqualified from such due to their immigration status (where still liable post objections and appeal rights): for 12 months after the penalty was issued (without a fine) or of the fine being imposed (1(d))
  - For not paying an outstanding civil penalty for employing an illegal worker (1(e)) or for giving a residential tenancy to an adult disqualified from such due to their immigration status (1(f))
  - For having been issued a civil penalty in relation to the Appendix C offences (see above where we address the bars on making further applications) (1(g))
- **Criminality**: for the unspent criminal convictions listed (1(h))
- **Regulatory issues**:
  - For being legally prohibited from becoming a company director subject to one of the exemptions (i.e. unless only being such because of being an undischarged bankrupt or subject to a Debt Relief Order) (1(i))

- Having previously had a Sponsor licence revoked (in the last 12 months: i.e. this refers to the post-revocation "cooling-off" period) (1(j))

➢ **Application failures**:

- Where there was a refusal in the last six months for not meeting a relevant requirement in the category applied under, sending a false document, lacking relevant processes to comply with Sponsor duties, having an unspent criminal conviction, a legal prohibition from being a company director, or having no UK trading presence (1(k))

- Because the application was sent by a representative rather than the would-be Sponsor (1(l))

- Where a further supporting document is sought but not supplied (1(m))

These are the Annex 2 discretionary refusal reasons:

➢ **Regulatory issues**:

- The OISC having removed the authorisation of the applicant or of an organisation in which they were involved (2(c))

- Receiving a penalty for not paying VAT or duty (2(e))

- Receiving sanctions from the EU or UN (2(j))

- Having on board a business owner, director or authorising officer of a Sponsor institution that has been ordered to pay costs to the Home Office in legal proceedings which have not been paid (2(k))

- The conduct of associated persons, such as responsible employees not directing, financing or being key personnel, will not be routinely assessed, but the Home Office reserve the right to ask for information about them

➢ **Sponsorship failings**:

- Previous history of poor or non-compliance with Sponsorship duties or work permit arrangements (2(a)) – depending on its seriousness, how long ago it took place and any mitigating circumstances, the involvement of associated persons who have been employed or associated with an organisation that has lost its Sponsor licence in the last five years, and previous criminal conduct having a bearing on suitability

- Failing to provide requested information (2(b))

- Previously being named as key personnel at a Sponsor organisation whose licence was revoked in whole or part in the last 12 months (2(i))

- **Civil penalties**:
  - For receiving a charge or penalty for employing one or more illegal workers in the last five years (2(g))
  - For a civil penalty for giving a residential tenancy to an adult disqualified from such due to their immigration status in the last five years (2(h))
- **Criminality**: having an unspent conviction for an offence considered relevant to Sponsor duties (2(f))

Document checking

There is a standard procedure for verifying documents, with the issuing organisation, and with other government departments in the UK and overseas. A standard form is used to record the results, and the Home Office will wait for up to three weeks for the information to be forthcoming. They may decide that a compliance officer should make a visit. The possible results of their enquiries are that the document checks:

- Confirm it as genuine; in which case the application will be considered as normal
- Confirm it as false; in which case the application will be refused, whether or not the document is essential to the application
- Are inconclusive; in which case the document will not be taken into account, and they may revert for further supporting documents

Sponsor ratings

Section 9 of the Guidance gives an overview of the sponsor rating system; section 18, addressed in Chapter 8: *Tier 2 and 5 Sponsors – Compliance Issues*, deals with downgrading. A Sponsor will be A-rated when their application is granted: indeed, if they do not achieve this ranking, the application will not be granted. If evidence subsequently comes to light that they are no longer able or willing to meet their Sponsor duties, the Home Office may take action, including downgrading them to a B-rating. Normally the rating is the same for all tiers in which the Sponsor is registered, although exceptionally there might be a partial B-rating.

Ratings are assessed by a scoring system, against the criteria of

- **Human resources systems** indicating the leave status of migrants and systems in place for monitoring attendance at work
- **Convictions and civil penalties** – unspent criminal convictions and having received a civil penalty
- **Migrant compliance** – ensuring migrants are not in breach of any requirements of their leave (e.g. students working excess hours)
- **Employment** – for Tier 2 (General), whether the work offered is genuine employment meeting the appropriate skill level with the appropriate pay rate (the examples in the Guidance are small businesses with no history of filling the skilled role for which a licence is now sought)

Any failing on these points will lead to refusal.

When the decision is made, it will confirm the application's approval or refusal, the reasons for a refusal, and the maximum number of CoSs that may be assigned. Where the Sponsor is uncertain of whether it will actually recruit migrant workers, then the CoS allocation will be set at zero.

The Guidance lists the precise circumstances where an application will be refused – not meeting the relevant Sponsor requirements for the category applied under, sending false documents, not having the necessary processes in places to meet the Sponsor duties, having a relevant unspent conviction, being legally prohibited from becoming a company director, or having no trading presence in the UK.

Cooling-off periods

There are a series of bars on making further applications (10.4) (including the situation where an application that would have been likely to be refused is withdrawn pre-decision):

- In general, a six month cooling-off period before a new application can be made

- Following a refusal because a previous sponsor licence was revoked from 6 November 2014, or surrendered after that date following notification of compliance action, then the cooling-off period is 12 months

- Refusal for having a civil penalty results in a 12 month cooling-off period before another application is made

- Appendix C to the Guidance lists civil penalties for certain *charges or penalties* of particular severity; refusal on some of these grounds means that no further application should be made for five years. These matters are: carrying clandestine entrants or passengers without proper documents (sections 23 & 40 of the Immigration and Asylum Act 1999; and bringing a passenger to the United Kingdom in breach of an authority to carry scheme (Reg 24 of the Counter-Terrorism and Security Act 2015 and the Authority to Carry (Civil Penalties) Regulations 2015)

- There is no cooling-off period where the refusal is because the application was sent by a representative or requested documents were not provided within the stated deadline for reasons beyond the Sponsor's control.

Example

Aardvark Enterprises has made a Sponsor application which has been refused. The Directors seek advice as to how long the cooling-off period will be.

It is first essential to identify the reasons for refusal, of course: they tell you that they were informed the application was refused because of human resource systems failures.

Essentially the firm has been refused because they do "not have the processes necessary to comply with your Sponsor duties". This carries a six month ban. The period runs from the date of the letter refusing the application.

However, when you take full instructions, it transpires that the firm had previously held a licence which was suspended nine months ago and which they had then surrendered during the subsequent enquiry. As this is post-November 2014, the ban runs from a year from the date UKVI confirmed they were accepting the licence's surrender, so there must be a few months still to run.

Error correction requests

Decisions sent after 1 April 2016 attract a review process on the *Error Correction Request Form.*

- The request must be made within 14 calendar days of the refusal letter's date, and the Home Office aim to respond within 28 working days of its receipt

- The process concentrates on whether there has been simple caseworker error (e.g. miscalculation of the six month cooling off period) or on whether documents have been overlooked – it is restricted to the evidence sent with the application, and will not look at any further evidence

- Where such an error is identified, the applicant will need to make a new fee-paid online application, albeit that the fee will be refunded on receipt

- The reconsideration will not necessarily result in a grant, merely a decision free from the error that was identified

Premium and priority services

Two fee paid services offer speedier or tailored assistance:

- The premium customer service allocates a dedicated account manager to provide tailored advice and support

- The priority change of circumstances service gives faster consideration of those requests

The Sponsorship Management System (SMS)

Section 11 of the Guidance explains the SMS – there are also a whole set of SMS user manuals which give very detailed instructions on its use. The SMS records

- The Sponsor's users and their access levels

- News and messages sent to Sponsors

- Changes of circumstances duly reported by the Sponsor

SMS users must never share their password with anyone else.

Changes of circumstance

Reporting changing circumstances via the SMS

Section 12 of the Guidance lays out the processes for reporting changes of circumstances; section 13 goes on to explain the reporting of changes to the organisation including mergers and takeovers. The level 1 user must use the *request changes to Sponsor details* function on the SMS to report:

- Changes to the name, address, and the identity or details of the key contact or authorising officer (licence name changes are important because they may bring a need for a new licence, e.g. where there is a merger or takeover) – note that it is necessary to change the working address for key personnel separately from the firm's change of address

- Changes to the structure: e.g. more branches/sites, new linked entities here or overseas (where licenced under Tier 2 (ICT)); or to the organisation, e.g. takeovers and mergers, sales of all or part of the business – and changes to business size from small to large, or vice versa (this change was introduced in January 2018)

- Changes to the status of any necessary registration by a governing body

- Convictions of relevant offences: these are those listed in the box in Annex 5, essentially all offences under the immigration legislation, plus espionage/terrorism, dishonesty (theft, corruption, deception and fraud), tax or excise duty avoidance, bribery, proceeds of crime and money laundering

- Licence changes: e.g. adding or removing a representative, surrendering the licence

Example

Emerald Enterprises, a licensed Sponsor, changes its main workplace. It records this on the SMS, however the contact details for named SMS users are left unaltered, although they moved to the new office.

The firm is in trouble if it is audited for compliance before this is corrected. It may seem like a minor error, but combined with other failings, it might be relied on to justify compliance action.

Oasis Enterprises recently opened a new subsidiary in Armenia. They decide to transfer a key employee from that overseas company to the UK. They check with their lawyer whether this is feasible.

One important thing to check is whether the new subsidiary has been reported on the SMS: were UKVI to learn of it only at the same time an application is made for a restricted CoS, they would be unimpressed.

Some changes may need to be accompanied by a signed declaration, e.g. surrendering the licence or replacing an authorising officer.

Reporting via the change of circumstances form
Sometimes it will not be feasible to report a change of circumstances, e.g. replacing the level 1 user, key contact or authorising officer when the person who has just left was the only SMS user. Accordingly the change of circumstances form must be used.

The submission sheet and supporting documents
However reporting is done, the Home Office may require a submission sheet to be completed, for the signed declaration and any supporting documents to be provided. This must all be done within 10 working days.

Insolvency, voluntary and debts arrangements
Where a firm enters administration or receivership, it is necessary to inform the administrator/receiver that the firm is a Sponsor, and to notify the Home Office within 20 days of entry into the process. The insolvency professional appointed to the administrator/receiver role must be appointed as the new authorising officer, either by the level 1 user making the change if the administrator/receiver is happy for them to retain that role, otherwise by using the *change of circumstances* form, marked clearly that the firm is now "*in administration*". The same form should be used for recording other changes.

Where a firm enters a company voluntary arrangement (CVA), it must inform the Home Office within 20 days, including whether this results in a change of ownership.

- If there is an ownership change, then the licence will be revoked, the matter being treated as if the business had been sold; the new owner must apply for a Sponsor licence within 20 days of the takeover if they wish to do so

- If the CVA represents an agreement with creditors without an ownership change, then the firm may keep its licence; if it was previously insolvent, it may now remove the administrator from the authorising officer position and replace them – the same applies with debt management/arrangement plans

Where a firm enters liquidation or sequestration, the Home Office must be told within 20 working days of ceasing trading, via an email to the Sponsor Compliance team if the SMS can no longer be accessed.

Where sole traders enter into an individual voluntary arrangement or debt arrangement scheme, they must tell the Home Office within 20 working days. The same rules apply regarding sale of the business: they must notify the Home Office of the sale within 20 working days, but if they are retaining ownership, they may keep their licence. Where a sole trader goes bankrupt, they must notify the Home Office on the same basis, and email the Sponsor Compliance team, whereupon their licence will be revoked.

Mergers, takeovers, etc.

If the Sponsor is involved in a change of ownership, it may have to make appropriate arrangements for its licence.

It is necessary to report ownership changes, mergers, takeovers and de-mergers. A failure to report can lead to action being taken both against the Sponsor and the migrants, whose leave might be curtailed.

The level 1 user must report the change via the SMS; or the new level 1 user where the Sponsor has been taken over, or merged into, another organisation which has a Sponsor licence. Where there is a change in direct ownership, as where it is sold as a going concern or shares are sold to a new owner, then the Sponsor licence will be revoked, unless sponsored migrants are moved over to another Sponsor's licence in whichcase it will be made dormant.

If TUPE or similar (e.g. certain public sector arrangements) protection is triggered when a sponsored worker moves to an existing Sponsor, the latter takes up full responsibility for them and must meet all relevant duties. Where sponsored workers move to an employer without a licence (or without one covering this tier/category of worker), the new employer must apply for one within 20 working days of the move. Failure to take this step or the refusal of the application for a licence will mean that workers have their leave curtailed to 60 calendar days.

Sponsored workers do not need to make a new application for leave in this situation, and the new Sponsor does not need to assign a new CoS to them, unless

- There is no TUPE or similar protection

- The migrant changes their job

Where there is a **complete takeover or merger**, then a Sponsor which is being subsumed must

- Report the change within 20 working days via the SMS, including all details of sponsored migrants moving to a new organisation

- Report any sponsored migrants who are not moving: their leave will be curtailed to 60 days

- Confirm whether they are surrendering their Sponsor licence

The Sponsor taking over

- Must make a valid application for a Sponsor licence within 20 working days
- Use the SMS to apply for an increased CoS allocation if their licence lacks sufficient CoSs to absorb the new sponsored migrants
- Report the change via SMS within 20 working days (limited access to the former Sponsor's SMS may be provided so the new Sponsor can report relevant migrant activity)

Where there is a partial **takeover or merger**, then the existing Sponsor must report the change within 20 working days including details of migrants moving to the new organisation, and confirming whether it wishes to surrender its licence. If it wishes to keep its options open for the future, the Home Office will reduce the CoS allocation to zero. The new Sponsor must conduct the same steps as above for full mergers. They will have to report on their new sponsored migrants via an email to the Tier 2 and 5 Migrant Reporting Team, having no SMS record for them, providing the old Sponsor organisation's name, licence number, details of migrants and any essential migrant reporting.

There are some useful flowcharts in Annex 8 giving further help on mergers and takeovers.

Sponsor duties

The duties begin from the time a licence is granted and end upon its surrender or revocation. In this Chapter we introduce the relevant duties; Chapter 8:, *Tier 2 and 5 Sponsors – Compliance Issues*, gives a much more detailed account of the consequences when things go wrong.

The key objectives of the Sponsor duties (Guidance section 14) are to

- Prevent abuse of assessment procedures
- Capture early patterns of migrant behaviour of concern
- Address possible weaknesses in processes
- Monitor compliance with the Immigration Rules

The Sponsor's responsibility for a particular migrant ends when:

- They notify UKVI they are no longer sponsoring them for any reason
- They leave the UK and their leave lapses
- They are granted further leave to remain with another Sponsor or they enter another immigration category meaning they no longer require sponsorship

Record keeping duties

There is a general obligation to keep records of the sponsored migrants' details (15.1-15.5):

- A photocopy or electronic copy of the passport/worker authorisation or UK immigration status document and biometric residence permit (where available: BRPs were introduced in 2008) showing their entitlement to work and period of leave
- Contact details (telephone including mobile, UK residential address)

- Records of the recruitment practices under which they were recruited, including evidence such as the Resident Labour Market Test – including details of any third party intermediary involved in assisting the Sponsor in recruitment (or the Graduate Entrepreneur selection process where the sponsor is a higher education institution endorsing a person in this category)
- Parental consent letters if the migrant is aged under 18 (for the child's application, travel, reception and care arrangements)

Casework Tip

Although employers need to be vigilant about why they employ, they must always remember they are subject to discrimination law. Under the Equality Act, it is unlawful to discriminate against a job applicant or employee on the basis of their race, which includes: colour; nationality (including citizenship); ethnic origin; or national origin.

So a firm with truly robust policies will ensure that its staff engaged in recruitment do not wrongly exclude candidates because of suspicions are that discriminatory.

Certain documents must be retained (Guidance section 16):

- There is no proscribed method for so doing so long as they are available to UKVI on request
- This includes such documents as are necessary to avoid employing those not entitled to work
- As a document holder, the Sponsor will have obligations under the Data Protection Act
- Documents must be retained for the shorter period of (a) one year from the date sponsorship ends or (b) the point at which a compliance officer examines and approves them once the migrant is no longer sponsored (Appendix D)

The full Guidance on retaining document copies is found in *Appendix D: keeping documents guidance for sponsors*. Copies must be kept of the following documents:

- Current passport pages showing stamps recording leave, or an immigration status document recording entitlement to work for the Sponsor; if there is no evidence of the entry date, then other evidence such as a boarding pass or ticket should be kept (documents need not be retained where the migrant works for less than a day for the Sponsor)
- The biometric residence permit
- A Croatian national's Purple Registration Certificate showing their right to work for this Sponsor (however special arrangements for Croatian nationals ended on 30 June 2018, so these will only be of interest for past periods of employment)

- One formal document recording their national insurance number, e.g. from DWP, HMRC or a wage slip
- A history of their contact details by way of residential address, telephone numbers
- Appropriate consent letters for a child migrant
- Disclosure and Barring Service check where required
- Records of absences, electronically or manually
- Any other document set out in the relevant code of practice
- For Tier 5 (Temporary Worker) International Agreement to sponsor Contractual Service Suppliers or Independent Professionals, contracts for the supply of services and evidence of how the contract was awarded, via tender or otherwise

Additionally, evidence must be retained showing the adequacy of the RLMT:

- Sufficient documents to prove that a rolling recruitment was operated, where applicable including the period of the recruitment exercise
- Copy of journal or newspaper adverts clearly showing the title and date of the publication and the closing date for applications
- For university milkrounds, a letter from each university, on their headed paper, confirming the milkround, the dates it was conducted and method used, e.g. presentation and/or interviews
- Copy of the contents of the job advert including the job title, its location, the main duties and responsibilities including the skills, qualifications and experience needed, an indication of the salary package or salary range and the closing date for applications
- For website adverts, a screenshot showing the website name, URL, date, advert contents and the application closing date – if the website is not the Sponsor's own, evidence showing they placed the relevant advertisement via invoice or letter from the website
- For Jobcentre Plus/Online adverts, a screenshot showing the logo of the government website hosting it, advert contents, the Job ID number or Job Reference number, the date, the closing date of the recruitment, and the URL for Find a Job vacancies
- A screenshot for any advertising required by the Financial Conduct Authority
- The governing body endorsement for sportspeople under Tier 2 or Tier 5
- For a sponsored researcher under Tier 2 (General), evidence of the competitive process that took place
- For all recruitments, all shortlisted applications including CVs, emails and application forms including personal details, the names and total number of applicants short listed for final interview, and for

each settled worker who was rejected, interview notes which show the reasons why they have not been employed

And these records must be kept for records of earnings:

- Payslips, clearly showing the name, NI number, tax code, any allowances paid and deductions made – or records of drawings and profit-share for partners

- Evidence corroborating receipt of those earnings, e.g. outgoing bank statement transfers in their name (unnamed transfer records are not sufficient) (this evidence is not required for contractual service providers)

- Contracts of employment or for services, showing names and signatures of all parties involved, start and end date, details of the job/work in question, and an indication of pay

- Allowances must be recorded if part of the salary package, via the contract, or payslips, or via other evidence showing their value (Appendix D gives examples of paying for accommodation: if owned by the Sponsor, an independent valuation of the rental value is needed, if paid for by the Sponsor, a statement from the landlord of the rent paid) – the provision of rent-free accommodation is a benefit in kind which must be included in the sums set out in the CoS (see for example Manzay Ltd [2016] EWHC 2582 (Admin))

- Any document required by the relevant Code of Practice

These records must show the skill level:

- A detailed and specific job description outlining the duties and responsibilities of the post including the skills, qualifications and experience required for the post (unless the job advert contains all this information) (this requirement is for CoSs allocated from 19 November 2015)

- Copies of any qualifications required for the skill level in question (though not for Contractual Service Suppliers or Independent Professionals sponsored under Tier 5 (Temporary Worker) International Agreement)

- Where no RLMT was conducted, confirmation of the qualifications showing they had the appropriate skill and experience, which may include previous employer's references (from 19 November 2015)

- Copies of any registration and/or professional accreditation documents and/or any confirmation letter, e.g. GMC registration for doctors, and sports bodies endorsements for sportspersons

- Details of the migrants' technical or specialist skills for those coming to the UK under the entourage provisions in the Creative and Sporting sub category of Tier 5

- Copies or originals of the evidence underlying the selection process and assessment of a Graduate Entrepreneur endorsed by the Sponsor

Casework Tip

Ensure that HR departments look at the background to an appointment. Here are a couple of "red flags" to look out for:

- **If a person is appointed having previously been present as a Tier 1 Entrepreneur, bear in mind that the expectation when they were granted that visa was that they were setting up their own business to make a contribution to the UK economy, not that they were going to become a full time sponsored worker: their circumstances may have changed, or this job may be temporary and a legitimate step on the road to gaining the experience they need, but either way, explanation may be needed**

- **If the appointee to a job at RQV level 6 had in fact been originally called for interview for a less highly skilled post, a Home Office decision maker may well look at their circumstances with some cynicism, so it would be advisable to keep records of even clearer evidence on the failure of an advertising campaign to produce a settled worker than is otherwise the case**

UKVI is entitled to request any of these documents and take action against the Sponsor if they are not supplied (15.1). This in fact was one of the reasons why the Sponsor in Raj and Knoll [2016] EWCA Civ 770 came unstuck: they had used a recruitment consultant for the advertising. Given that the use of such an intermediary will mean that the adverts do not show the Sponsor's name, it is essential that documents are provided, such as contracts or invoices, to link the Sponsor to the advertising.

Reporting duties

There is a duty to report certain events using the SMS, giving full contact details for the migrant including any known name and address for a new employer, and confirming whether, and why, sponsorship is continuing, where the sponsored migrant (15.6-15.7):

- Does not turn up for their first day of work

- Has their contract of employment or for services terminated before the date provided in the CoS, e.g. due to resignation or dismissal

- No longer requires Tier 2 sponsorship because they move to an immigration route that does not require one

- Is absent for work without pay for four weeks or longer (subject to the reduction in salary provisions) (though not if their absence is due to involvement in lawful strike action)

- Is affected by TUPE or similar protection, as in the case of a merger or demerger

- Is a person to whom information comes to light suggesting they may be breaching the conditions of their leave

- Is absent from work for more than 10 consecutive days without permission (which must be reported within 10 working days of the 10th day of absence)

- Undergoes a significant change of circumstances as to job title, core duties, salary, or location of employment

- Is a Graduate Entrepreneur who has been endorsed, in which case there must be contact at least once very quarter within a 12 month period, and if there is an unpermitted failure by the migrant to maintain contact, this must be reported within three months of the failure

These reporting requirements are taken seriously by UKVI and the courts: for example in Country Court Care [2015] EWHC 2054 (Admin) failing to report the fact that several workers had moved on was treated as "a serious breach of your sponsor duties and severely hinders UKVI in its duty to maintain effective immigration control." In that same case, the Sponsor had recorded that a significant number of care workers worked at its head office: when this was investigated by the Home Office, it transpired that they in fact often worked at the various individual care homes. Their response that they had considered it unrealistic to report individual movements between care homes was considered disingenuous, particularly given that it had represented that "all of the addresses at which they work" were recorded on their CoS.

The Sponsor must report significant changes to their own circumstances, such as selling all or part of the business, stopping trading, entering administration, substantially changing their business's nature, or being involved in a merger/takeover, within 20 days of the event in question (15.7).

A migrant who gives reason to suspect them of criminality or terrorism must be reported to the police.

Complying with the law
The references below to restricted CoSs relate to these migrants:

- Tier 2 (General) workers currently abroad who will be paid less than £159,600 a year and are not in an inward investment post

- Family members (dependants) of Tier 4 migrants who are switching to a Tier 2 visa

There are various stated requirements for complying with the UK's immigration laws:

- Only employing migrants appropriately qualified, registered or experienced for the job, or will be (in the case of Tier 2 migrants) by the time they commence work

- Keeping registration documents, certificates and references confirming this, and providing this on request

- Not employing migrants where they lack experience or permission (including where they no longer have permission) to do the job in question

- Not assigning CoSs where there is no *genuine vacancy* meeting the sponsorship criteria

- Only employing migrants on a shortage occupation list under Appendix K

- Only employing migrants where they intend and are able to fulfil the role in question

- Only assigning a CoS for a role at or above the appropriate skill level identified in the Guidance

- Only allowing the migrant to undertake the specific role identified in their CoS and only assigning a CoS where the migrant is likely to comply with all relevant conditions

- Disclosing the assigning of a CoS to a family member of the business's owner with the sponsor organisation if it is a small or medium sized business (the latter being defined at 24.15 as those with under 250 employees), and to anyone else's family member where it is a large business

- Complying with employment law, e.g. National Minimum Wage and paid holiday entitlement

- Holding suitable planning permission or Local Planning Authority consent to run their business at their trading address, where required

- Being registered with or approved by the appropriate food authority

- Complying with any conditions on a work permit such as rate of pay

- Only employing a migrant who has had a Disclosure and Barring Service check where this is required (generally speaking, when working with children or vulnerable adults, see generally the Regulated activity (adults) guidance)

Example

Oasis Enterprises holds a licence for Tier 2 workers. It has just begun to issue CoSs.

The firm should think carefully about its record-keeping regime. Relevant considerations are:

- **Automating human resources processes**
- **Auditing those processes against the information that must be retained**
- **Training personnel staff about the relevant requirements and how strictly they are interpreted**
- **Finding a rational and accessible way of storing the relevant information, possibly via secure online cloud facilities**
- **Ensuring there is a system in place for updating itself as to changes in the Immigration Rules and the Guidance for Sponsors, because the requirements may subtly alter**
- **Ensuring there is a system in place to update records when a sponsored worker's visa is due to expire, and on the anniversary of their employment date to make sure there are no surprises**

Genuine vacancies
These are defined as those which require the jobholder to perform the specific duties and responsibilities for the job, and for a role matching the period stated in the CoS, and does not include dissimilar and/or lower-skilled duties (15.13). Examples of improper vacancies include those which are

- Exaggerated or feature incorrect job descriptions that deliberately make it seem the job meets the tier and category requirements, when it does not

- For a role that does not exist, in order to enable a migrant to enter or reside in the UK

- Advertised in a way that is tailored to exclude resident workers

Example

Minerva beauty salon wishes to obtain a Sponsor licence so it can employ two Tier 2 General migrants as business development managers.

In order to persuade UKVI that these are genuine vacancies, the firm must show a real business case for this scale of business development. And it must always remember that a compliance visit in a couple of years may well require that work records are shown that prove that the staff in question are wholly engaged with business development work, not helping out in more mundane activities. Indeed you can read about just this kind of case in <u>Singhar Beauty Clinic Ltd</u> [2016] EWHC 2703 (Admin).

Co-operation with the Home Office
Sponsors must permit UKVI staff full access to any premises or site under their control or demand (15.14). A visit may be prearranged or unannounced. Abusive or insulting behaviour will not be tolerated.

Specific duties under Tier 2 (General) and Tier 2 (Intra-Company Transfer)
Those migrants who are subject to an annual limit on numbers can only be sponsored via a restricted CoS. Other migrants can be issued an unrestricted CoS. Sponsors must not assign a restricted CoS for a role requiring an unrestricted CoS, nor vice versa; and they must assign a restricted CoS for a job other than described when applying for it (15.16).

Tier 2 (General) Sponsors are giving a warranty that they assign CoSs only where one of these applies:

- The RLMT was carried out under the rules at the relevant time (and the migrant will be paid at the advertised rate, being the appropriate rate, set out in Table 11AA of Appendix A to the Rules, including specific permitted allowances, and the job is a genuine vacancy)

- The job was exempt from the RLMT at the relevant time

- The job was on the UK-wide, or as appropriate Scottish, shortage occupation list in Appendix K to the Rules on the date the CoS was assigned

Surrendering the licence
Surrender is addressed at section 21 of the Guidance. The licence fee will not be refunded, in whole or part. The licence may be surrendered for all tiers and categories and sub-categories, or just some of them. The decision is communicated as a change of circumstance via the SMS.

The Sponsor should confirm, with evidence, they no longer have responsibility for any sponsored migrants; any that are still sponsored will have their leave curtailed.

A licence may be surrendered during compliance action, but the appropriate "cooling-off" period will then ensue.

Renewing the Sponsor licence

Section 22 of the Guidance deals with renewal. The licence start and end date, and the date when a renewal application can be made, all appear in the *Licence summary* function in the SMS. If the licence expires without renewal, the Sponsor loses it and will be unable to assign further CoSs, their sponsored workers' leave will be curtailed to 60 calendar days, they will disappear from the Sponsor register, and they will be unable to access their SMS account.

The Home Office will issue reminders (five times, from 120 days down to 14 days, on the timetable at 22.7) as to the renewal date but Sponsors must nevertheless apply in good time; otherwise a delay may cause a last-minute application to stray over the expiry point, potentially bringing the adverse consequences just mentioned. Timely applications also give the chance to make a further application if the first one unexpectedly fails.

A Sponsor which lets its licence expires, deliberately or not, may apply for a further licence in the future, but it will then be treated as a new Sponsor, and would have to carry out RLMTs (where required) for issuing CoSs to existing employees (22.24).

If a Sponsor is B-rated and thus on an action plan at the time of renewal, the decision will be deferred until the action plan period expires. A B-rated Sponsor can no longer add branches to its licence (5.2) nor new tiers for sponsoring migrants (11.8).

Where a firm gains access to a dormant Sponsor licence due to some restructuring, they need not renew the licence: they will be able to access it until the leave to remain of the last sponsored migrant expires.

Renewal requires

- Checking the Guidance to ensure any relevant changes are addressed, e.g. to the requirements for SMS users

- Checking the fees: there are tables showing the various fees according to the type of licence sought, Tier 2 or Tier 5 or a mixture, giving different fees for small or charitable sponsors and for medium or large sponsors *UK Visa Sponsorship for employers* (that link explains that a firm will be a small business if its annual turnover is £10.2 million or less or it has 50 employees or fewer)

- Accessing the renewal function via a level 1 user, working with the approval of the authorising officer

- Complying with any checks that the Home Office request: for example they may ask for further documents listed in Appendix A, and may make a visit: any of the adverse compliance measures, downgrading, suspension or revocation, could ensue, if the subsequent interviews and examination of documents and records are found wanting

Chapter 8: Tier 2 and 5 Sponsors – Compliance Issues

Introduction

This chapter explains the system for sponsoring workers from the Sponsor's perspective with regards to compliance issues, including the consequences and possible remedies when things go wrong. Chapter 7: *Representing Tier 2 and 5 Sponsors*, gives a detailed overview of the process, including an introduction and discussion of the recurring concepts of the Sponsorship system. Chapter 5: *Tier 2 Sponsored Workers*, looks at things from the migrant worker's immigration perspective.

Compliance is a critical part of the sponsorship regime. It is understood there were some 15 licence revocations every week in late 2017, so it represents an important aspect of commercial immigration practice.

A Sponsor may be visited at any time during the currency of their licence, with a view to verifying the information they originally provided when their application was originally approved and checking that they have adequately kept up with their record-keeping and reporting duties. Those visits may involve the questioning of migrant workers, their colleagues and managers, with a view to ensuring they are working in line with the job details given in their CoS. Compliance visits may well arise when an application has been made for a licence extension – and unannounced visits are becoming more common generally.

If the findings of the compliance visit makes UKVI suspect there have been failures to adequately follow the Sponsor's duties, they risk a downgrading of their sponsorship rating, or suspension or revocation of their licence. Malpractice in employing workers subject to immigration control may also lead to civil penalties. The more serious the failing, the more dramatic the UKVI intervention is likely to be.

Downgrading will cause the Sponsor lose the typical benefits of participation in the scheme, including no longer being able to endorse Graduate Entrepreneurs. An action plan will be provided which must be complied with within three months, to avoid further action being taken.

The compliance regime exists entirely within Home Office Guidance: presently this is *Tiers 2 and 5: guidance for sponsors* (Version 07/18; effective from 7 July 2018). The Annexes to the Guidance itemise the various failings which can lead to downgrading, suspension and revocation. They overlap to a certain degree. They range from dishonesty (usually via suspicions of having supplied false information or failing to provide necessary information, during the application process or otherwise), to regulatory failings such as losing the necessary accreditation or registration, to receiving civil penalties. All kinds of sponsorship failings can also result in compliance action: allocating CoSs without properly complying with the Resident Labour Market Test (RLMT) or not paying the appropriate salary, failing to assign a new CoS when needed, or failing to establish that the job is in reality involves work at the claimed skill level.

The Home Office look for whether the Sponsor poses a serious threat to immigration control in order to determine what action to take. Other government departments and agencies may be involved in the process. As there is no remedy by way of appeal or administrative review, the only way to challenge decisions is to activate the judicial review process.

The compliance process and compliance visits

Section 17 of the Guidance addresses compliance generally. Chapter 7: *Representing Tier 2 and 5 Sponsors*, deals with the general reporting and record-keeping duties.

A Sponsor who has concerns as to whether their practices are fully compliant with Home Office requirements may always make enquiries to the Business Helpdesk on BusinessHelpdesk@homeoffice.gsi.gov.uk or telephone the helpline on 0300 123 4699.

Compliance checks may be made via a site visit in order to ensure that a Sponsor has given complete and accurate information, and that they are offering genuine employment, genuinely trading in the UK, pose no threat to immigration control and are complying with Sponsor duties (17.1). These may well be unannounced. They may be random, so do not necessarily imply any concerns held prior to the visit, and they may be part of the application process, or take place at any time following the issue of a Sponsor licence. At a compliance visit Home Office staff may (17.5):

- Question migrant workers (including former sponsored workers), employees who were involved in their recruitment, and management

- Verify information given on the Sponsor application and in support of sponsored migrants' indefinite leave to remain applications

- Check compliance with Sponsor duties including record-keeping

- Check the status of other workers to ensure illegal working obligations are met

Staff will not confirm their assessment of compliance with Sponsor duties during the visit itself. A decision will be made based on all the information previously provided plus the intelligence gathered from the visit. Action may be taken based on any of the information gathered, including prosecution of the Sponsor, an employee, or a representative, who has attempted deception. Allegations of abuse of Sponsorship will be treated in confidence (they may be emailed to the Business Helpdesk).

If a Sponsor is notified of a compliance visit, it is a good idea to take the opportunity to be thoroughly prepared. A diligent Sponsor might:

- Ensure their authorising officer is on site, and perhaps their legal advisor too

- Check the contents of all sponsored migrants' files to ensure the documents required by Appendix D are all present – if there are missing records, then it is worth checking if this is a one-off aberration or represents some systemic failing that can be speedily rectified for other files too

- Ensure any documents requested by UKVI are available, particularly if they have to be retrieved from off-site or downloaded

- Brief sponsored workers to answer all questions they are asked honestly, and to carefully check their interview records are accurate (and that the records provide a complete account showing that their role is skilled to the relevant level and reflects their job description)

- Request a complete record of the notes taken by the UKVI compliance team during their visit

Casework Tip

Typical issues that may arise during a compliance visit include:

- **Whether sponsored migrants are truly carrying out the duties referred to in their CoS: concrete evidence must be available, by way of records of their work, performance assessments and liaison with senior management, that clearly links the migrant in**

question to the performance of relatively highly skilled activities. It is important that their line manager and the human resources department is clear on the migrant's actual duties, as they may be interviewed.

- **Whether their work is sufficiently skilled to meet the relevant SOC code, and whether they are they filling a genuine vacancy? Is there evidence on their file which casts doubt on the actual work they do – for example, in the case of Birds Hill Nursing Home [2015] EWHC 2241 (Admin) the fact that Public Relations Officers had been the subject of a Criminal Records Bureau check raised suspicions that they were caring for patients rather than carrying out public relations duties, as did the fact their names appeared on a staff rota for care duties**

- **Is their pay consistent with the appropriate rate for the job?**

- **Is the record-keeping up to scratch and are migrants being tracked in line with sponsor duties?**

- **Is the relevant information being reported to the Home Office in time?**

- **Did the migrant's role require a RLMT and, if so, do the personnel files contain all the documents and information listed in Appendix D to the Guidance?**

- **If a RLMT was not required (e.g. where a Tier 4 student was switching into Tier 2, is the justification for the exemption clear from the CoS?**

- **Has the Sponsor notified the Home Office of any relevant changes to its business such as a change of owners, a change of address, the addition of new branches where sponsored migrants will work? Are sponsored migrants actually working at the addresses provided to the Home Office?**

- **Are the positions of Authorising Officer, Key Contact, Level 1 User and Level 2 User held by suitable persons?**

- **Do all the Sponsor's employees have the right to work in the UK and is the Sponsor conducting right to work checks in accordance with the rules?**

The best way of preparing for a compliance visit is probably to get a specialist legal advisor to conduct a mock audit, to assess how the systems work under stress.

Sanctions for non-compliance

Non-compliance may be sanctioned by steps of varying severity. Normally suspension would precede revocation, with an opportunity to make representations. This is the range of options available to UKVI:

- Revocation (if the Sponsor is considered to constitute *a serious threat to immigration control*, this may follow the compliance assessment without a suspension stage)

- Suspension (where there has been a number of breaches which are themselves minor, or sustained non-compliance over time, which indicates serious or systematic failings)

- Downgrading to B-rating with an action plan

- A reduction in the number of CoSs that may be assigned

- Civil penalties may follow if illegal migrant workers have been employed, of up to £20,000 per worker, and there may be criminal prosecution and disqualification as a company director in serious cases: the Guidance sets out the full list of sanctions at 17.21, and other government agencies such as HMRC and Gangmasters Licensing Authority may be contacted if UKVI considers it necessary

Where the breach is considered minor, and the Sponsor is able and willing to correct it, then an action plan is likely to be required explaining the essential steps to retain the licence.

Downgrading the licence rating

Downgrading to a B-rating is one of the options that might be taken where there are Sponsor failings (section 18 of the Guidance).

The Criteria for downgrading

The mandatory downgrading criteria are found in Annex 3:

- A migrant claiming benefits with the Sponsor's knowledge, the latter having certified they would not do so

- Using procedures that are not fully compliant with Sponsor duties

- Failing to provide a document or information within the given time limit

The discretionary downgrading criteria are found in Annex 4:

- Sponsoring more than 20 migrants in the Tier 2 ICT Graduate Trainee category with start dates in the same financial year

- Failing to provide a document or information listed in Appendix D (i.e. the record-keeping requirements for sponsored migrants) within the specified time limit

- Failing to comply with Sponsor duties

Features of the process include:

- Downgrading may result from various scenarios, including suspicion of having provided false statements or information (18) – the process may involve reference to agencies including a compliance officer, other law enforcement agency, government department, local authority or a foreign government, at least once representations have been received (18.7)

- 20 days' notice is given when downgrading is being considered for a written response, that period being extendable if a request shows exceptional circumstances; the response may include witness statements and documentary evidence (18.6)

The consequences of downgrading

There are various consequences following downgrading:

- A downgraded Sponsor loses their ability to participate in the Graduate Entrepreneur scheme – migrants endorsed by them will have their leave curtailed to 60 days

- The customer services benefits package for Premium and SME+ "A-rated" Sponsors is lost

- An action plan will be provided, for which there is a fee – typical requirements are improvements to recordkeeping, improving control over staff assigning CoSs or improving communication between different branches

- No further CoSs may be assigned during B-rating status until the action plan fee is paid and the Home Office accept that commitment to improvements is shown by signing up to the measures therein

- The steps in the action plan accompanying downgrading must be successfully implemented within a time limit of three months (18.13)

- A Sponsor confronted with an action plan must make payment within 10 working days using the SMS (18.11) in which case licensed sponsor status continues

- If the Sponsor declines to pay the fee by reporting this decision on the SMS, they may surrender their licence, and will be treated as doing so if they fail to make payment within 10 working days – if they take no action, the licence will simply be revoked (18.11)

- During an action plan period, no new CoSs can be assigned, except for migrants already sponsored under Tiers 2 or 5 who are extending their leave to remain, or who are switching from a Work Permit (18.12)

- The Home Office reserve the right to make further compliance visits during the action plan period – if CoSs are assigned to new migrants, the licence will be revoked (18.16)

- At the end of the action plan period, UKVI will visit to see if the requirements are met:

    - if not, the licence will be revoked;

    - if the plan is met and there are no other concerns, an A-rating will be awarded and the CoS allocation threshold will be reviewed if new migrants require sponsorship;

    - if the plan is met, but there are some new concerns, then a further action plan and extension of the B-rating may ensue (18.13) – however there may only be two action plans during the validity of a Sponsor licence (i.e. four years) (18.17) and a licence will be revoked if there are further concerns after this (18.18). If an action plan extends into a new licence period, then it will be treated as one of the two tolerated plans over the span of that licence (18.19)

- A confident Sponsor can request a visit before the three months are up to demonstrate compliance with the action plan before the full period expires, though the Guidance indicates there will only be one compliance visit (18.14)

Example

Aardvark Enterprises receives a compliance visit. Although most of their record keeping is found to be satisfactory, the compliance officers raise worries with regard to the fact that one of their sponsored migrant's contact details are not up-to-date.

It would be open to UKVI to state that they were "not satisfied that you are using a process or procedure necessary to fully comply with your sponsor duties" (Annex 3 reason (b)) and to propose an action plan. If they proposed stronger action than this, such as a suspension of the licence, then the firm might try and negotiate on the basis that downgrading would be a more proportionate response.

Suspending the licence

The suspension regime is set out at section 20 of the Guidance.

The procedure for suspension

There are two processes, which both allow for representations to be made following notification of suspension. It appears the difference between them is that Process 1 applies where UKVI consider they already have enough evidence for suspension without further investigation, whereas Process 2 applies when UKVI thinks that there is sufficient evidence to suspend, even though a full investigation is still pending.

These are the two procedures for suspension:

- Under Process 1 (20.7ff), which applies where UKVI thinks it has sufficient evidence to suspend the licence without further investigation, they will write giving reasons, providing 20 working days to respond via representations and evidence; the period may be extended if exceptional circumstances are given

    - During this period UKVI may interview or question sponsored migrants

    - If any additional reasons arise in the investigation, a further 20 days will be given to provide a response

    - Other government bodies and foreign governments may be notified and asked to supply information

    - A final decision will be given within 20 working days of receiving the Sponsor's response unless the case is "exceptionally complex" or information is still pending from another body, and is based on the papers without any oral hearing

    - The decision takes effect from the date it is sent

- Under Process 2 (20.13ff), there will be no suspension pending further investigation: UKVI will write notifying the Sponsor of the fact of a pending investigation, giving reasons, providing 20 working days to respond via representations and evidence; the period may be extended if exceptional circumstances are given

- The length of investigation will be a matter for UKVI: they will give regular progress reports

- When it finishes, the UKVI will write again, repeating the original reasons for suspension and adding any further reasons and information gleaned from their investigation which may include interviewing or questioning sponsored migrants

- 20 days will be given to provide a response

- The consideration process will resume, with the same recourse to third parties and timetable as above (i.e. 20 days unless "exceptionally complex")

- The decision takes effect from the date it is sent
-

At the end of either Process, appropriate action will be taken: reinstating the licence with an A- or B-rating (with the concomitant action plan: there is no further period given for making representations against downgrading), and/or stopping further CoS assignment or revoking the licence.

The consequences of suspension.
These are the consequences of suspension:

- No further CoSs can be assigned during suspension

- All Sponsor duties must be fully complied with during suspension

- Applications from sponsored migrants for further leave to remain will be put on hold pending suspension, unless they fall for refusal for some other reason (e.g. that the job is not a genuine vacancy)

- If the Sponsor is part of the Graduate Entrepreneur scheme, migrants endorsed by them will have their applications put on hold unless falling for refusal on other grounds

- The Sponsor's name will be removed from the Register of Sponsors

Casework Tip

Once a licence is suspended, the clock is ticking for appropriate action to be taken. Bear in mind:

- **This is usually the last chance to state a really strong case before the licence is revoked (occasionally further evidence provided alongside a Pre Action Protocol letter post-revocation may be considered: but this is wholly at the discretion of the Home Office)**

- **So it is very important indeed to ensure that all available evidence in support of the contentions being made is provided, whether or not the Home Office has requested it**

specifically: any assertion made in representations that is not backed by evidence is likely to be rejected

- **Further evidence provided, whether or not requested, may be scrutinised by UKVI for additional reasons for revoking a licence: so look at any further documents critically, bearing in mind the issues known to antagonise the Home Office, such as those listed above**

- **It may be advisable to put forward an action plan of the Sponsor's own devising to demonstrate that there is the willingness and ability to correct any procedural failings of the past**

- **Always make sure that ALL further information and documents requested have been provided: failure to do so may itself become a reason for further compliance action**

- **The deadline for the representations will only be extended if there are exceptional circumstances – so do not delay**

Revoking the licence

Section 19 of the Guidance addresses revocation.

The criteria for revocation

The mandatory revocation criteria are found in Annex 5. There are rather a lot of them, and as always there is no substitute for reading them for oneself. Nevertheless, in outline they are as follows:

- **Dishonesty**:
    - Providing false information during the Sponsor licence application that would have led to its refusal had the correct information been given (5(a))
    - Knowingly providing a false statement or false information, or not providing required information (5(k))
    - Giving false information on a CoS application (5(q))
- **Stopping trading or operating** altogether or in the UK for any reason, including sale, liquidation, bankruptcy or sequestration (5(b))
- **Regulatory failings**:
    - Losing accreditation or registration (5(c))
    - Failing to hold appropriate planning permission or consent for the type of business (5(w)) (in Sivayogam [2017] EWHC 2575 (Admin) a failure of a religious charity to obtain planning permission for the accommodation of their resident priests was successfully relied upon by UKVI)
    - Failing to meet the Safeguarding children requirements (5(x))
    - Failing to hold appropriate food business approval or registration (5(z))

- **Receiving a civil penalty**
  - Those listed in Appendix C (we list these above where we deal with the cooling-off period under Sponsor ratings) (5(d)), though not for illegal migrant workers or giving a residential tenancy to an adult disqualified from such due to their immigration status
  - For employing one or more illegal workers where the fine was at the maximum post objections and appeal rights (5(e))
  - A business owner, director or authorising officer, for giving a residential tenancy to an adult disqualified from such due to their immigration status (5(f))
  - For a first time offence of employing an illegal worker or giving a residential tenancy as above, where the fine is below the maximum but not paid within 29 days of notification of liability and the appeal process expiring (5(g)(h))
  - Breaching the conditions of an agreed payment instalment plan for a civil penalty fine (5(i))
- **Convictions of relevant offences**: essentially all offences under the immigration legislation, plus espionage/terrorism, dishonesty (theft, corruption, deception and fraud), tax or excise duty avoidance, bribery, proceeds of crime and money laundering (5(j))
- Failing to meet a requirement of the action plan for a B-rated Sponsor (5(l)) or failing to pay the action plan fee within 10 working days (5(n)) or being identified for some adverse compliance action that would have resulted in a further action plan had two not already been awarded (5(m))
- **CoS misdemeanours**:
  - An SMS user assigns a CoS to a family member or partner (5(o))
  - A B-rated Sponsor uses a CoS to sponsor a new migrant (5(p))
  - Assigning a CoS where the salary stated on the CoS (including any sponsor note on the CoS) is different from the amount paid including allowances (5(s)) (in Sivayogam [2017] EWHC 2575 (Admin) a failure to include the allowances and a goodwill payment in the payslips of employees was one of the factors held sufficient to justify revocation)
  - Using a CoS to fill a vacancy other than that given on the assigned CoS (5(t))
  - Assigning a CoS where the RLMT was non-compliant or not carried out, or the vacancy was wrongly stated to be a shortage occupation (5(u))
  - Wrongly stating the job was exempt from the RLMT (5(v))
  - Assigning a CoS for a non-genuine vacancy, e.g. because the job description is exaggerated, or for a role that does not truly exist (5(ee))
  - Failing to assign a new CoS via an RLMT where a change of employment application was appropriate (5(ff))

- The role undertaken does not match the Appendix J job description associated with the role in the CoS, or their role does not match the CoS description (5(gg))

- Assigning a CoS without the right endorsement from the appropriate governing body for a sportsperson or coach (5(ii))

➢ **Job failings**:

- Employing a migrant in a job not meeting the skill level requirements (5(r))

- Acting as an employment agency or business and providing a sponsored migrant as labour to a third party (5(y)), or being an employment agency or business than assigns a sponsored migrant for one of its own employees as labour to a third party (5(cc))

- Failing to employ a qualified resident worker for the job (5(hh))

- Employing, or applying to employ, a migrant under the shortage occupation provisions without meeting one of the Sponsor criteria for those provisions (5(ii))

➢ Not having (or ending) an operating presence in the UK (5(bb))

➢ Failing to send a document or information within the given time limit (5(dd))

➢ Sponsoring a Tier 5 International Agreement migrant as a Contractual Service Supplier or Independent Professional to service a contract the Sponsor has not told UKVI about, or UKVI has not confirmed a CoS can be issued in connection with that contract or UKVI has set it does not meet the Guidance's requirements (5(aa))

➢ Assigning sportsperson/coach CoSs without a current endorsement from the appropriate governing body, or overpaying expenses to a Tier 5 temporary worker migrant (5(jj) and (kk))

➢ Artificially inflating salary payments to assist a migrant obtain indefinite leave to remain (5(ll))

And these are the **discretionary revocation criteria**, found in Annex 6:

➢ **Losing authorisation from the OISC** (i.e. the immigration legal services regulator for non-solicitors and barristers) (6(a))

➢ **Sponsorship failings**:

- Failing to comply with any Sponsor duties (6(f))

- Not having adequate procedures in place to meet Sponsor duties (6(i))

- Failing to have a level 1 user in place meeting the relevant requirements (6(g))

- Having no SMS users in place (6(h))

- An SMS user disclosing their password to another person (6(o))

- Having no authorising officer in place meeting the Guidance's requirements (6(q))
- Failing to provide a requested document within the specified time limit relating to a change reported via the SMS or the *Change of circumstances form* (6(r))
- Being named as key personnel at an institution whose Sponsor licence has been revoked in the last year (6(u))
- Paying a migrant in cash (6(v))
- Failing to comply with a compliance visit or activity (6(w))

➢ **CoS failings**:

- Assigning a CoS under Tier 5 Temporary Worker Graduate Authorised Exchange scheme for a longer period than authorised that has successfully supported an application for leave to remain (6(n))
- Sponsoring more than 20 migrants in the Tier 2 ICT Graduate Trainee category with start dates in the same financial year (6(p))
- Assigning an unrestricted Tier 2 (General) CoS to a migrant for a restricted job (6(z))

➢ **Regulatory failings**:

- Becoming legally prohibited from being a company director (6(d))
- Becoming an undischarged bankrupt (6(e))
- Receiving a penalty for failing to pay VAT or duty in the last five years (6(s))
- Having been subject to United Nations or international or EU sanctions which will be broken if the licence continues to be held (6(x))
- Having on board a business owner, director or authorising officer of a Sponsor institution that has been ordered to pay costs to the Home Office in legal proceedings which have not been paid (6(y))

➢ **Civil penalties**

- Receiving any penalty not listed in Annex 5 (i.e. other than those bringing mandatory revocation) (6(k))
- Receiving more than one civil penalty for employing an illegal worker during the licence's validity, the decision being upheld following objection and on appeal (6(l)) – or an owner, director or authorising officer receiving one for giving a residential tenancy to an adult disqualified from such due to their immigration status (6(m))

- **Employment failings**:

    - Failing to pay the appropriate rate for the sponsored job under Appendix J and the Guidance (6(b))

- **Record-keeping failings**:

    - Failing to provide an Appendix D document, or evidence required for recruiting to shortage occupations under Appendix K (6(c))

- **Immigration failings**:

    - Having a sponsored migrant who does not comply with the conditions of their leave or worker authorisation in the UK where the Sponsor has not been following good practice guidance from the Home Office or a relevant sector body (6(j))

The revocation procedure
This is the procedure:

- The decision maker will consider the criteria just set out, addressing revocation on a mandatory basis (Annex 5) and a discretionary basis (Annex 6)

- A Sponsor may survive revocation where the grounds for it arising a discretionary: if there is evidence of "robust processes and procedures in places and have taken all reasonable steps to verify information that you are required to obtain and hold" (19.5) the licence will be suspended (19.6). In Sivayogam [2017] EWHC 2575 (Admin) §56 counsel representing the Home Office indicated that a failure to notify a change of address (envisaged as a temporary move by the Sponsor) might be thought a "technicality"; however, in Raj and Knoll [2016] EWCA Civ 770 the Court of Appeal noted that failures to report a change of business address, and the working address of employees, were breaches of sponsor duties that gave rise to "serious disquiet"

- The test that is applied is essentially whether the Sponsor is a threat to immigration control: this does not mean that UKVI has to show actual breaches of immigration control, only that the Sponsor's conduct creates a *threat* – judges on judicial review are likely to find that a failure to maintain the required processes and procedures to ensure compliance is itself sufficient to constitute a threat to immigration control

- There is no right of appeal against revocation: the only remedy is judicial review

The consequences of revocation
The consequences are:

- No further Sponsor application can be made until the cooling off period has expired (set out in the Guidance at 10.4, dealt with in Chapter 7: *Representing Tier 2 and 5 Sponsors* under the heading *Cooling off periods*), thereafter the application will be treated as would any other application (19.16)

- Sponsored migrants will have their leave curtailed (19.8):

- Immediately where the Home Office believes they were actively and knowingly involved (complicit) in the reasons for revocation (e.g. if they agreed to a non-existent job being held out for them) (they will be expected to leave the country at this point too, 19.9)

- To 60 calendar days if they have more leave than that remaining, otherwise their leave will be left intact; either way they must leave the country if they have not made an another application in a category of leave for which they qualify (19.9). If they do not depart, the usual mandatory bans for overstaying will bite on future entry clearance applications (r320(7A) of the Rules)

- Sponsored migrants en route to the UK will be refused leave to enter, and those with entry clearance who have not yet travelled will have that clearance cancelled (19.13)

- Any CoS assigned becomes automatically invalid, so any pending applications by sponsored migrants will face refusal

➢ The Sponsor loses their ability to participate in the Graduate Entrepreneur scheme – migrants endorsed by them will be treated in line with sponsored workers (19.10)

The general approach of the courts is summed up by these words from the judge in London Reading College Ltd [2010] EWHC 2561:

> It has to be remembered that the primary judgment about the response to breaches of a College's duty is the Defendant's and the Court's role is simply supervisory. It has also to be remembered that the underlying principle behind this scheme is that the UKBA entrusts to Colleges the power to grant visa letters on the understanding, and with their agreement, that they will act in a manner that maintains proper immigration control. The capacity for damage to the national interest in the maintenance of proper immigration control is substantial if Colleges are not assiduous in meeting their responsibilities. In these circumstances, it seems to me that the Defendants are entitled to maintain a fairly high index of suspicion as they go about overseeing colleges and a light trigger in deciding when and with what level of firmness they should act.

Steps to take when a licence is under threat

There is no right of appeal to an independent judge against any decision by the Home Office in relation to a Sponsor licence. So the only remedy will be negotiation, and the threat and possible issue of judicial review proceedings.

The ideal solution would be to negotiate to bring the matter to a satisfactory conclusion for both parties: UKVI being content that the issues that caused them concern are properly addressed, and the employer retaining their licence.

There are a number of possible strategies in a case like this:

➢ Providing further evidence that demonstrates that UKVI's first impression was wrong – and while there is still an opportunity to do so by making representations, then this is an important option, and one that should be used wisely

- Ensure that the evidence answers every feature of the UKVI criticisms: for example, if the skill level of a job is questioned, then evidence should be put forward addressing each aspect of the job description on the CoS

- Remember to ensure that any representations is *consistent* with the information and arguments given in earlier correspondence, otherwise one may generate more, rather than fewer, future reasons for revocation

- Also, always ensure that *evidence* is provided, by way of witness statements and/or documents: any *assertion* made in representations which is not backed by independent evidence is effectively worthless. Equally, witness statements will generally be providing context and plugging the odd gap in the evidence: if evidence which could reasonably be expected to back up the witness statement is not produced, then UKVI are likely to reject the claims made

- Piles of evidence that are not expressly and clearly linked to the role of the sponsored worker in question are unlikely to be given much weight

- The Sponsor's defence needs to be clearly explained and presented: one cannot expect the Home Office to do the running in terms of making sense of documents or linking up arguments and evidence over a lengthy period of correspondence

➢ Admitting wrongdoing (ideally, relatively minor wrongdoing) and explaining that this was down to oversight, and perhaps providing an "action plan" of the advisor's own invention demonstrating that any procedures so far found wanting have been thoroughly reviewed and robust solutions put in place – this runs with the idea expressed in the Home Office guidance that

Where the breach is a minor issue, you are willing and able to correct it, and pose no continuing threat to immigration control, we will in most cases support you in making the relevant improvements by issuing an action plan, which sets out the steps you must take in order to retain your licence.

Emphasising that any wrongdoing is minor and relates to refusal grounds which are discretionary rather than mandatory, such that it would be *disproportionate* to refuse having regard to all the circumstances of the case.

➢ Seeking disclosure of any material on which UKVI are relying which the Sponsor has not so far seen: a judge on judicial review will probably accept that facts asserted as true by the Home Office are indeed reliable, unless they are challenged early on in the process (a judge might be more sympathetic to a Sponsor if a UKVI assertion is undermined by documentary evidence)

➢ Regarding any issues where further negotiation is not possible, identifying evidence that has been overlooked or misunderstood by UKVI: this may found a successful judicial review challenge down the line, and a reasonable decision maker may appreciate their own failings and offer to reconsider rather than risk losing court proceedings

Beware:

➢ Simply apologising for misdemeanours is unlikely to satisfy UKVI: that amounts to accepting the allegations they have made

➢ Experience suggests that is relatively rare for a Sponsor to be wholly in the right and UKVI to be wholly in the wrong: accordingly the tone of correspondence is best kept polite and contrite, rather than unduly confrontational. The judges in Raj and Knoll expressed their surprise at the non-conciliatory tone of correspondence in that case, finding that the

> solicitors … adopted a wholly inappropriate and unjustified confrontational stance which can have done nothing to allay [UKVI] concerns and indeed can only have contributed to them

It is vital that the documents and arguments advanced at each stage of the process are assembled in a clear and comprehensible way: much time can be wasted where pre-revocation and post-decision evidence are muddled together.

Mandatory and discretionary revocation
It is important to be aware of those Guidance breaches which lead to mandatory revocation of a licence (i.e. automatic revocation), and those which are discretionary (i.e. depending on all the facts of the case).

Automatic revocation can take place for many reasons, though in practice it tends to involve gross or multiple failings, or dishonesty. However it also includes some sponsorship duty breaches, such as employing a migrant worker at an inappropriate skill level or failing to pay the salary indicated in the CoS.

Where a particular failing leads to discretionary revocation, then the decision maker has to consider all relevant factors arising in the case as a whole, rather than just automatically revoking because of the particular problem; any mitigating circumstances must be balanced against the seriousness of the failing.

Example

**Following a compliance visit, Aardvark Enterprises, are told that as they have failed to pay a Tier 2 migrant the appropriate rate for their job, their licence is being suspended.
They now have 20 days to make evidence-backed representations as to why this is an aberration. This is a discretionary reason for revocation (Annex 6, reason (b)) and so UKVI must take account of all the circumstances of the case, such as the general robustness of the firm's procedures.**

Judicial review as a remedy against revocation of a licence

The remedy of judicial review is very closely focussed on the arguments and evidence before the original decision maker. In general it is not permitted to put forward further evidence, and it is very rare for oral evidence from live witnesses to be admitted.

So it is very important to ensure that the right points are made before the case gets to the Pre Action stage: i.e. during the representations process following notification of the problems by the Home Office to the Sponsor. This goes both for evidence, and for the actual arguments that are made. Litigation involving the Points Based System generally is littered with arguments being added to the process too late to get real traction. The key case in this area is Raj and Knoll [2016] EWCA Civ 770, where the Court of Appeal summarises the principles that have developed in the earlier cases – several involved colleges sponsoring Tier 4 students, hence the occasional references to CASs as well as CoSs:

- The essence of the system is that the Secretary of State imposes "a high degree of trust" in Sponsors granted licences in implementing and policing immigration policy in respect of migrants to whom it grants a Certificate of Sponsorship ("CoS") or Confirmation of Acceptance ("CAS")

- The authority to grant a CoS is a privilege which carries great responsibility: the Sponsor is expected to carry out its responsibilities "with all the rigour and vigilance of the immigration control authorities"

- The Sponsor"must maintain its own records with assiduity"

- There is no need for UKBA to wait until there has been breach of immigration control caused by the acts or omission of a sponsor before suspending or revoking the sponsorship, but it can, and indeed should, take such steps if it has reasonable grounds for suspecting that a breach of immigration control might occur

- The courts should respect the experience and expertise of UKBA when reaching conclusions as to a Sponsor's compliance with the Guidance, which is vitally necessary to ensure that there is effective immigration control

Reading this, you will immediately understand that the courts apply rather a light touch in their supervision of UKVI decision making when it comes to Sponsor licences. Various attempts have been made over time to argue that the serious commercial consequences of revocation for licensed Sponsors should mean that judges review adverse decisions with particularly close scrutiny. However, so far the judges have indicated that they do not think this is appropriate, given the courts have no special expertise in the immigration regulation system.

In order to succeed in a judicial review application, it is necessary to show more than just a single flaw in the decision. Lord Neuberger MR held in the case of <u>FDA</u> [2012] EWCA Civ 332 that

> Where a decision-maker has taken a legally irrelevant factor into account when making his decision, the normal principle is that the decision is liable to be held to be invalid unless the factor played no significant part in the decision-making exercise ... Even where the irrelevant factor played a significant or substantial part in the decision-maker's thinking, the decision may, exceptionally, still be upheld, provided that the court is satisfied that it is clear that, even without the irrelevant factor, the decision-maker would have reached the same conclusion.

The Home Office is permitted to provide witness statements giving further information about the reasoning underlying their decisions after judicial review proceedings have been launched. Basically it is allowed to do so "to explain the thought processes which informed its decision". However it is now allowed to try to plug a real gap in a deficient decision by inserting reasoning which was clearly not in the mind of the original decision maker.

Promising arguments
A number of grounds for judicial review could potentially succeed:

- **Unfair procedure**: for example

  - Failing to interview sponsored migrants or their managers before coming to conclusions on the nature of their work – given the opportunity usually given to provide representations and further evidence before a licence is revoked, it may be hard to establish unfairness in this sense

  - Failing to give sufficient opportunity to respond to a particular issue, perhaps by being unclear as to precisely what criticism is being made of what evidence

- Failing to take account of evidence of improvements following the imposition of an action plan

- Thus we see the judge in Burnley Training College Ltd [2011] EWHC 2928 (Admin) say:

It may well be that the defendants are entitled to maintain a fairly high index of suspicion, but that does not mean that they can disregard established laws of natural justice or ride roughshod over a person's reasonable expectations in conformity with the tenor of the guidance they themselves have issued that appropriate enquiries will be made ... the applicant has in turn a right to expect a degree of fairness from the defendant in its dealings and an equal measure of trust that its application and considerations connection with its application will be dealt with seriously, carefully, responsibly, properly and, above all, fairly

➢ **Factual error**: e.g. failing to correct an earlier statement of concern notwithstanding that evidence of compliance has now been put forward on that particular issue. However, it is necessary to show that the factual error has a significant impact on the overall decision if it is corrected before the final decision is made, or if there are multiple other reasons. Always remember a judge will step back and read the decision letter as a whole having regard to the heavy duties imposed on Sponsors, meaning this argument may not be sustainable

➢ **Misconstruing Guidance**: if the Guidance is open to more than one interpretation, a judge may accept that the UKVI understanding is not the only way of reading it.

  - For example, there seems scope for confusion as to the extent to which IT consultants can be subcontracted to other firms by a Sponsor: time-limited secondments where the Sponsor maintains control over their actions are permitted according to the Guidance, but UKVI compliance officers seem to take a tough line on these cases, often suspecting them of involving the prohibition on supplying labour or acting as a recruitment agent

  - Goldsmith International Business School [2014] EWHC 1232 (Admin) is a case where the Home Office misunderstood the application of its own Guidance to a particular form of qualification; in Leeds Unique Education Ltd [2010] EWHC 1030 (Admin) the decision maker misunderstood the requirements of an accrediting body

Unsuccessful arguments
The reported cases are littered with failed arguments.

➢ Technical arguments designed to show that the Sponsor Guidance has been wrongly interpreted often fail, because they fail to engage with the onerous duties with which Sponsors are expected to comply, or with the basic objectives of protecting the domestic labour force

➢ The fact that the Home Office may not have picked up on a particular failing when granting a licence or its extension in the past is not really relevant; see for example Sivayogam [2017] EWHC 2575 (Admin) §56 and Singhar Beauty Clinic Ltd [2016] EWHC 2703 (Admin)

➢ Disputing conclusions of the Home Office when no relevant evidence has been overlooked or misinterpreted. Judicial review is not a merits appeal, so the judge is not entitled to make up their own mind about whether revoking a licence was the best option; they are simply supervising the Home Office decision, from a starting point that Parliament has put UKVI in charge of a relatively technical area of immigration control in which the courts have no particular expertise. This is how one judge puts it, in the Singhar Beauty Clinic Ltd case:

> this is a very high threshold to overcome. It is not sufficient that the court may disagree with the defendant's decision or even take the view that most people would disagree with it ... [it is] only if the decision is one "so outrageous in defiance of logic or accepted moral standards that no sensible person who had applied his mind to the question could have arrived at it" will the decision be held to be unlawful.

- Questioning the relevance of a particular requirement of the Guidance (because judges generally accept that the content of the scheme is entirely a matter for the Home Office)
- Claiming another part of the Home Office held the relevant information that should have been reported to UKVI in the appropriate way, so there was no threat to immigration control raised on the facts of the failure in question (see for example Manzay Ltd [2016] EWHC 2582 (Admin))
- Challenging the contents of interview records when there is no independent evidence or explanation for any claimed misunderstanding of what was said
- Giving explanations which simply demonstrate that the importance of accurate and exhaustive record-keeping are not understood, or are not taken sufficiently seriously
- The fact that a decision maker did not expressly consider whether the case was an *exceptional* one justifying departure from the normal course to which the Guidance pointed, e.g. Country Court Care [2015] EWHC 2054 (Admin)
- Arguing that the failings are the result of innocent mistakes rather than active dishonesty

The private life of persons receiving care
Some judicial decisions have looked at the impact on residents of the loss of migrant workers:

- One judge has recognised that the loss of a nursing home's Sponsor licence might impact on the care received by its elderly residents, Birds Hill Nursing Home [2015] EWHC 2241 (Admin):

> for frail, elderly residents (such as the 2nd Claimant) the continuing ability to live in the nursing home to which they have become accustomed is an important part of their private lives to which Article 8 of the ECHR is directed.

- However, unless there is an individual relationship between particular staff members and residents, one would need clear expert evidence, for example from an accountant, that the roles in question were essential to the survival of the business: as the judge remarked in Country Care Ltd [2015] EWHC 2054 (Admin) §74: "It is remarkable how often dire predictions prove ill-founded once put to the test."

  Furthermore, in Country Care Ltd, the judge decided that the commercial pressures on the Sponsor would be likely to prompt them into finding suitable alternative labour – and in any event, the potential disruption to the lives of care-receivers was an inevitable feature of the system, and a proportionate consequence given the dangers to immigration control that would otherwise ensue

The judicial review application process
These are the various stages in the process. As the application is brought in the Administrative Court, the parties are known as Claimant and Defendant.

(1) The deadline for bringing a judicial review application is three months from the date of decision. Before making the application, a Pre Action Protocol letter must be sent giving the Defendant (usually) 21 days to respond. The idea is that this gives the Home Office formal notice that their decision will be challenged in the courts if it is upheld notwithstanding the notice of dissatisfaction given formally by this letter. The letter gives the Defendant a chance to concede before a Sponsor incurs significant legal costs in taking things further.

(2) The Home Office always reply to that letter with a Response, though sometimes not until it has been necessary to lodge the judicial review application to avoid running out of time.

(3) Presuming the Home Office maintain their revocation after the pre-action exchange, a judicial review application must be lodged, in the Administrative Court.

(4) The judicial review application will be the subject of a *permission* decision just based on a judge reading the papers. Before that decision, the Home Office will produce an Acknowledgment of Service with summary grounds of defence, giving the grounds on which they wish to uphold their decision. Sometimes they concede that they should reconsider the case at this point, though this is relatively rare.

(5) If permission is refused, it is possible to "renew" the application so there will be an oral hearing. Usually a skeleton argument will be produced, summarising the issues and giving an answer to the reasons provided in the permission refusal. These hearings tend to be relatively short – though a number are listed at the same time, usually 10:30am, so there can be some waiting around.

(6) If permission is refused at the oral renewal hearing before the Administrative Court, it is possible to appeal to the Court of Appeal. The merits of such an application entirely depend on how strong the grounds for judicial review are, and how well they have been dealt with by the judge refusing permission. The process involves a further paper application; there is unlikely to be a further oral hearing. The Court of Appeal has the power to reverse the permission refusal and send the matter back to the Administrative Court. It rarely retains cases in this situation, unless some major issue of principle is involved.

(7) If permission is granted at the oral renewal hearing before the Administrative Court, then the application will eventually be listed for a full substantive judicial review hearing in the Administrative Court (this can be a long process, one sees cases take more than 18 months to get from lodging to full hearing). Both sides will produce further written arguments for that hearing. The judge "hands down" their decision: this may involve reading out their judgment on the spot, or scheduling a further hearing to give it, in the latter case often giving the option to the parties not to attend.

(8) The Home Office might reconsider the case when permission is granted: this happens in a significant proportion of cases. It depends on what they assess their chances of success in defending their decision to be, taking into account any comments made by the judge granting permission.

(9) If an application for judicial review ultimately succeeds, then the Home Office may be ordered to pay the Claimant's legal costs, of legal advice and representation and court fees.

(10) Judicial review is not a merits appeal – it only leads to a reconsideration of the case, in line with any relevant rulings from the court. So a successful outcome requires the Home Office to reconsider their decision. This may well lead to a reversal of the original decision, depending on how much margin the judge's decision leaves them with.

(11) If a judicial review application ultimately fails, then the Claimant will probably be ordered to pay the legal costs of the Home Office (i.e. their legal team's fees, based on their hourly rate and the number of hours put in, both those of the Government Legal Department liaising with UKVI, and their barrister). This may or may not be in line with the Claimant's own legal team's fees, depending on the hours of work they put in. Failing to pay legal fees following an unsuccessful judicial review claim can itself lead to future Sponsor applications being refused.

Interim relief during the judicial review process

The loss of a licence may of course have a significant impact on a Sponsor's business: sponsored workers may move elsewhere following a licence being suspended because of their uncertain status, and once the licence is revoked their lawful residence is likely to be curtailed to 60 days.

It is possible to request *interim relief* as part of the judicial review application. This is an application for the court to order that the revocation decision be suspended until the judicial review application is finally determined, to avoid the Sponsor's business suffering unduly before they manage to get to a hearing where they show a judge that they have a winning case.

Such an application needs to be backed by impressive and detailed evidence showing that the sponsored workers are key to the business's operation and perhaps even its survival, explaining how it is that settled workers could not manage to fill the gap even for a limited period of time.

The judge looking at the application must decide if the arguments put on the judicial review claim

- Raise a *serious* issue (i.e. that the Sponsor has a reasonably strong claim) and that

- The *balance of convenience* favours the Sponsor: i.e. that it is more of a disaster for the firm to lose its licence during the judicial review process than it is for the Home Office (and the British public) to face an arguable threat to immigration control by having a Sponsor employ migrant workers whose compliance with Sponsor duties is debated.

Chapter 9: Tier 5 Temporary Workers and Youth Mobility Scheme Temporary Migrants

Overview of Tier 5 Temporary Workers

This route is for certain types of temporary worker whose entry helps to satisfy cultural, charitable, religious or international objectives including volunteering and job shadowing (r245ZM). There are five sub-categories:

- **Creative and sporting** – for people coming to the United Kingdom to work or perform as sports people, entertainers or creative artists for up to 12 months (subject to further extension)
- **Charity workers** – for people coming to the United Kingdom to do voluntary work and not paid work for a charity
- **Religious workers** – for people coming to the United Kingdom to work as religious workers. Duties may include preaching, pastoral and non pastoral work
- **Government authorised exchange** – for people coming to the United Kingdom through approved schemes that aim to share knowledge, experience and best practice
- **International agreement** – for people coming to the United Kingdom under contract to provide a service that is covered by international law; for example the General Agreement on Trade in Services

Each of these routes is partially explained in the Guidance. Indeed it is rather difficult to understand the route by simply reading the requirements in the Rules, so it is probably best to read the Guidance first. As usual, there are two sets of Guidance: one for Home Office staff deciding applications (Version 18.0 effective from 5 January 2017), one for applicants when putting together their application (Policy Guidance for applications from 29 August 2017).

As usual for much of the PBS, a person applying for entry clearance or leave needs a Sponsor. They will be issued with a Certificate of Sponsorship (CoS) that provides certain specified information – it must match with the information held by the Certificate of Sponsorship Checking Service (CoSCS). They then use the CoS to obtain their visa; there are certain requirements for the CoS to be (and stay) valid, such as being used within three months of its issue and no more than three months before the employment commences.

Non-visa nationals entering the UK for periods of no more than three months may travel and enter without having entry clearance, so long as they can satisfy the immigration officer at the port of entry that they can meet the requirements of the Rules.

The general rationale of CoSs granted under the temporary worker route is that the individual will not be basing themselves in business here or posing any threat to the resident labour force (e.g. Guidance for applications, para 102ff). As always applicants are susceptible to having their application assessed for its genuineness, where there is reasonable suspicion as to their ability to fulfil the role in question. For this reason, the role must be a *supernumerary* one in most of the sub-categories – i.e. one that is beyond the usual requirements of the employer and which they would not otherwise be recruiting to fill. This ensures that the Tier 5 migrant is not filling a genuine vacancy that should have be made available to a settled worker.

There are intricate provisions addressing the precise period of entry clearance/leave to be granted. The Guidance addressing *Periods of Grant* explains that creative workers may extend their leave for up to 24 months if they remain with the same Sponsor. A non-visa national may apply at the port of entry where seeking to enter for three months or less, so long as they have a CoS. Those wishing to take advantage of this possibility should ensure they carry relevant evidence to establish they meet the Rules and contact details for their Sponsor.

There is no English language requirement (thus the Rules contain no cross-reference to Appendix B and there are no English speaking requirements in Appendix A).

There are few ways by which a person present under Tier 5 can extend their stay in the UK in another category of the Rules because, when one looks at the switching controls found in the "leave to remain" component of the various routes under the Points Based System, we find that Tier 5 is rarely listed. An exception is that an applicant may switch out of Tier 5 (Temporary Worker) Migrant where they are sponsored in the Government authorised exchange sub-category in an exchange scheme for sponsored researchers (r245BD(c)(iii)).

It is also difficult to switch into Tier 5; visitors conducting permitted activities in the creative and sporting sub-routes, and from Tier 4 for those in Government authorised exchange programmes from UK recognised bodies/higher education institutions, are the only modern candidates. So generally this is an entry clearance only route.

Tier 5 is not in general a settlement route (though there is a dispensation for those present in the route under the sub-category for private servants in a diplomatic household under the Rules in place before 6 April 2012).

Creative sector

Those in the creative sector may obtain a single CoS for a series of engagements with no more than 14 days between them if they have a single promoter; if they have multiple promoters during a single trip then each must be a Sponsor in their own right, and the applicant must ensure that there are no gaps exceeding 14 days between periods of engagement. Otherwise they must leave the country and seek further entry clearance. A Group CoS may be obtained so as to include a creative person's entourage.

Creatives enjoy a dispensation as to the place from where they may apply for entry clearance: they may apply to an entry clearance post where they are residing at the time of the application, provided that the relevant post is one which has been designated as appropriate for this route, and the applicant lives there lawfully and works in a role consistent with their planned activities in the UK (r28A).

Sportspeople

Those in the sportspeople category must be internationally established at the highest level and set to make a significant contribution to their sport's development at that level in the UK. The Guidance makes it clear that it is not for those who have previously entered the UK under permit free concessions for entertainers and sportspeople, as they have specific provision made for them under sub-categories of the visitor route. The route is not for those wishing to play for professional clubs.

A professional footballer in the creative and sporting sub-category may switch into Tier 2 General within the sportsperson migrant category (r245HD(e)).

Charity workers

This route is for those wanting to undertake unpaid voluntary fieldwork (i.e. activities which would not normally be offered at a waged/salaried rate which does not include work ancillary to the charitable purpose, such as routine administrative work, retail/sales work, fund-raising and maintaining the office: Guidance para 117) contributing directly to the Sponsor's charitable purpose in the UK. Accordingly the CoS requirements demand an assurance that no remuneration will be received, as statutorily defined.

Religious workers
Religious workers will be performing religious duties, via work within or directed by the Sponsor's organisation, which may include preaching, pastoral work and non-pastoral duties: these duties must be outlined. If the organisation is a religious order, the applicant must be a member.

Government authorised exchange
This route is for those coming to the UK through approved schemes aiming to share knowledge, experience and best practice via work placements, whilst experiencing the wider social and cultural setting of the UK. It must not be used to fill job vacancies or import unskilled labour.

The central idea is that individual employers and organisations cannot act as Sponsors, with the exception of schemes for sponsored researchers approved by the Department for Innovation, Universities and Skills, and Government Departments and their Executive Agencies. So applicants must identify and apply to the appointed overarching body, which in turn must have the support of a UK government department. These bodies oversee numerous schemes, and range from the Bar Council to BAE Systems, and are listed in Appendix N.

There are four schemes within this sub-category:

Work Experience Programme – volunteering, job-shadowing, internships and approved work experience programmes

Research Programme – only those working on specific scientific, academic, medical or government research projects at UK higher education institutions or other research institution operating under the authority and/or financial sponsorship of a relevant government department

Training Programme — only those receiving formal, practical training in the fields of science and/or medicine, those receiving training by HM armed forces or UK emergency services, or those who obtained a UK degree at Bachelors or Masters level during their last grant of leave who are sponsored for required postgraduate training/work experience in that degree's field who are not filling a permanent vacancy in the sense that the Sponsor would be aiming to employ them in that role at the training's end

Examples

You can see an example of the various processes for the College of Optometrists here, which gives some idea of the importance of ensuring that the steps are taken in the right order: an applicant from the right kind of educational institution may switch from Tier 4 once they have obtained a degree of the right quality, obtaining a pre-registration place may be necessary before the CoS is issued, and then the CoS can be used to support an application for leave to remain, before the placement is taken up.

Jane, who is present in the UK under Tier 4, wants to take up an internship that she has been offered with a law firm once she completes her studies.

Potentially this may be feasible under Tier 5 as the Law Society is one of the overarching bodies within the Government Authorised Exchange programme in Appendix N of the Rules. Of course, if the internship is short, she may be able to complete it under the terms of her Tier 4 leave. Otherwise she may be able to switch into Tier 5, as that is feasible for a Tier 4 student entering a Government Authorised Exchange who obtained a degree during their last period of stay. The law firm does not need to be a Sponsor with the power to issue a CoS – it

is the Law Society as the overarching body which does this, and thus the Law Society will need to assess the vacancy in question, ensuring that there is a detailed training plan and that the role is supernumerary – i.e. it is not filling a genuine vacancy that should be made available to a settled worker.

Overseas Government Language Programme – schemes that are fully or partially funded by overseas governments or government sponsored organisations, for those undertaking development placements to build and/or enhance foreign language skills and foster good cultural relations in the UK.

International agreement
There are various sub-routes here.

- Private servants in diplomatic households

- Employees of overseas governments and national organisations (the Sponsor must guarantee the migrant will not try to change to a different sub-category within the international agreements after entering the UK)

- Via an international agreement, i.e. the General Agreement on Trade in Services, or equivalents such as the EU-Andean multiparty trade agreement, the EU-Chile trade agreement and the EU–CARIFORUM agreement

There are precise requirements as specified in Appendix A to be provided in each case. There is a specimen employment contract for overseas domestic workers set out in the Guidance.

Those entering under international agreements will either be

- **Contractual service suppliers** – who have been an employee of the company for at least 12 months with a degree level qualification (unless providing services as identified below when we address the precise CoS requirements), employed by a company based in a country with a relevant trade agreement under which they are supplying services, which has no commercial presence in the European Union with a contract to supply appropriate services under that agreement, or

- **Independent self-employed professionals** – their business must be established on the territory of the country which is signatory to the relevant trade agreement under which they are supplying services, they must be a national of that country with a degree level (university or technical) qualification and they must hold any specific professional qualifications that are required, and hold six years' professional experience.

They may not spend more than six months in any 12-month period in the UK with leave under this route (r245ZO(h)).

Recurring concepts within the temporary worker route

Entry clearance not required for some short stays
Entry clearance is required (r245ZN(a)) unless the migrant meets the requirements of the route (r245ZN(b)) and

- has consecutive engagements which are in total three months or less or

- has a single engagement of no more than three months

- is not a visa national, or
- is within the creative and sporting sub-category

Consecutive engagements
There is no need for entry clearance where the migrant has consecutive engagements which are in total three months or less. These are defined as engagements within the creative and sporting sub-category where each has its own CoS reference number and there are no gaps of more than 14 days between the periods of engagement – those periods are those given in each CoS for the start and end dates of the employment (r245ZM(b)).

Example

Raymondo is a renowned magician. He is booked to perform in the UK for short seasons with three different promoters over a four month period.

As Raymondo has different promoters, each needs to be a Sponsor issuing their own CoS. These are potentially consecutive engagements, so long as there is no more than 14 days between the employment start and end dates in each CoS.

Entering the UK
A person with entry clearance can enter the UK up to 14 days before their start date under the CoS: this being the pre-arrival grace period customarily given as part of the conditions of leave.

Change of employment
Migrants present as temporary workers may change their employment, within the currency of their leave. They will need to obtain a new CoS with a licensed Sponsor. A change of employment will not permit them to extend their stay beyond the maximum the category allows, and nor can they switch out of their sub-category under Tier 5 (Guidance paras 162-166).

There are specific provisions regarding private servants in a diplomatic household whose entry clearance was granted under the Rules from 6 April 2012. They may not change their employment in general – however they may change their employer so as to move to another household, as part of the general policy to avoid abuse of those working in this category r245ZP(f)(iii)(5)).

Example

Maryam is present working as a private servant in a diplomatic household. She entered the UK with entry clearance six months ago. She has been abused by her employers and is looking for options; she is supporting her family back in her country of origin and does not want to travel back yet.

So long as she can find a new employer in a diplomatic household then she can switch her work to them, filing an appropriate change of employment request. If she cannot, she will have to consider leaving the country unless she has another immigration route open to her. She may be a victim of trafficking in which case she could request a referral to the National Referral Mechanism.

Registering change of circumstances

Migrants may amend their records regarding their personal or dependents' details, criminal convictions, contact or representative details, via the *Change of circumstances* form.

Private servants in a diplomatic household

There are specific provisions addressing their situation (r245ZO(f)-(g)). If sponsored in the international agreement sub-category as a private servant in a diplomatic household where the employer is a diplomat or an employee of an international organisation recognised by Her Majesty's Government, who enjoys certain privileges or immunity under UK or international law, they must

- Be at least 18 years of age at the application date *and*
- Provide evidence that their terms and conditions of employment are consistent with the National Minimum Wage provisions under Appendix 7 (which provides a statement of the terms and conditions of employment of which two copies must be provided, completed and signed by the employer and the overseas domestic worker) and that the wage will truly be paid throughout their stay *and*
- Confirm they are not related to the employer or employer's spouse by blood or marriage
- Confirm that the post does not comprise work as set out in para 57 of the National Minimum Wage Regulations 2015, i.e. that they are not a member of the employer's family living in the family home sharing in the family's tasks and activities – this is required for leave to remain applications too (r245ZQ(o))

They are under a specific regime for changing employer which we address above under *Change of employment.*

These are the only individuals within the temporary worker migration route who can access settlement, if they were present in the route under the sub-category for private servants in a diplomatic household under the Rules in place before 6 April 2012, and they have only short breaks in their employment due to changing employer. They may then count that time towards a settlement application (r245AAA(b)). They must stay within this route during their time in the UK, not fall foul of the general refusal reasons, pass the life in the UK and English language requirements of Appendix KoLL, not be an overstayer incompatibly with r39E, and must provide a letter from their employer detailing absences and periods of annual leave; non-work absences must be explained in a letter from the applicant (r245ZS).

Restrictions on Contractual Service Suppliers and Independent Professionals in the International Agreement sub-category

Where the CoS is for one of these roles, then the grant of leave must not lead to them receiving leave for a cumulative period exceeding six months in any 12 month period during the period of leave granted (r245ZN(h))

Visitors switching into the route the sports or creative sub-category

This class of visitors may switch into the route where they were visiting and conducting permitted activities in the sports or creative sectors and entered the UK after they have been allocated the relevant CoS. Para 16 of Appendix 3 to Appendix V of the Rules allows artists, entertainers and musicians who are visiting the UK visitors to give performances as an individual or as part of a group, take part in competitions or auditions, make personal appearances and take part in promotional activities, or take part in one or more cultural events or festivals on the list of permit free festivals in Appendix 5. They may also take a paid engagement if they have been invited by a creative (arts or entertainment) or sports organisation, agent or broadcaster based in the UK (Appendix 4 to Appendix V).

Example

Rudolph, a violinist, is present in the UK as a visitor with a view to taking part in the Aldeburgh Festival. He has found out about the Tier 5 temporary worker route and is wondering if he can remain for longer, given that he is famous as a virtuoso with unparalleled command of the Paganini caprices.

In theory Rudolph might seem to be able to switch into the temporary worker route, as he is taking part in permitted activities in the creative sector: the Aldeburgh Festival appears as one of the permit free festivals (see V16(d) read with Appendix 5 to Appendix V). However, when we look at the Part 6A Rules, we see that he would have had to have had the CoS allocated to him before he travelled, so a spur-of-the-moment switch like this is not available to him.

Students joining the government authorised exchange sub-category

Certain students can join this sub-category. These are those who previously held leave in Tier 4 General and were last sponsored by a UK recognised body or a body in receipt of public funding as a higher education institution, or an overseas higher education institution, to undertake a short-term study abroad programme in the United Kingdom. They may do so where the CoS shows that they are sponsored in the government authorised exchange sub-category, lawfully obtained a UK recognised degree level plus qualification (only a degree, not an equivalent) during their last grant of leave, and are being sponsored to undertake a period of postgraduate professional training or work experience which is required to obtain a professional qualification or professional registration in the same professional field as that qualification (r245ZQ(b)(vi)).

Genuineness testing

There is a genuineness test as is routinely found in PBS routes. For those seeking entry clearance, it focuses on whether (r245ZO(i))

- They are genuinely able to undertake (and intend to undertake) the role in the CoS
- They will not be taking employment in the UK other than as permitted under the route: i.e. as specified in the CoS and the various provisos addressed below
- If in the private servant in a diplomatic household sub-category, the National Minimum Wage will be paid

An applicant may be requested to provide further information or attend an interview, providing such further information within 28 days of the request being sent, on pain of refusal if the material is not provided, or if the interview is not attended absent a reasonable explanation (r245ZO(j)). No points are awarded under Appendix A if genuineness is not established (r245ZO(k)). Again as is routine under the PBS, the decision maker does not have to carry out this assessment where the application falls for refusal for other reasons, but reserves the right to do so in any reconsideration (r245ZO(l)).

There are a similar set of provisions for those seeking leave to remain (r245ZQ(k)-(n)).

The guidance explains that the decision will be made on the balance of probabilities taking into account the interviewee's knowledge of the role, relevant experience relative to skills required, knowledge of the Sponsor, explanation of how they were recruited, and any other relevant information.

Example

You can see the considerations in play in Singh (IJR) [2015] UKUT 538 (IAC). There the applicant for entry clearance was applying to work as a priest at a Southall Gurdwara, and their application was refused because they were considered to know very little about the role they were taking on. The UT upheld the Home Office decision on the basis that it was not unreasonable to think that an applicant would have some knowledge of their planned working conditions.

Multiple periods of employment in UK
A multiple entry CoS may be issued for those needing to enter the UK regularly. This is not required simply for normal overseas travel for personal or business purposes (see generally Guidance 169-173).

Leave lapses where a person leaves the Common Travel Area (i.e. the UK, the islands and Ireland) having entered the UK without entry clearance or having been granted leave for less than six months. Accordingly they would have to re-apply for entry clearance with a new CoS to return. Those with entry clearance or leave more than six months do not lose their leave and so can travel more freely.

Key criteria for the route

The migrant must:

- Not fall foul of the general refusal reasons (r245ZO(a), r245ZQ(a))
- Have 30 points under Appendix A (A105-112) (r245ZO(b), r245ZQ(c))
- Have 10 points under Appendix C (C8-9) (r245ZO(c), r245ZQ(d))
- If under 18, have the usual consents from their parent/legal guardian to the application and to their travel, reception and care arrangements (r245ZO(d)-(e), r245ZQ(f)-(g))
- If sponsored in the international agreement sub-category as a private servant in a diplomatic household, meet the relevant requirements discussed above (r245ZN(f-g))

- If a Contractual Service Supplier or Independent Professional in the International Agreement sub-category, not spend more than six months of any 12 month period with leave for this purpose (r245ZN(h), r245ZQ(j))

- Satisfy the decision maker that they genuinely intend to undertake the job in question and not work other than is permitted (r245ZN(i))

For those seeking leave to remain, there is permission to switch into temporary worker from these routes (r245ZQ(b)):

- Temporary worker (i.e. extending leave in the same category)

- Visitors in the sports or creative sub-category where conducting the relevant permitted activities we have addressed above

- From Tier 4 General where they have an appropriate Sponsor and are applying for the government authorised exchange sub-category with a UK recognised degree or higher degree obtained during their last leave for the purpose of a period of postgraduate professional training or work experience which is required to obtain a professional qualification or professional registration in the same professional field as that qualification

- The Guidance (page 21) also states that people on some rather old immigration routes (Overseas Government Employees, Qualifying Work Permit Holders and Students from the pre-Tier 4 regime) may switch into the route

To extend leave as a temporary worker within the route, the CoS must be issued for the same sub-category as previously. For those who entered the route from 6 April 2012 within the private servant in a diplomatic household sub-category, they must remain with the same employer and confirm they have worked under the appropriate terms and conditions (set out above) (r245ZQ(e)).

A student (including Tier 4 migrants, a student resitting their course, writing up their thesis, student nurses and student union sabbatical officers, and postgraduate doctors/dentists) switching into the route having previously been sponsored by a government or international scholarship agency now or within the last 12 months must confirm that the Sponsor agrees to them remaining in the UK (r245ZQ(h)).

They may not be overstaying inconsistently with the provisions of r39E (r245ZQ(i)).

The Appendix A requirements

As usual a CoS must be valid in order to found the award of points (A108), and to be so its reference number must link to a valid reference with the Certificate of Sponsorship Checking Service (CoSCS) (A109). Further requirements for validity are (A109A):

- The CoS was **assigned no more than three months before the immigration application**, unless the applicant is applying for leave to enter having previously been granted leave to enter on the basis of the same CoS number

- The application is **made within three months of the employment start date** given in the CoS

- The CAS reference number has **not been cancelled** by the Home Office or the Sponsor

- The Sponsor must be an **A-rated Sponsor unless this is an extension application** within the Tier 5 Migrant route

- Where the CoS records more than one individual engagement, there **is no more than 14 days between each successive engagement**

- The CoS must not be issued on the basis of the provisions under Mode 4 of the General Agreement on Trade in Services relating to intra-corporate transfers (A112)

Each CoS may only be used once (A110).

There are then a series of criteria to be satisfied for a CoS depending on the sub-category the applicant is applying under:

- **Creative and sporting (A111(a))**

  - The CoSCS must record the issue of a unique endorsement number showing endorsement in line with published criteria by a sporting Governing Body listed in Appendix M

  - The endorsement letter must be supplied from that Governing Body confirming the player/coach is internationally established at the highest level and will make a significant contribution to the sport's development at the highest level in the UK, and that the post could not be filled by a settled worker

- **Creative worker (A111(b))**

  - Where there is a relevant creative sector Codes of Practice existing in Appendix J, the Sponsor has complied with I (the Guidance lists these as those operating in dance, theatre and film/television (para 102)); or

  - The job appeared on the Appendix K shortage occupation list when the CoS was assigned; or

  - The Sponsor has otherwise taken account of the resident labour market needs in that field, and the work could not be carried out a settled worker (the Guidance para 102 suggests recruitment activity, written support from an industry-representative body, or sector labour market information, as suitable evidence)

- **Charity workers (A111(c))**

  - Where the work sponsored is for voluntary fieldwork contributing directly to the Sponsor's charitable purpose

  - The applicant must not be paid or otherwise remunerated, including receipt of benefits in kind, save for reasonable expenses permitted under the National Minimum Wage Act section 44

  - The applicant must not be filling an a permanent position, including on a temporary basis

- **Religious workers (A111(d))**

  - The applicant must be sponsored to perform religious duties, via work within or directed by the Sponsor's organisation, which may include preaching, pastoral work and non-pastoral duties: these duties must be outlined

- The applicant must be a member of a sponsoring religious order

- The applicant must receive pay and conditions at least equal to those given to settled workers in the same role

- The remuneration must comply with National Minimum Wage regulations or be exempt from them

- Details of how the resident labour market test has been complied with, or why the role is exempt from the test (A92A requires that the CoSCS confirms that a role is supernumerary, i.e. over and above normal staffing requirements, or involves living within and being a member of a religious order, or is for a Sponsor holding a national register of all settled workers who might fill the role)

➢ **Government Authorised Exchange (A111(e))**

- The CoSCS entry must show that the work, volunteering or job shadowing being sponsored meets the requirements of the individual exchange scheme, set out in Appendix N and does not fill a vacancy in the workforce

- The role is skilled to RQF level 3 under the Appendix J codes of practice

- All relevant regulatory UK and EU legislation is complied with, i.e. the National Minimum Wage Act and Working Time Directive

➢ **International Agreements – Contractual Service Supplier or Independent Professional (A111(f))**

- The CoSCS entry must show that the work is pursuant to a contract to supply services to the Sponsor in the United Kingdom by an overseas undertaking established on the territory of a party to the General Agreement on Trade in Services or a similar trade agreement which has been concluded between the EU and another party/ies and which is in force, and which has no commercial presence in the European Union

- The service which that undertaking is contracted to supply to the Sponsor in the United Kingdom falls within the scope of the sectors specified in the relevant commitments in respect of Contractual Service Suppliers or Independent Professionals as set out in the GATT or other agreement

- The Sponsor has, through an open tendering procedure or other procedure which guarantees the bona fide character of the contract, awarded a services contract for a period not exceeding 12 months to the applicant's employer

- The Sponsor will be the final consumer of the services provided under that contract

- The applicant is a national of the country in which the overseas undertaking is established

- An applicant who is under the Independent Professional sub-category must provide a university degree or technical qualification demonstrating knowledge of an equivalent level (the qualification must be provided showing their course title/award, its duration and completion date plus their name), proof of relevant professional qualifications required by the law, regulations or requirements in force in the UK, and have six years' professional experience in the sector concerned; unless they are in the International Agreement sub-category and retain the same Sponsor and are applying for the purpose of the same contract to provide services as was the case when previously granted entry clearance or leave

Example

Your client wants to enter the UK with a view to taking up a job offer with the company that has issued them with a CoS to work as a Contractual Service Provider.

One of the things to check is that the contract was offered to their employer under an open tendering or other suitable procedure. Failure to carry out steps like this may mean that the CoS is deemed inadequate when a Home Office decision maker reviews it.

➢ **Contractual Service Suppliers (A111(f)(vi))**

- The applicant must have been employed by the service supplier for at least one year before the application

- The applicant must possess a university degree or technical qualification demonstrating knowledge of an equivalent level (the qualification must be provided; the Guidance sets out that the certificate must clearly show their course title/award, its duration and completion date plus their name)

- Possessing any relevant professional qualifications for the role in question

- Three years' experience in the sector concerned

- However, those requirements are waived where the individual is working in one of the following areas and has three years' professional experience and provides the certificate of the relevant qualifications:

    - Advertising and translation services

    - Management consulting services

    - Technical testing and analysis services

    - Fashion model and entertainment (but not audio-visual) services

    - Chef de cuisine services, an advanced technical qualification and six years' professional experience

- If within the International Agreement sub-category other than as a Contractual Service Supplier or Independent Professional, the entry must confirm they are being sponsored as an employee of an overseas government, or of an international organisation established by international treaty signed by the UK or European Union, or as a private servant in a diplomatic household under the provisions of the Vienna Convention on Diplomatic Relations 1961 or in the household of an international organisation recognised by HM Government, enjoying certain privileges or immunity and UK or international law

Specified documents for Contractual Service Suppliers

These individuals have to provide a particular set of documents (A111-SD(a)):

- Payslips by employer showing the employer's name *or*

- Payslips plus a letter from the employer on headed notepaper signed by a senior official confirming their authenticity *or*

- Personal bank/building society statements for the full specified period clearly showing applicant's name, account number, the date of the statement (the most recent must be dated no earlier than 31 days before the application date), the financial institution's name and logo, and transactions by the service supplier covering the full specified period

    - these statements must be printed on paper bearing the bank/building society's letterhead or bearing the official stamp on every page, or accompanied by a supporting letter from the issuing bank/building society confirming their authenticity; they must not be from an ATM

- *Or* a building society pass book, clearly showing the applicant's name, account number, institution's name and logo, and transactions by the service supplier covering the full specified period

Period and conditions of entry clearance and leave

r245ZP addresses the length of leave granted, and its conditions. The essential conditions are

- No recourse to public funds (r245ZP(f)(i))

- Police registration if r326 requires this (r245ZP(f)(ii))

- Study is permitted, subject to meeting the ATAS requirements in Part 15 of the Rules for those who are aged 18 or will reach that age during this period of leave (r245ZP(f)(v))

- Only employment as specified in the CoS (r245ZP(f)(iii)) save for

    - Supplementary employment save for those in the international agreement sub-category working as a private servant in a diplomatic household, or as a Contractual Service Supplier or Independent Professional (for no more than 20 hours a week – Guidance para 157; there is no need to advise the Home Office of supplementary employment (para 160); no additional work save for work meeting these criteria is permissible (para 160))

    - For those in the Government Authorised Exchange sub-category, work, volunteering or job shadowing authorised by the Sponsor

- In the creative and sporting sub-category, performing as a sportsperson for their national team while that team is in the UK, playing in British University and College Sport (BUCS) competitions and Temporary Engagement as a Sports Broadcaster
- In the International Agreement sub-category as a private servant in a diplomatic household, employment as a domestic worker in a household other than that specified

ENTRY CLEARANCE AND LEAVE TO ENTER FOR TEMPORARY WORKERS	
Type of applicant	**Leave granted**
A person arriving without entry clearance who has consecutive engagements (r245ZP(a))	The shorter of (a) a period starting 14 days before the first engagement and ending 14 days after the last one finishes (b) 3 months
A person arriving without entry clearance who a single period of engagement (r245ZP(b))	The shorter of (a) a period up to 14 days before the engagement starts and ending 14 days after it finishes (b) 3 months
For those arriving with entry clearance, with CoSs in the Creative and Sporting, Government Authorised Exchange for a Work Experience Programme, or the Charity Workers sub-categories (r245ZP(c))	The shorter of (a) a period starting 14 days before the engagement starts and ending 14 days after it finishes, or if there are consecutive engagements, before and after the first and last engagements (b) 12 months
For those arriving with entry clearance, with CoSs in the religious workers, Government Authorised Exchange subcategory for a Research Programme, Training Programme or Overseas Government Language Programme, or other than as a Contractual Service Supplier, or Independent Professional, in the international agreement subcategory	The shorter of (a) a period starting 14 days before the engagement starts and ending 14 days after it finishes (b) 2 years

(r245ZP(d))	
For those arriving with entry clearance, with CoSs in the Contractual Service Supplier, or Independent Professional in the International Agreement sub-category (r245ZP(e))	The shorter of (a) a period starting 14 days before the engagement starts and ending 14 days after it finishes (b) 6 months The Guidance explains that they may only apply for a maximum of 6 months in any 12 month period

The arrangements for extensions of leave are found in r245ZR.

LEAVE TO REMAIN FOR TEMPORARY WORKERS **Note that leave will be refused if the calculation given results in a figure of zero or less**	
Type of applicant	**Leave granted**
Visitor conducting permitted activities in the sports or creative sector r245ZR(c)	The shorter of (a) The period of engagement plus 14 days, or if there are consecutive engagements, from the first day of the first engagement until 14 days after the last day of the last one (b) 12 months
In the international agreement sub-category as an overseas government employee, employee of an international organisation or a private servant in a diplomatic household where in the case of the latter they entered the UK with a valid entry clearance in that capacity under the Rules in place before 6 April 2012 (r245ZR(d))	The shorter of (a) the period of engagement plus 14 days (b) 24 months UNLESS the applicant has spent more than 4 years with leave as a temporary worker in which case leave granted will be the shorter of (c) the period of engagement plus 14

	days (d) a period of 6 years less the period already spent as a temporary worker
In the international agreement sub-category as a private servant in a diplomatic household to work in a domestic capacity in the household of a named individual where the applicant entered the UK with a valid entry clearance in that capacity under the Rules in place from 6 April 2012 (r245ZR(e))	The shorter of (a) the period of engagement plus 14 days (b) 24 months UNLESS the applicant has spent more than 3 years with leave as a temporary worker in which case leave granted will be the shorter of (c) the period of engagement plus 14 days (d) a period of 5 years less the period already spent as a temporary worker
In the creative and sporting sub-category as a creative worker extending leave with the same Sponsor as last time (r245ZR(f)-(g))	The shorter of (a) the period of engagement plus 14 days (b) 12 months UNLESS the applicant has spent more than 1 year with leave as a temporary worker in which case leave granted will be the shorter of (c) the period of engagement plus 14 days (d) a period of 2 years less the period already spent as a temporary worker

If being sponsored in the Government Authorised exchange sub-category for a Work Experience Programme where the initial grant of leave was granted under the Rules in place from 6 April 2012, or the Creative and Sporting or the Charity Workers sub-category (r245ZR(b)(ii)(1))	The shorter of (a) the period of engagement plus 14 days or (b) the difference between the period spent in the UK already and 12 months
If being sponsored in the Government Authorised Exchange sub-category where the initial grant of leave was made under the Rules in place before 6 April 2012 or for a Research Programme, Training Programme or Overseas Government Language Programme, the Religious Workers subcategory, or the International Agreement sub-category other than as a Contractual Service Supplier, or Independent Professional (r245ZR(b)(ii))(2))	The shorter of (a) the period of engagement plus 14 days or (b) the difference between the period spent in the UK already and 2 years
If being sponsored in the International Agreement subcategory and is a Contractual Service Supplier or Independent Professional (r245ZR(b)(ii)(3))	The shorter of (a) the period of engagement plus 14 days or (b) the difference between the period spent in the UK already and 6 months

Overview of Tier 5 Youth Mobility Scheme Temporary Migrants

This route is for sponsored young people from participating countries and territories who wish to live and work temporarily in the UK – to experience life here, as the Guidance puts it. It is probably the simplest of all routes within the PBS to understand, as the Rules are less intricate and the criteria rather easier to understand and fulfil than elsewhere in the system.

Applicants must be from either an Appendix G country, or be a British Overseas Citizen, British Overseas Territories Citizen or British National (Overseas). There are a certain number of places reserved for each of the Appendix G countries set out therein, so it is always necessary to be alive to how many places remain available at the relevant time. Some countries are subject to the *Invitation to apply arrangements* addressed below. Government statistics recorded that 50% of the Youth Mobility visas issued in 2016 were to Australians, followed by 18% for New Zealanders and 15% for Canadians.

Applicants must also be below the age of 31 at the date of application, and over the age of 18 by the time they will be travelling. They may not have any dependent children, either living with them or financially dependent on them.

Entry clearance is given for two years; there is no possibility of extending leave within the route, which unsurprisingly does not lead to settlement. As always there is Guidance under the scheme which explains how the Rules operate.

Recurring concepts within the youth mobility scheme

Invitation to apply arrangements
These arrangements (G3-4) permit the Home Office to manage applications from countries specified in Appendix G – presently Japan and Taiwan. Applicants must submit an expression of interest under the published process.

The Home Office keep a record of all such expressions of interest and randomly select those who are to be invited. They may place a time limit on the period within which expressions of interest are submitted and determine the number of invitations to be issued in any calendar month, provided that the invitations issued are no less than the annual allocation of that country.

Deemed Sponsorship status
Nationals from countries with this status may simply make an application without further ado, whereas citizens of other countries eligible for the route but which are not deemed Sponsors must obtain a CoS to support their application.

Annual allocations
Each territory receives an annual allocation of places on the scheme. Applications will be accepted for consideration only up to the point that this is filled. If the annual allocation is reached a notice will be released to notify customers of this. The notice will be published on the relevant UK Embassy, High Commission or Diplomatic Post website.

There is no annual allocation for applications from British Overseas Citizens, British Overseas Territories Citizens and British Nationals (Overseas).

Example

James is present under the Youth Mobility route. He wishes to switch to Tier 2 General.

Part 6A of the Rules addresses all the PBS categories and Youth Mobility is not named as a candidate to switch into Tier 2 General: indeed, it is not named anywhere else in Part 6A, showing that one cannot switch out of the route. It would be necessary to return abroad and apply for entry clearance.

Key criteria for the route

It is an entry clearance only route; i.e. a visa is always required before travelling, otherwise entry will be refused (r245ZJ). Applicants enjoy a dispensation as to from where they may apply for entry clearance, in that they may apply to an entry clearance post (designated as appropriate for this route) where they are living lawfully at the time of the application (r28A).

An applicant can apply for a visa up to six months before travelling.

Only some nationalities qualify (r245ZK(b)):

- An Appendix G country (to be established by presenting the relevant passport)

  - Those with deemed Sponsorship status (Australia – 35,500 places, New Zealand - 13,000 places, Canada – 5,500 places, Japan – 1,000 places, Monaco– - 1,000 places, and Taiwan – 1,000 places)

  - Those without deemed Sponsorship status (South Korea and Hong Kong - 1,000 places each)

- A British Overseas Citizen, British Overseas Territories Citizen or British National (Overseas), as defined by the British Nationality Act 1981

Applicants may establish their entitlement to use the route (r245ZK(c)):

- From countries with deemed Sponsorship status, simply by possession of the relevant passport, in which case they may apply at any entry clearance post in the world; however they must be resident there for at least six months under the general requirements of the rules

- For countries without deemed Sponsorship status, they must hold a CoS issued by that country's authorities and apply from within its territory

For example, in 2017 the Hong Kong Labour Department accepted applications for the route from 20 February to 3 March.

The CoS will be valid only if issued within three months of the entry clearance application and where it has not been cancelled by the time it is relied upon (r245ZK(ca)).

The other requirements are

- Scoring a minimum of 40 points under paragraphs 101 to 104 of Appendix A (r245ZK(d))

- Scoring a minimum of 10 points under paragraphs 6 to 7 of Appendix C (r245ZK(e))

- Having no children under the age of 18 who are either living with the applicant or for whom the applicant is financially responsible (r245ZK(f)

- Not previously have spent time in the UK as a Working Holidaymaker or a Tier 5 (Youth Mobility Scheme) Temporary Migrant (r245ZK(g))

  Where the applicant is a national of a country whose annual allocation of places available under this route is subject to invitation to apply arrangements operated under Appendix G, they must have been issued with an invitation to apply, and have made their application within the period of time specified on the invitation (r245ZK(h))

The Appendix A requirements

These are exceptionally slight (A101-A104). Essentially the applicant must simply provide a valid passport showing that they are the citizen of a country or rightful holder of a passport issued by a territory listed in

Appendix G or are a British Overseas Citizen, British Territories Overseas Citizen or British National (Overseas).

Additionally they must be aged 18 or over on the date their entry clearance becomes valid for use, and under the age of 31 on the date the application was made.

If they satisfy these two requirements, they receive 40 points.

Period and conditions of entry clearance and leave

Entry clearance will be granted for two years subject to the following conditions (r245ZL):

- No recourse to public funds
- Registration with the police if required by r326
- No employment as a professional sportsperson (including as a sports coach), or as a Doctor or Dentist in Training, unless the applicant has obtained a degree in medicine or dentistry at bachelor's level or above from a UK institution that is a UK recognised or listed body, or which holds a sponsor licence under Tier 4 of the Points Based System, and provides evidence of this degree
- No study subject to the conditions in Part 15 of the Rules: i.e. they must obtain an ATAS clearance certificate if wishing to study for a postgraduate qualification in a sensitive subjects area, knowledge of which could be used in programmes to develop weapons of mass destruction
- No self employment, except where:
    - The migrant has no premises which he owns, other than his home, from which he carries out his business
    - The total value of any equipment used in the business does not exceed £5,000, and
    - The migrant has no employees

Acknowledgements

Many thanks go to Mark Symes for his editorial flare, creativity and incredible knowledge of the Points Based System. Thank you to Melanie Porte and Melanie Chrysostomou for their valued help and support. Special thanks go to Androulla Demetriou for her design flair, her patience and hard work in producing the printed edition.